Chasing Africa

Chasing Africa

Fear Won't Find Me Here

A MEMOIR

Lisa Duncan

RMB

For information on purchasing bulk quantities of this book, or to obtain media excerpts
or invite the author to speak at an event, please visit rmbooks.com and select the
"Contact" tab.

RMB | Rocky Mountain Books Ltd.
rmbooks.com
@rmbooks
facebook.com/rmbooks

Cataloguing data available from Library and Archives Canada
ISBN 9781771605816 (paperback)
ISBN 9781771605823 (electronic)

Design: Lara Minja, Lime Design
Cover photo: Shutterstock/Xavier Sanchez Criballes

Printed and bound in Canada

We would like to also take this opportunity to acknowledge the traditional territories
upon which we live and work. In Calgary, Alberta, we acknowledge the Niitsítapi
(Blackfoot) and the people of the Treaty 7 region in Southern Alberta, which includes
the Siksika, the Piikuni, the Kainai, the Tsuut'ina, and the Stoney Nakoda First
Nations, including Chiniki, Bearpaw, and Wesley First Nations. The City of Calgary
is also home to Métis Nation of Alberta, Region III. In Victoria, British Columbia,
we acknowledge the traditional territories of the Lkwungen (Esquimalt and Songhees),
Malahat, Pacheedaht, Scia'new, T'Sou-ke, and W̱SÁNEĆ (Pauquachin, Tsartlip,
Tsawout, Tseycum) peoples.

We acknowledge the financial support of the Government of Canada through the
Canada Book Fund and the Canada Council for the Arts, and of the province of
British Columbia through the British Columbia Arts Council and the Book Publishing
Tax Credit.

For E.M.M.,
the best adventure I could ask for.

I never travel without my diary.
One should always have something sensational to read in the train.

—OSCAR WILDE, *THE IMPORTANCE OF BEING EARNEST*

"Here's to all your adventures around the world," said Puddle.
"Here's to all your adventures right at home," said Toot.

—HOLLY HOBBIE, *TOOT & PUDDLE*

Prologue

THERE IS ONE MEMORY from my African journey that is embedded in my mind like a recurring dream. It floats around in isolation, refusing to conform to chronology. There are no photos in my vast slide collection that capture this night. The pages of my journals cannot validate its existence, nor can I recall precisely who I was with at the time. I'm confident it happened somewhere in Malawi or Zimbabwe. But I would be hard-pressed to say exactly where.

I wish I could extract more details from the depths of my brain, but these unknowns remain elusive. Mysterious. Yet the memory is real. An experience so visceral it can never be forgotten.

I close my eyes and *I am there.*

It's after dinner. I'm walking with a few backpacker friends. All traces of the sunset glow have long been absorbed by the darkening night sky. Stars flicker alive. The balmy air caresses my bare arms and legs. I feel safe, warm. *Unworried.*

We're ambling along a dimly lit, unpaved path away from the centre of town. In less than a hundred metres, we arrive at a desolate road. A few locals trail behind us. Sounds of their laughter and lively chatter fill the muggy air. I turn around. In typical African fashion, they extend their warmth to us. Within seconds we are walking and talking together as friends. Their timing must be fortuitous. Prior to their arrival, we were aimlessly wandering. It feels as though they've shown up to lead us to our unlikely destination.

Compared to the opaque darkness of the sky, the ultraviolet light spilling out of the gas station is blinding when we first approach. As we get closer, I have to squint before my eyes adjust to the bright and baffling scene. Instead of customers gassing up cars, several men and women are gathered around the gas pumps, moving about under the harsh lighting of the shelter. From afar, their actions look quick and precise. Only when I get up close and stand next to them do I understand their motivation for coming to the petrol stand: they're catching grasshoppers for food.

In the day, the gas station is nothing more than a requisite stop for the rare car owner or truck driver. By nightfall it has been transformed into a small mecca bursting with energy and excitement. The artificial lighting is a magnet for the insects, making them easy prey for the local trappers. At least a hundred light-green grasshoppers are swarming all around us, flying and bouncing in every direction to evade capture. The frantic snapping and crackling sounds are nothing like the symphony of chirping grasshoppers I revered as a child during my visits to the dyke near my family home.

I stand there, smiling in awe, observing the insect collectors' finely tuned techniques. They make it look so easy. After several minutes, I decide to give it a go, but I'm completely out of my element. The grasshoppers move too fast – each time I bend down or reach up high to grab one, they mock me and jump away. I move quickly. They move quicker. My failed attempts make the expert collectors chuckle. My uncontrollable laughter makes my belly ache, threatening to burst my bladder.

Always up for a challenge, I'm not about to concede defeat. *Not yet.* I persevere a bit longer, but they keep getting away. Then I catch one. I cup it in my hands gently so as not to crush it to death. Now the grasshopper's fate is sealed unless I decide to release it.

Its movements tickle my palms. Before I have time to think, it slips out my hands and leaps to freedom. Despite its quick escape, everyone cheers after seeing my small victory. *Just one grasshopper.* That's all it took for the locals to act like I'd scored a goal in a soccer match.

Once again, among new friends, I experience the joy of expecting the unexpected. It's a gift to be part of a true human connection.

I can't stop smiling.

The unplanned grasshopper "hunt" at the gas station has always stood out for me. My recollection remains imperfect and devoid of some major details – the who, where and when – yet the experience carries a sense of wonder, a sense of connectedness to those around me.

Two decades later, this cherished memory remains vivid. The night reminds me of the immense pleasure found in simplicity. I wasn't worrying about family illnesses or dreading future outcomes. It didn't matter whether I could catch a grasshopper or not. The important fact was that I was *trying*. And that I wasn't doing it alone. This rare gathering reminds me that when darkness is lurking, it is vital for me to seek out the light. To let others in to reveal it.

Africa taught me extraordinary things will happen when I find the courage to set fear aside. There have been some dark days and many sleepless nights when I have forgotten her simple wisdom. Rather than succumbing to the darkness in my life – fear, guilt, illness, death – I choose to move away from it, fight it, even when it is looming and inescapable. I refuse to live by the "learn to suffer" maxim of my family name. Instead, I have learned to *endure*. Learned to be brave and create the light necessary to heal my heart and mind.

One

I LAY WIDE AWAKE AGAIN, a regular occurrence I had come to expect and dread. *Don't look at the time*, I reminded myself. *It only makes falling asleep worse.*

Despite the wee hour, my mind was lucid. *I'm going to Africa.*

I'd made up my mind. And, as usual when I made a major decision, there was no looking back. The only thing left to do was tell them.

On cue, the tossing and turning drill began. I turned onto my left hip. Within a minute, I switched to my right side, but changing my position rarely proved effective. In the daytime, I maintained my mom's calm, cool demeanour. At night, I couldn't switch off my brain and fretted like my dad, worrying myself sick about things I couldn't control or change.

My alarm clock's glowing digits were a formation of beady bat eyes staring me down. I caved. 1:07 a.m. I reached over and turned the alarm clock toward the wall. *Out of sight, out of mind. Right. You can do this.*

I was desperate to sleep but felt their presence like skulking bullies in a playground. Fear and Worry arrived on their tandem bike of torment, racing through my body and mind. Fear was in control, navigating up front. Worry pedalled quietly at the rear, keeping the wheels in motion. They cut a spiral path through my chest. The mounting pressure moved back and forth, side to side, up and down, a wooden rolling pin pressing dough into submission.

The tightening sensation percolated up to my throat. I sat up in bed and took a deep breath. *Leave me alone,* I implored. I was frustrated and angry they'd shown up again, intent on plaguing my night with trepidation.

My pulse quickened. A flash flood of panic rushed to my stomach, twisting it into crampy, painful knots: Guilt had joined the dynamic duo tonight.

Leave me alone, I repeated. *I want to be free. Is that too much to ask?*

Fear piped up first. *You can't leave now. What if they get worse while you're away?*

I had played out this reality a hundred times in my head. I knew there was a good chance they *would* get worse while I was in Africa. But it would happen whether I stayed or not.

Dad wasn't counting on a cure for Parkinson's. His bleak prognosis and failing body gave him little to look forward to. Russ had little hope of his MS symptoms retreating. His 28-year-old body was wobbly, his words slurred like a drunk's. He'd already transitioned from a cane to a walker. A wheelchair was just a matter of time. Neurologists never handed my dad and brother expiry dates, just said the demise of their bodies was inevitable. How quickly or severely, they couldn't really say.

I don't think it was death I feared – their diseases wouldn't kill them anytime soon. It was all the unknowns that kept me up at night. Having two family members with two different neurological diseases was rare. *Of course,* the possibility that I had a similar curse had crossed my mind. After all, there hadn't been any obvious signs prior to Dad and Russ getting sick. At least not any I observed.

Despite all this, I couldn't stay. Going to Africa was the only thing that seemed like mine. A selfish act for me and no one else. I was determined not to let anything – or anyone – interfere with my plans. I *needed* to go. I needed to remind myself who I was before illness and grief eroded my identity and muddled my path.

Fear and Worry came to a halt. Guilt weighed in, one last attempt to get me to change my mind. *It's not fair for you to take off and go traipsing around Africa while your mom is forced to look after them. You're being really selfish.*

I stood my ground. I had to rid myself of their clutches.

I need to be free, I repeated. *At least for a little while.*

I PULLED UP TO MY PARENTS' HOUSE Sunday afternoon and parked behind Russ's uninsured Mazda RX7. His prized silver sports car hadn't moved from the driveway in over three years. The chance of him ever driving again was slim, but no one dared suggest he sell it.

We moved into that house in 1972 when I was 6 months old: it was the only family home I had known. Our stucco shoebox-shaped house was perched on a spacious corner lot. It lacked architectural finesse, but its bright turquoise exterior made it stand out among the 1960s split-level homes in their Richmond neighbourhood. To my discerning eye, the house wasn't true turquoise but a greenish, less attractive aquamarine hue. I had never seen the paint fade or peel: Dad was meticulous. I assumed the hardware store would one day discontinue his preferred paint swatch. But for almost 20 years, Dad had kept it the same colour. Now thick drips of dried paint were visible on the wood siding and white and turquoise fence boards: his last attempt to touch up had proved challenging for his unsteady body.

Unless I was away for the weekend, I made regular visits to see Mom, Dad and Russ. I got along fine with my family, but it was more obligation than affection that brought me home each week. After three or four hours, I was eager to return to the salmon-coloured character home I rented with my best friend in Vancouver, 35 minutes away by car.

I walked up to the house and gazed up at the towering twin maple trees in the front yard. Against the pale slate sky, the bare branches looked more silver than brown and seemed to shiver in the winter chill. I opened the front door. It was usually left unlocked during the day, but in the last few months there had been a few unnerving instances when Dad's med-induced paranoia kicked in and I arrived to find the house locked with additional security latches and deadbolts.

The sweet aroma of Mom's freshly baked bran muffins greeted me in the entryway. My mouth watered. I kicked off my shoes and called out hello. Breeze, Russ's black lab retriever, bolted down the stairs, his tail wagging like a propeller.

"Hey, Breezer. How you doing, boy?" I rubbed his head and ears and ascended the stairs.

Mom met me at the top of the stairs, wiping her hands on a tea towel. "Oh hi, love. Happy belated birthday," she said with her usual warm smile. "Russ is lying down. We'll have some cake later when he gets up. I'm just making some coffee. Want a cup?"

Of course, I accepted. Three things I could never refuse at home were a cup of Mom's strong coffee, her little raisin bran muffins and a round of competitive Scrabble. The effortless way she played and often won, you'd never know English was her third language.

I went upstairs. Dad was in the living room. The plastic Christmas tree was already set up, but the decorations were still in boxes on the floor. A lone red poinsettia plant sat on display in front of the main living room window. Despite its cheerful colour, I felt sorry for it: another month or so it would dry up then be discarded.

"Hey, Dad. How are you?" I took my usual seat on the chesterfield.

He barely looked up from his book and mumbled, "Oh, hi, Lis. Fine. How ya doing?" *Lis. Wies. Breeze.* When Dad projected his weakened voice, the first consonant was often inaudible, making our names indistinguishable. Dad's increasingly incoherent ramblings annoyed Mom, but it gave Russ and me a good laugh whenever she and I would both answer "Yeah?" as Breeze ran into the room.

I reached across the coffee table for the *Vancouver Sun* newspaper, in search of the arts section. I glanced at Dad. He was dressed in his favourite teal knitted vest on top of a thin, white undershirt. His navy jogging pants looked two sizes too big with the drawstring pulled in tight around his skinny waist. Dad's black hair had turned silver a decade earlier, but it was still thick and wavy.

He was seated in his favourite brown upholstered armchair, its spindly, wooden legs shaped like his bony calves. This was the same chair he'd sat in when I was a young child. When I got up to use the bathroom at night, I could see him from the bedroom I shared with my older sister Sue. Dad sat in that chair with his head buried in his hands, grappling with something too big for him to bear. Seeing him like this made my tummy feel strange. Sickly. In her calm voice, Mom had told me to leave him be, explaining Daddy needed time alone.

This was the same chair that had toppled over when the fighting turned physical. I was around 6 or 7, asleep in bed when a loud thud startled me awake. I ran down the hall to the living room. Dad and Mike were on the floor, wrestling, punching one another. Dad looked dishevelled, his eyeglasses on the carpet. I screamed at them to stop, hoping to erase what I'd seen and heard. But I never forgot the violent look in my father's eyes. Or the hurtful words that spilled out of his mouth into the ears of my oldest brother. It was around that time the shame of family secrets started to weigh me down, keeping me up at night.

Dad looked statuesque and typically focused: lips pursed tightly, neck and shoulders stooped forward, his slim torso leaning slightly to the left. He was reading a medical book. A lined notepad with some notes he had jotted down sat on the corner of the coffee table. Before Parkinson's, Dad's cursive writing had been a flawless work of art. I loved the way he would raise up his pen to make a few circles in the air before committing his signature to paper. Now his words looked shaky and were devoid of the precision they once held.

Last month Dad immersed himself in literature related to the positive effects of primrose oil on MS patients. So far it had proven unsuccessful in slowing Russ's decline. Studying the merits of vitamin and mineral supplements to help offset the severity of Parkinson's had become his latest preoccupation.

Lumbar puncture. Myelin sheath. Primary progressive. Spasticity. Blood brain barrier. Dopamine. Neurotransmitter. Sinemet. L-DOPA. Dyskinesia. None of these medical terms had been in my vocabulary five years before. Now we couldn't escape the weight of these words after they jumped off the pages of medical brochures and out of doctors' mouths and invaded our lives.

Dad's left forearm and hand shook uncontrollably as he read. He took his meds precisely every three hours from the time he woke up until bedtime. The involuntary tremors only occurred when he sat still, and stopped the second he turned the page. A mild symptom, though, compared to the stiffening of his gait and increasingly erratic behaviour that hinted at an unstable mind.

Diagnosed at 57, Dad had snuck extra meds to mask his symptoms at work. Over time, the increased dose of synthetic dopamine messed with his head. Two years later, he was forced to retire. When he lost his driver's licence, his morale and psyche suffered further. A year earlier, on Christmas day, Dad had confided, "I wish I could kill myself. But that wouldn't be fair to Russ, would it?" He never uttered these words again to me, but his confession was a noose around my chest and stomach and added to my mountain of worries.

Mom emerged from the kitchen carrying two tiny mugs of coffee, humming along to the faint classical music playing on her CD player. She passed me the one with the Frisian flag pattern. Cream, no sugar for me. Mom drank her coffee with heaping teaspoons of sugar and coffee whitener. Aside from the odd migraine, eczema and unsightly varicose veins, Mom had always been a beacon of health. She didn't drink or smoke. This sugary fix was one of her few vices.

Mom returned to the kitchen to retrieve buttered muffins, not much bigger than large eggs. She set them on the coffee table and sat down in her easy chair. I'm not sure what it is about the Dutch and their small portions, as if they need to prove they're capable of practising self-restraint. I ate the warm muffin in four bites. Then I reached for another.

"So how was your birthday? Do anything special?" she asked.

"It was good. I climbed at the gym after work, then went out for sushi." I paused for a moment and took a sip of coffee. "The best part of my week was booking my flight to Johannesburg. I'm leaving for Africa on my own in February."

Dad looked up from his book and peered at me over his dark-framed bifocals, shaking his head in disbelief. "Why *on earth* would you want to go to Africa?" he asked incredulously, his mouth wide to reveal his silver premolar fillings. It was more a statement than a question. He acted as if I had just told him I was heading off to the Nile to master the art of crocodile wrestling. For someone so serious, Dad could be a real drama queen sometimes.

I rolled my eyes. *Who wouldn't want to go to Africa?*

I'd been saving up for over a year to go travelling. It took me a solid month of waffling to decide backpacking in Africa on my own wouldn't be too daunting. Even though I'm the youngest, I had been the first to move out when I was 19. I wasn't seeking my parents' permission. But I had hoped to see something in their expressions that would alleviate my guilty conscience about leaving.

Dad's curt reaction didn't surprise me. We didn't see eye to eye on most topics. He didn't share my love of world travel. Nor did he understand my excitement when I left home at age 17, with Mom's full support, to study in Japan for a year. After I had declared my art history major, Dad deemed my decision impractical, "a waste of money and time." He would have preferred me to study engineering, despite the fact I had never, *ever*, shown any interest or skill in the field.

Dad had dropped out of high school to work when his mom became ill. University had never been in the cards for him: it was a luxury he couldn't afford. My arts degree had seemed frivolous to him. After four years, I had student loans to pay off with no exciting job prospects related to my fine arts and Japanese language studies. I'd been working as a letter carrier for the last 14 months – definitely not a path I had envisioned for myself at age 24. At least the pay was decent and kept my legs in fantastic shape.

I'm sure Dad saw my going to Africa as just another pointless undertaking. But the great thing about him was that, after stating his opinion, he didn't try to stop me from pursuing my goals. Even if he had tried, I was too set in my ways to listen to his "advice."

"I've always wanted to see giraffes and elephants in the wild," I answered proudly.

Dad couldn't argue with *that*. As a child, I loved thumbing through our family's stacks of *National Geographic*: the photographs of animals in the savannah and the barren deserts intrigued me the most. Heck, with his yearly subscriptions, Dad could have taken credit for igniting my curiosity in the continent.

"Well, I think you're crazy, especially travelling there on your own," he replied.

Mom had a much better understanding of my ever-expanding travel bug. At age 28, she had boarded the SS *Ryndam* in 1961 with her best friend, leaving her family behind in the Netherlands. The ship sailed across the Atlantic, arriving two weeks later in Nova Scotia. They continued west to British Columbia and, after a few months, bused it all the way to Mexico City before returning to Vancouver for work.

I sometimes wondered if Mom had ever planned on having more adventures before settling down and having kids. Now, decades later, instead of enjoying the freedom of her 60s, she was tethered to Dad and Russ as their caregiver.

Mom smiled upon hearing my news. I sensed she was relieved to know my journey would begin in South Africa, where her eldest sister lived. "I'll have to give Tante Atje a call and let her and your cousin Rika know you'll be visiting. How long will you be away?" she asked.

"I'll be back in June," I replied.

I'd thought about staying on for a few months after my money dried up, to teach. But there was no need to make my parents think I'd be away longer than planned. Besides, three and a half months – more than a full season – seemed like a long enough time to be away. My sister Sue and her husband lived 40 minutes away by car and made regular visits to see Mom, Dad and Russ. After Dad became ill, the tension between him and my brother Mike had lessened. But Mike had been living in Toronto and was moving to Australia within a few months. Even with Sue around, I wasn't sure if I could handle the guilt of being away for longer.

I got up for more coffee when Russ's slurred voice called out from downstairs. "I need some help." Mom got up from her chair. I stopped her. "It's okay, Mom. I'll go."

I went downstairs with Breeze at my heels. Russ, who looked like a young Tom Berenger, was halfway across his room, inching his walker forward across the thin beige carpet with his unsteady legs shuffling behind the wheels.

"Hey, Russ. How's it going?"

"Okay. Hockey game's on in a few minutes. Wanna watch?"

"Sure. You know how much I *love* hockey," I replied, my voice thick with sarcasm. Who knows? Maybe I would have liked hockey more if I hadn't been dragged to the ice arena at dawn for Mike and Russ's practices when I was little.

Russ threw me a goofy smile. He maneuvered his walker out of his bedroom. I followed him around the corner, down the linoleum-tiled hallway and into the small bathroom. He parked the walker in the corner and tightly gripped the thick PVC pipe mounted on the wall.

As he shuffled his stiff legs across the floor, I studied the faded cream wallpaper. I was never sure if the ochre-and-forest-green pattern, featuring the Ol' Squire Inn, willow trees and a portrait of a long-haired, bearded nobleman was supposed to evoke romantic notions of travel. But I found the wallpaper tacky and depressing.

Russ positioned himself in front of the toilet. He placed his left hand on the small white sink while his right hand held onto the diagonal wall mount. His quads quivered as he lowered himself onto the toilet seat. In one swift move, I pulled down his track pants to his knees. I placed my hands against his upper back to prevent the full weight of him from crashing down onto the toilet, keeping my gaze averted to give him some dignity.

I closed the bathroom door and walked down the hall to the rec room. I sat on the sofa next to Breeze, turned on the TV and switched the channel to CBC: *Hockey Night in Canada*'s theme song was already in full swing.

I would wait until intermission to tell my brother about Africa.

I NEVER TOLD MY FAMILY the other reasons that motivated me to travel to Africa beyond my desire to see exotic wildlife. Trips to Europe and Japan had ramped up my appetite for adventure and ignited my wanderlust. But going to Africa was much more than a new notch in my travel belt. By age 20, I had become captivated by the cinematography I saw in *Baraka* and *Out of Africa*. The raw beauty of the African landscapes fed my curiosity, but it was the stories about primatologists Dian Fossey and Jane Goodall that deepened my desire to travel to this distant land. I longed to be half as brave as these bold women and admired their ability to put their own goals and desires before anyone else. Over the years, I watched with envy as friends, boyfriends and school acquaintances left to pursue their goals. Instead of feeling bold and brave, I felt like I was being left behind. Stuck. Directionless.

Four years earlier, during my second year of university, I had flown to Toronto to attend an interview for a bachelor's program in interior design. I was enthralled by the aesthetics of architecture, but I think my real passion for this field stemmed from a subconscious need to create my *own space*, a place where I could thrive.

I beamed with pride the morning I tore open my acceptance letter. But by then I'd already decided not to go. Future job prospects in interior design were uncertain. The thought of incurring student loans for another four years was daunting. But those reasons were convenient excuses – my main reason for not going was family. I couldn't in good conscience move 4000 kilometres across the country. The guilt and worry would have been too much for me.

When I had moved to Japan after high school, nothing had stopped me. It never occurred to me that one day I'd feel compelled to consider others when paving my path. Sure, I was satisfied with the way my university life turned out. But my decision not to study in Toronto set a precedent. One where I made compromises instead of going after my dreams.

Graduating from university in the spring of 1994 brought me a sense of finality and accomplishment, but also an overwhelming feeling of, *Okay, now what the hell should I do?*

My life took a wonderful turn when my best friend and I signed up for a rock-climbing course a month later. I nurtured this new-found love like a zealot. Road trips to the climbing meccas of Squamish, Skaha and Smith Rock fulfilled my adventurous spirit and passion for the outdoors. Dad's and Russ's prognoses were depressing, but there was nothing wrong with *my* body. Climbing made me feel powerful. In control. It forced me to focus on the present while distracting me from family worries.

After returning home from my adrenalin-filled trips, though, the gravity of my family circumstances always set in. The short-lived thrill of my outdoor adventures was bittersweet. When I went home to visit, I kept my mountain escapades to myself. Describing a pristine alpine hike or recapping how I lead-climbed up a technical rock face made me feel like I was flaunting my healthy body and freedom.

Before Dad and Russ got sick, I had always envisioned myself travelling for longer periods and maybe working overseas. Now the prospect of being away for more than a week or two made me anxious and fearful. I needed to step things up a notch, get away for longer on my own. Backpacking in Africa seemed like a logical step toward reclaiming myself. I needed tangible proof I could become the version of myself I always thought I'd become: Brave. Adventurous. Unwilling to compromise or give in to fear.

This would be *my* trip of a lifetime.

Two

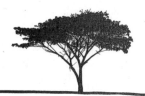

MY HEART FLUTTERED as I glided into the Vancouver airport the morning I left for Africa. I was no stranger to YVR. During my undergrad, I'd worked at the airport's foreign exchange for four years to pay rent and offset my student loans. At first it was fun to put my Japanese fluency to use in an environment where people were starting their own adventures. It didn't take long until the novelty of counting thick wads of 10,000-yen notes wore off. With my degree complete, I quit that job, vowing *never* to go back to the airport unless I was getting on a plane.

February 20, 1996, was the day I fulfilled that promise to myself. Half a dozen jet planes were spinning out of control in the pit of my stomach. Exhilaration. *Fear.* Courage. *Guilt.* Anticipation. *Worry.* This flurry of emotions messed with my head as I waited for the first leg of my long journey to begin.

I'd walked on air the day I bought my *Lonely Planet Africa* guidebook along with an 80-litre backpack: these purchases solidified my plans. However, my mounting excitement had clouded my judgment. I was lured by the pack's sale price and overlooked its poor fit and excessive space. Even with my linebacker shoulders and the pack's waist belt cinched up tightly, it was two sizes too big for my five-foot-seven, compact frame. I packed only essentials: clothes, toiletries, climbing shoes, harness, two journals, a Nikon camera, a dozen rolls of slide film, a first aid kit, my sleeping bag, mattress pad and water purifier. The pack still had plenty of room.

I made my way to the luggage check-in. As my pack disappeared down the conveyor belt, the emotional load that had been weighing me down vanished. I wandered around feeling carefree, savouring those final rousing moments before boarding when anything seemed possible. *I'm doing this. I'm actually going to Africa on my own.*

I had imagined this day for months. Now the moment of leaving everything – and everyone – behind had arrived. It was impossible to contain the excitement surging through my body.

THE DEAFENING WHIRRING of the engines subsided to a dull vibration. I craned my neck to look out the tiny window. The plane flew westward before it looped around and travelled over the marshland near my parents' neighbourhood one kilometre below.

Despite my unwavering desire to escape suburbia as a teen, I was fortunate to grow up where I did. Our family home was a short walk from the dyke located in the northwestern region of Richmond, a suburb south of Vancouver not far from the airport. From the age of 4, my connection to these local surroundings was profound. Growing up close to the dyke in the '70s and '80s introduced me to a wondrous ecosystem of plants, insects and birds nestled between farmland, marsh and ocean: nature's playground was right in my backyard. In small but significant ways, my childhood explorations served as preliminary prep work for Africa.

As children, Mike, Russ, Sue and I often walked or biked to the dyke with Mom and Dad. I only had to pedal a few minutes, northbound, along the dyke's wide gravel path before briny scents of marsh, mud and ocean reeled me in, inviting me to set my bicycle down and explore on foot. To my left, looking westward, a hazy outline of Vancouver Island hovered above the marshy expanse that hugs the Pacific Ocean. Nearby, low-lying blackberry bushes, groves of white-barked trees and clusters of bulrushes punctuated the grassy marshland's uniform canvas.

My explorer legs led me along the seemingly endless collection of sun-bleached logs that had delicately settled below the edge of the dyke. Each log was a one-of-a-kind sculpture. The perfectly long cylinders, polished and creamy gold like butter, were solid as stone and easy to walk across when it was dry but were slick in the rain. The smaller, irregularly shaped logs wobbled like teeter-totters and made my heart jump. Some were fragile and crumbled underfoot. Others had been charred by fire with rusty spikes poking out. The odd log had been soaked in creosote – a smoky, tar-like smell I grew to love – with black, oily beads glistening in the sun.

Few logs had bark still attached. Instead, they were speckled with patches of moss and flaky, yellow-orange lichen and sprouted tufts of green grass from cracks and holes. The logs pockmarked from wood-boring beetles and the ones that looked like beached sea creatures captured my imagination the most.

I loved exploring on my own, meandering back and forth, carefully planting my feet from one log to the next to avoid any gaps that might cause me to lose my balance and fall. When I lost my footing, it was a relief to land on a desiccated layer of flattened, straw-coloured grasses that blanketed the thick muck and decay. This disturbance caused tiny spiders to appear and scurry away like miniature crabs.

It seemed my legs could travel along these logs forever, or at least until the log clusters thinned to nothing but thick mud. The further I went out, the larger the gaps grew between the logs. My imagination ran wild: I was convinced the mud was quicksand. A fear of slipping, and visions of getting stuck knee-deep, prevented me from straying too far.

Mike or Russ would interrupt my solitary exploration, calling out to me using my nickname: "Hey, Bird! Over here." Sometimes Dad would gather us for a story. I can't recall the details of his storytelling, but I'll never forget the calming effects of the natural surroundings. I studied the tall, proud bulrushes, fascinated by their sponge-like texture and gravity-defying strength. The soothing sounds of a grasshopper choir filled the air as little sparrows and starlings darted between wild grasses swaying in the gentle breeze. Off in the distance above the horizon, a flock of 50 geese took flight and filed into their V formation.

I felt free and unworried. The dyke was my sanctuary, a peaceful setting in which to lose myself for an hour or two. Despite its tranquility, it also served as a window into other parts of the world. I couldn't ignore the thundering airplane overhead as we sat perched like blue herons. I gazed up toward the sky and wondered if the passengers in the plane could see us wandering below like tiny ants. I waved my little hand, hoping they would acknowledge my presence.

Over time, my longing to fly away in one of those departing planes grew stronger.

Please take me with you.

Twenty years later, I looked from the plane's window down toward the length of the dyke and my old stomping grounds. As a child, the logs I used to balance upon seemed to go on forever. Now they looked so small and insignificant to my adult eyes. My childhood fears of falling into the mucky marsh paled in comparison to the real grown-up fears that had taken hold of me – fears of getting stuck: emotionally, mentally and geographically.

As I set out for my African journey, I scanned the dyke one last time in search of human specks among the logs and bulrushes. If by chance a young, curious girl were waving up toward me, I would be sure to wave back.

AFTER A NINE-HOUR FLIGHT to Frankfurt, it would be another 16 hours until I arrived in Johannesburg. Trying to fall asleep on planes usually proves futile for my active mind. I popped a Gravol anyway, hoping this time might be different. The only time these pills had worked was when I was 14, coming home from my first trip to Japan. After downing a double dose of Gravol, I had passed out during the nine-hour flight from Tokyo. My body sat slumped sideways, calves dangling over the armrest into the aisle like baseball bats. Forty-eight hours later, I landed in the principal's office, where I was accused of underage drinking.

As predicted, during the Frankfurt flight I sat wide awake. It felt luxurious to stretch my legs across the two vacant seats next to me. For the first hour I pored over my guidebook as though it were Scripture, mine to devour with unfaltering devotion. It was easy to visualize my trip. With each turning page, the carefree act of daydreaming pushed away thoughts of family. I'd written most of my itinerary in pencil with the help of my guidebook maps: South Africa. Namibia. Zimbabwe. Malawi. Tanzania and Zanzibar. Maybe even Kenya. The prospect of seeing all these countries made me burst at the seams.

I had arranged for my cousin Rika to pick me up at the airport in Johannesburg. Despite my commitment to being a solitary backpacker, this arrangement put my parents at ease. They knew I'd be safe and sound after my arrival with a place to crash for the first few days.

In the summer of '95, I met four rock climbers from South Africa. With his confidence, quick wit and rugged good looks, Thomas was the leader of the pack. He invited me to visit him in Joburg and promised to take me to some local crags. The thought of going climbing in South Africa with Thomas thrilled me. I couldn't wait for the adventures to begin.

A few hours into the flight, a petite blonde around my age, sitting two aisles over, stood up to stretch her legs and stopped to say hello. The woman was heading to Germany for a work trip. We made an instant connection when I discovered she knew my cousin in Kamloops. She sat down in the empty seat next to me to chat. Her eyes lit up after hearing about my travel plans. Then a look of concern washed over her face when I told her I'd be backpacking alone.

"Aren't you worried about travelling all by yourself?" she asked.

"No, not really. I've always enjoyed doing things on my own," I assured her.

I've often found it easy to be myself around strangers. And yet I couldn't tell her I was more afraid of staying behind, getting stuck in a life that no longer seemed like mine to design.

Three

I LOVE THE ANTICIPATION of arriving somewhere new. I was amped to have a bit of time to explore Frankfurt before flying to South Africa. I was hoping for a little adventure to set the tone for my Africa journey, even if it was just a few hours between flights.

As soon as I walked outside, freezing temperatures and the heavy presence of smokers crushed my enthusiasm. After setting out to explore the city, my heart sank: all the shops and museums were closed because of a festival that was taking place outside the city.

I meandered from one nondescript *strasse* to another in my untarnished dark brown Blundstones, in search of something, *anything*, to lift my spirits. My carrot-coloured shorts and favourite cotton moss-green sweater added some much-needed colour to the swatches of grey that painted the city streets. The dark, cloud-filled sky appeared ominous. It felt like the shadow of dread had followed me across the Atlantic, ensuring I wouldn't forget about everything I had left behind.

It wasn't only my family situation that was grey. My love life hadn't been particularly rosy either. Up until my departure, I'd been seeing a buff, intelligent climber for two months. I had always embraced my independence and didn't mind being single. But the Christmas season and winter months had a tendency to bring my spirits down – a few relationship breakups and Dad's and Russ's illnesses had that effect on me. This was the first time I'd dated someone because the companionship offered a much-needed distraction from my family situation.

I enjoyed Ryan's easygoing company. But it wasn't love. At least not for me. Aside from our love of climbing, we didn't have a lot in common. I could overlook our dietary differences – he was vegan, I wasn't – but I found some of his views on sex almost as off-putting as his love of death metal.

Confronting my emotions rarely comes easy for me and I've always struggled with open, honest communication. Instead of breaking up with Ryan, I promised to write and phone, leaving him with the impression our relationship would continue. He seemed excited about my return: I didn't see the point of ending it, nor could I summon the courage to do so.

When my skin could no longer tolerate Frankfurt's winter chill, I ducked into a colourful curry house with fluorescent lighting and a friendly host. I made notes in my guidebook, nibbling on a samosa and sipping a mango lassi.

I had to be patient.

HALFWAY THROUGH the 11-hour flight to Johannesburg, my fingers danced like little puppets. I didn't care if the cloud cover blanketing Central Africa made me conjure up images on my own. I closed my eyes and let my mind wander. I saw giraffes galloping across the grasslands like slow-motion horses, a band of mountain gorillas grooming each other under a thick canopy of trees, herds of elephants cooling off in shallow pools of muddy water, lazy lions grazing under shady patches of umbrella trees.

Hours later, I was immersed in my guidebook when I heard the pilot's announcement: we were flying over Zambia. I peeked out the window. My heart sped up when I saw the cloud curtain had parted to reveal wide open plains, lush green with streaks of amber, mountainous hills and drier, ochre-stained slivers of land. I had barely slept in the last 20 hours, but my body tingled with electricity as soon as the meandering Zambezi came into focus. The sun's rays illuminated the river's metallic hairpin curves, revealing its unexpected rapids and abrupt changes in direction, foretelling the coming months of my unpredictable journey.

My hand gripped the armrest tightly. As the plane flew over Lusaka, Lake Kariba shimmered silver in the sunlight, signalling that in less than three hours I would be stepping onto African soil. Sure, I was thousands of metres up in the sky, but I was here – in Africa. My heart pounded like a fearless lioness.

SOMEHOW RIKA and I missed each other at arrivals. Luckily, we both had the sense to page one another and met at the info booth. I recognized my cousin by her short dark hair and thick-framed glasses. Her tall swimmer's physique was clad in mid-thigh athletic shorts and a faded cotton T-shirt. She waved excitedly and didn't hesitate to pull me in for a big hug. Despite our 15-year age gap, and the fact we were practically strangers, my older cousin's friendly nature made us mesh from the get-go.

"Welcome to South Africa, Lisa! Are you tired? You *must* be really tired." Rika studied my face. "Wow. You sure look like your mother."

With blue-eyed parents, I somehow ended up with golden-ringed green eyes. I had my light-brown, shoulder-length hair cropped to my chin, losing my natural highlights. Mom envied my thicker, wavy locks and always had her short, fine, chestnut hair permed. But one look at our jawlines and cheekbones and there was no mistake: I was my mother's daughter. The only traits I'd seemed to inherit from my raven-haired father were his dry sense of humour, poor eyesight and a predisposition to worry.

"Yeah, I get that a lot. And, yes, I *am* tired. But I doubt I can sleep."

It was a comfortable 20 degrees Celsius outside. I shed my sweater and threw my backpack into the trunk of Rika's Toyota with a thud.

Her home in the suburb of Roodepoort was 30 kilometres outside of Johannesburg. During the drive, I assumed Rika would inquire as to how Mom, Dad and Russ were doing. To my relief, she began discussing the political climate that had unfolded in South Africa following Nelson Mandela's 1990 release after 27 years of imprisonment.

"Since Mandela became president, it's a pretty exciting time to be living here. Lots of South Africans are worried about how the country is changing under his rule. But so many of us are ready for positive change."

Rika's optimism made me hopeful about the country's post-apartheid future. It was a relief knowing she held liberal-minded views on what could have been an awkward and contentious topic.

While driving along the highway from the airport, she began giggling to herself like a schoolgirl. She turned to me. "Oh my goodness. Do you remember the first time we met?"

"No, not really," I replied.

In 1974, I was 2 and a half years old the first time I boarded an airplane. My family travelled to the Netherlands to meet Mom's vast clan for a family reunion to commemorate my grandparents' 50th wedding anniversary. It seemed overpopulating the planet wasn't a concern for my extended family. Mom and her seven siblings all walked down the traditional path of marriage. Over two decades, two dozen grandchildren were born across four continents: I was the youngest tribe member.

It was in a quaint Frisian town where teenage Rika, clad in bell-bottom jeans and a geometric-patterned blouse, met me for the first time. Our relatives gathered from Canada, South Africa and New Zealand. The local newspaper snapped our photo and wrote an article about this rare family gathering – it was big news for this little dot on the map.

Even though this had been my first dose of international travel, I was much too young to remember the reunion. Nonetheless, the evidence of the trip, including local newspaper clippings, photographs of me strapped into a child harness and stories retold by my parents, left a big impact on me.

Rika chuckled away. "That day you met me, you had such an un-impressed look on your cute little face. You were *so* disappointed that even though I was *African*, I wasn't Black."

"What? Really?" I laughed back. "I don't remember that at all." I was surprised to learn that, at such a young age, impressions and stereotypes of Africanness had already formed in my mind. I'm sure I had *National Geographic* to thank for that.

We pulled up to Rika's driveway. Her spacious property was buffered by large shady trees and tall tropical plants. She led me around back to a concrete patio in full sun. My jaw dropped when I saw the open, grassy backyard and pristine outdoor below-ground pool. By my Canadian standards it wasn't extravagant, but compared to my family's humble, above-ground, solar-heated pool, Rika's looked like the Hilton.

French doors from the patio led us into a warm interior of teak furnishings. Well-placed windows let in streams of sun onto the hardwood floors, casting a perfect blend of light and shadow onto the cream-coloured walls. The house's cozy, open-concept style was in stark contrast to my parents' dated home. I was impressed by the living room, decorated with African fabric wall hangings and animal sculptures made of hardwood and soapstone. Nothing about the home seemed excessive or pretentious – its tasteful design reminded me of the interiors I admired in architectural magazines. Of course, I was well aware that the majority of people in Joburg didn't live like this. Rika's home would have seemed like a castle compared to those living in the Black townships like Soweto that I had read about and seen in photographs.

I napped for a few hours then woke to the sounds of feet padding on hardwood floors. Hushed voices spilled out from the downstairs hallway as I went to the bathroom to put in my contact lenses. Rika's young son and daughter peeked around the corner from the kitchen and greeted me with huge smiles. In an instant, their initial shyness in meeting "the Canadian cousin" was replaced with curiosity. They looked adorable holding a printed map of BC, my home province. They placed it on the kitchen table and asked me to show them where I lived.

I had been in Africa less than five hours and I was already talking about home.

THE NEXT MORNING RIKA TOOK ME on a drive through the outskirts of her neighbourhood. My skin and tongue were parched from the dry air gusting through the open windows of the car, but I revelled in the warmth. I watched a few tumbleweeds bounce, hesitate, then somersault across the road. They reminded me of suicide squirrels back home. We were somewhere in between the suburbs and the countryside. The accumulation of subtle differences – indigenous grasses, giant cacti plants, exotic trees, the lower humidity, signage in both English and Afrikaans, and the fact we were driving on the "wrong" side of the road – made me feel excited about being away from home.

After picking up my anti-malaria pills from the pharmacy, Rika took the kids and me to the Sterkfontein caves northwest of Joburg. Located in the "Cradle of Humankind," these famous lime caves are known for their fossils and hominid discoveries.

When we entered the visitor centre, I briefed myself on the history. The two-million-year-old skull of "Mrs. Ples," along with the three-million-year-old skeletal remains known as "Little Foot," were the most famous discoveries found inside the caves. Reading about fossils and artifacts that are *millions* of years old is mind-boggling to me, almost as unfathomable as believing in the concept of a god or supernatural powers.

We descended a staircase into the first cave and joined the tour. Despite the guide's thick accent, I was able to surmise that paleontologist Robert Broom had discovered the fossilized remains of an adult man-ape at this location. Our guide led us to an open, artificially lit area where the ceilings extended upward over 30 metres. I gazed up in awe at the jagged white limestone walls and grottos. The damp, cool air felt primal and invigorating. Water dripped slowly from yellow-stained mineral clusters, creating playful echoes: *Plip. Plip. Plip.* It was hard to imagine what the cave would have looked like in its natural, unaltered state.

I turned around and noticed two tourists from Japan had joined our group. My propensity to speak to complete strangers – *especially* Japanese people – has always given me immense pleasure. In the late '80s and early '90s, I worked summer evenings as a tour guide accompanying tourists on yachts while they soaked up Vancouver's gorgeous ocean sunsets.

I had no qualms chatting with the two tourists at the Sterkfontein caves. I naturally fell into the role of informal guide, asking them about their travels in South Africa, and translating what I could given my lack of vocabulary related to stalactites and stalagmites. The Japanese couple gave me the usual, "*Waa, nihongo ga jouzu desu ne?*" (Wow, you're good at Japanese, aren't you?) – a reaction to which I had grown accustomed. I humbly replied, "*Iie, amari*" (No, not really), which made them praise me even more.

I felt proud showing off my fluency in front of my cousin: proof I could achieve a major goal without anything stopping me. It also reminded me that I never know where on earth I might end up using my Japanese skills. I was happy to discover that Africa was no exception.

THE FOLLOWING DAY I masked my disappointment when Rika took me to Pretoria, the administrative capital of South Africa. The design of the parliamentary Union Buildings combined a variety of styles, from neoclassical to Edwardian. Despite my studies in architectural history, I found the sandstone structures bland as boiled chicken: I just couldn't get excited about English-inspired gardens and overstated colonial architecture.

It was a huge relief that Rika kept the tour brief. During the one-hour drive back to Joburg, she told me owners of BMWs and

VW Kombis were often targeted for their cars. Once stolen, the vehicles were disassembled in minutes flat for parts and became impossible to trace.

I've never really cared what kind of car someone drives, unless it's a behemoth, gas-guzzling SUV. Rika explained her husband was expected to drive a higher-status vehicle to reflect his position as a bank manager. But he couldn't be bothered. It wasn't worth the risk, and neither he nor Rika felt the need to prove their social status by the brand of car they drove.

Rika went on to tell me how South Africa had changed over the last few years. "Since Mandela became president, there's been a big effort to employ more Black South Africans because of affirmative action, to right the wrongs of apartheid. But there are many whites worried about losing their jobs. A lot of them work long hours to prove their worth to employers."

She talked about an increase in cases of Black South Africans being hired for jobs and put into senior positions without sufficient skills, training or education.

It was hard for me, as an outsider, to have a balanced opinion on South African politics. I understood how whites would feel frustrated being replaced by someone less qualified. But I sympathized more with the Black majority and their need to feel empowered. After centuries of racism and oppression, who could blame them for wanting a better life?

BY MY THIRD DAY, I was growing antsy: suburbia wasn't what I'd had in mind when I set out to discover Africa. Staying at Rika's comfortable home offered me a glimpse into how some privileged white South Africans lived, but it prevented my identity as a bold, independent traveller from unfolding. Instead of letting her show me around, I wanted to tackle the open road on my own. I felt like a fraud, an imposter of the backpacker world. I had to get moving and travel on my own.

I still hadn't heard from my climber friend Thomas. It was a colossal relief when, four days after my arrival, his mom received my telegram message – a dated communication tool even for the '90s. She invited us over for tea, explaining that Thomas had gone climbing for the weekend but was due back the next day.

En route to Thomas's home, Rika and her husband took me on a quick drive-by tour of Johannesburg. I had few expectations of South Africa's largest city. Back home, I had read news stories about its staggering crime rate. My guidebook warned travellers about violent muggings, even in daylight. And yet, from the inside of a moving car, I couldn't see any evidence of its unfavourable reputation. A few eye-catching heritage buildings stood out, but Joburg's grid design, large stadium, shopping plazas and glass skyscrapers made it seem like I was visiting some random city in the American Midwest.

While driving through the Hillbrow district, Rika told me it wasn't safe for us to walk around. As someone accustomed to walking freely on the streets back home, I questioned whether or not there were any real threats. I thought perhaps suburbanites were cautious or overprotective. When we pulled into Thomas's neighbourhood, it looked perfectly safe to me. That was until I noticed the barbed wire attached to some of the fences.

Thomas's mom greeted us with warmth and openness as we gathered in her small kitchen. She raised her thick eyebrows. "You're not going travelling all by yourself, are you?"

"Yeah. I'm hoping to make it all the way to Kenya, assuming I don't run out of time…or money," I replied with conviction.

Nothing I had seen or heard up until then had made me question my solo mission. If anything, being in suburbia had made my desire to travel alone even stronger.

That evening, Thomas pulled up to Rika's driveway in his light-blue, vintage sports car. He looked amped from his recent adventure. His unshaven face glowed a deep tan, his grin was nonchalant and unworried, his dimpled chin exuded male confidence. He hopped out of the car, and I moved in to give him a quick hug.

"Yay! You're here. How's Africa so far? Looks like it suits you."

"I love it. But I really want to start backpacking."

"I hear you. First, you need to spend some time with me. I'll give you a taste of South Africa that you can't get in the city. I guess you haven't done any climbing since you got here?"

"No, not yet. I'd love to, though."

"Don't worry. I'll take you this weekend. I've arranged a trip with some friends."

My excitement grew as Thomas drove us over to the Yeoville district of Joburg. He parked his MG without the assistance of homeless parallel-parking assistants looking to earn some cash – a common sight I observed in the business district.

The sunset left a rosy tint in the sky. I did a quick scan of the block as we jaywalked across the quiet street. The neighbourhood storefronts were vibrant and edgy. It looked safe to stroll around in the early evening. I was relieved to see an ethnically diverse group of people walking in and out of artsy coffee shops and restaurants.

Thomas took me to Iyavaya, a local restaurant featuring authentic dishes from a variety of African nations. The dimly lit dining room had a minimalist décor – bare white walls with some framed artwork – yet the boisterous chatter and tantalizing aromas wafting from the kitchen created a warm, welcoming ambiance.

My mouth watered in anticipation of the seafood stew I'd ordered. While waiting for our meals to arrive, Thomas and I chatted about South African politics before moving on to some of his recent climbing escapades. It was hard to contain our laughter when he reminisced about his attempt to hitchhike from Vancouver to California with his climbing buddies using a cardboard sign.

"Oh, man. Everyone talks about how friendly Canadians are, but *no one* stopped for us. We must have waited for over an hour before this guy pulled over and told us we were standing on the wrong side of the highway," he laughed. Listening to Thomas's story made me eager for my own adventures to begin.

"I've got tomorrow off. You up for some caving?" I didn't need any convincing and agreed immediately. It was such a relief to be in his company and have someone share my love of the outdoors.

The server walked over and placed a steaming plate in front of me. I inhaled the succulent smell and felt a rush. This was my first time eating couscous: I had no expectations except that I hoped the delicious aroma matched its flavour. I scooped up a spoonful and blew into the mound before taking a mouthful. Instead of scarfing it down, I savoured my first bite: the couscous's nutty texture complemented the spiced sauce of the tender stew to perfection.

Finally. I am in Africa. I smiled and took another bite.

THE NEXT MORNING Rika drove me to Thomas's, where I would stay until I began backpacking.

"Thank you for everything, Rika," I said as I gave her a big hug.

"Pleasure. Call if you run into any problems, okay? And be safe," she said.

"Don't worry. I'll be fine. I'll send you postcards. See you in June."

As planned, Thomas took me caving in Mamelodi, 80 kilometres northeast of Joburg. During the two-hour drive, I looked over at Thomas seated behind the wheel and thought of Dad, who loved to travel in style in a string of MG sports cars in the late 1950s.

Dad had always been tight-lipped about his childhood. The shame he carried after his parents divorced in the 1940s lasted decades. I knew a few details. His father remarried while Dad and his sister lived with their mother, who suffered from "nervous breakdowns" and had no means to support them. Dad always told me she died when he was 14. Years later, my aunt revealed their mom had died from surgery complications when Dad was 18. I felt cheated by his deception. No wonder I carried my own sense of shame in matters of family: Dad had passed it down to me.

After his mother's death, Dad worked and studied hard despite leaving high school before graduating. During his two-year stint working at a pulp mill in Prince Rupert, he had his coveted pale-green convertible MG shipped on a barge back to Vancouver, before driving it more than 5000 kilometres to southern Mexico with his buddy.

The long road trip he took down south had always impressed me. I remember the photo of him seated at an outdoor patio in Acapulco, black horn-rimmed glasses framing the pure, infectious glint in his eyes. I was struck by how happy he looked. No illness. No worries. Just the open road, sandy beaches and sunny skies to look forward to – his reward for working in the cold, rainy climate of remote, northwestern BC.

It wasn't until I was older that I understood how much Dad loved cars and going on road trips. The loss of his driver's licence crushed his spirit. It seemed so cruel that he was not able to enjoy his well-deserved freedom after working hard his whole life.

"Have you done much caving before?" Thomas asked.

"Just once on Vancouver Island. There's some really cool caves at Horne Lake. But you can stand up in them, so it was pretty low key."

"Well, the caves we're going to, we won't be upright much. Be prepared to do some crawling on your belly," Thomas said with a laugh.

I buzzed with anticipation but couldn't stop biting my thumbnail. Thomas was a seasoned caver. I wasn't sure what I'd gotten myself into.

We exited the car. I followed Thomas toward the cave entrance. I stopped in my tracks when I almost stepped on a pair of thick-bodied, colourful insects. The two grasshoppers were perched upon a flat rock between tufts of grass. As big as baby feet, their bodies cast little shadows onto the russet clay soil. I studied their brilliant markings. One was avocado green with a cinnamon trim. The other boasted bright crimson markings on its head and legs and had a zebra-striped abdomen. Thomas turned round and saw the look of fascination on my face.

"Ah, yes. The mighty *koppie* grasshoppers…Gorgeous, aren't they? Don't be fooled. Those sneaky bastards produce a toxic foam. My friend's dog got really sick after it played with one of them."

Back home, the grasshoppers I had heard but rarely seen were tiny, the colour of dull pears. After seeing these unique foaming koppies, I *knew* I was in Africa.

Outside the cave entrance, we put on our helmets and clicked on the headlamps. We hadn't even begun spelunking, yet my palms were already sweaty. The prospect of crawling around in cramped spaces filled me with nervous energy.

The primal smell of concrete, like underground parking stalls, has always had a rousing effect on me. As soon as I entered the cave, I inhaled deeply, relishing its intoxicating mustiness, feeling the rush of pleasure like an addict.

Thomas and I got onto all fours and quickly began crawling onto our elbows, knees and bellies. We slithered through the first underground passage like a couple of swift-moving snails. It was thrilling to be underground, exploring a place so few people spent time in.

"Oh man, this is so freakin' cool!" I exclaimed, unable to contain my enthusiasm.

It didn't take long before the cave narrowed. My initial rush of adrenaline was replaced by mild trepidation: there was no quick exit if something went wrong. A feeling of unease swelled up in my throat when the top of my helmet scraped the shallow cave roof, sounding like an animal's claws against a cage door.

I had no choice but to keep moving and follow the soles of Thomas's boots into the dark void. When my hip brushed up against the wall of damp, hard sediment, my heart jumped out of my chest. The more I tensed up, the more difficult it was to steady my breathing. How was it I could tie into a rope, climb more than 20 metres up a rock face and not feel scared, but dragging my belly across a cave floor at a sloth's pace made me anxious? It wasn't as though there was a threat of a flash flood that would fill the cave and drown us. Nor was it likely the cave walls would spontaneously collapse and crush our bodies. Rationally, I knew we were quite safe: panicking served no purpose. Yet the more ground we covered, the more my mind raced – and the more trapped I felt.

I imagined this was how Dad and Russ must have felt: trapped, their movements inhibited, unable to see what lay ahead in the darkness. Of course, the crucial difference was their narrowing cave was inescapable. I could leave whenever I wanted to.

I needed to get a grip and calm myself down. Unlike the fear that had held me back before, this fear was different, a natural reaction to my immediate environment. Soon it would pass.

From my ragged breath and nervous mumblings, Thomas must have picked up on my discomfort. I was thankful to have his reassuring voice preventing me from freaking out further. "All right. That was the tightest section. This next passage opens up again just now."

A minute later, the cave widened enough to fit the two of us side by side, standing hunched over. I got up off the ground and looked around the cave without feeling constricted. My breathing returned to normal.

"Come over here and have a look at this," Thomas said.

He was shining his headlamp onto the moisture-laden floor to reveal some unusual discoveries: cow skulls, used candles, an unrecognizable rusted metal object, a ball of yarn.

I kneeled down for a closer inspection. "Ha. Weird. These sure are random. Maybe it's some kind of underground riddle for us to solve?" I joked.

Just then, a small colony of bats flapped and fluttered inches above our heads. Within seconds, they vanished into the dark abyss. I found their fleeting presence amusing and a welcome distraction. Seeing them made me wonder what other animals and life forms were lurking in the shadows.

I had finally started to relax again when Thomas announced, "Y'know, these caves are rife with bat shit. You gotta be careful. If you inhale too much of it, you can get cave disease."

I took a moment to absorb his words. *Why the hell are you telling me this now?*

"Thanks, Thomas. Definitely *not* what I wanted to hear right now."

He laughed it off. "Ha. I'm sure we'll be just fine. I haven't got it yet."

Thomas was probably right. But his crash course on histoplasmo-
sis left me feeling unsettled. In the days and weeks that followed,
anytime I had a tickle in my throat or coughed, I thought *maybe, just
maybe*, the spores of bat guano fungus had lodged themselves into
my lungs. If I got sick, my travel plans would be ruined. Or worse, I'd
have to return home.

We explored the cave for nearly two hours. The sun's rays were laser
beams to my eyes when we emerged from the darkness. Thick, dark-
brown muck covered us from our cheeks to our ankles. We dragged
ourselves over to the nearby watering hole to wash off, smirking at
one another's dishevelled appearances.

A group of locals around our age were sitting at the river's edge,
drinking some beers. They shot us looks of alarm and curiosity. Our
stained shirts and pants made us look like we had just finished up
a serious match of mud wrestling. But I didn't care. The last thing
on my mind was how I appeared to a bunch of strangers. I had just
survived my first *real* caving adventure. I was just happy to be outside
in the daylight again, surrounded by nothing but fresh air and the
infinite blue sky.

AS PROMISED, Thomas arranged a weekend of climbing and camping
with a group of his friends. Two days later he drove the two of us to
Waterval Boven, a popular sport climbing area 240 kilometres east
of Johannesburg.

Climbing wasn't just a distraction from my family worries – the
sport opened an entirely new world for me. Experiencing first-hand
the adrenalin rush of scaling geographical wonders and making
friends with strangers through a shared love of granite, sandstone
and basalt became addictive. Post-university, it was refreshing to be
away from an academic setting and have something exciting to balance my mundane work life delivering mail. It was a bonus that this

outdoor pursuit proved an effective way to meet people, socially *and* romantically.

A few months earlier at the climbing gym, the cover of a *Rock and Ice* magazine caught my attention. It featured a striking photo of the climbing route "Restaurant at the End of the Universe" in Waterval Boven. It was hard to believe I was now going to be in the same area, climbing in one of South Africa's most beautiful crags.

Thomas's climbing buddies weren't arriving until the morning. After setting up camp, we walked over to the humble campsite diner for supper. A stout, big-busted woman, whom Thomas unaffectionately referred to as Big Bertha, stood behind the counter and seemed to be the only one in charge.

Bertha threw us a nasty look and muttered something unintelligible in Afrikaans toward the kitchen. She watched us like a hawk as we took our seats at a table next to the window.

"You can't sit there," she scoffed. "*Dat* table is for six."

We looked around. There was only one other person in the diner. We moved to a table for two.

Boxy Bertha's eyes stayed on us as she stomped toward our table in matronly heavy-soled shoes. She set down two small glasses of water. My eyes locked with hers for a few seconds before I looked away. Her lips were pursed tightly like her short, permed curls. She had mastered the art of scowling with all the colours of the South African flag.

"Ve're sold out of *die potjies*," she blurted out with an air of annoyance.

Bertha walked away before we had time to ask her any questions about the slim menu of *potjies* (stews), sandwiches and soups. Clearly, hospitality wasn't her strong suit.

Thomas, a descendent of British blood, didn't hold back his aversion for this crotchety Afrikaner. When she returned to take our order, his demeanour turned surly. Like a bratty pubescent, he whispered, "Beerthaaa, Beeeerthaaaa," over and over, barely loud enough for her to hear.

Thomas spilled some toothpicks onto the table then flicked a few across the floor in her direction. I shifted in my seat and shot him a disapproving look. Sure, Bertha had been curt from the moment we walked in, but Thomas was being immature. I did little to stop him, however.

After she plopped down our soup and sandwiches, Thomas began crying out in an absurd, high-pitched voice. He sounded like an injured baboon. I laughed awkwardly, even though I was uncomfortable condoning his churlish behaviour. I didn't think Bertha deserved the extent of his provocation. But as far as Thomas was concerned, she had it coming.

I quickly discovered Thomas and I didn't always see eye to eye. Over supper, we had a heated conversation that really got my blood boiling.

"I think there would be less problems if more women were in power," I said casually.

"Well, there's a reason why there are so few women in positions of power," he replied.

"What do you mean?" I asked, keeping my voice steady.

"Women just don't have what it takes to be effective leaders. They always take things so personally and get so emotionally worked up."

I was blindsided and shocked by Thomas's statement. Seconds earlier, our discussion about African leaders and corrupt politicians had been nothing more than a cordial match of tennis. We'd been rallying back and forth, back and forth. Then, *bam!* Out of nowhere, he served a shot between my eyes. Now I was squirming in my seat, dreading the direction the conversation seemed to be taking.

I took a moment and paused before responding. Debating political or social issues had never been a forte of mine. Immediately I was dumped into a zone of discomfort and insecurity. All of a sudden, I felt like I had travelled back in time to one of my family dinners.

My family always ate meals together. Suppertime was fairly laid back, but my siblings and I all had to say grace before eating, always had to finish what was on our plate and always had to help with the dishes.

As I got older, it sometimes felt like I was dining with strangers. In my household, meaningful discussions at the dinner table were few and far between. Despite my strong resemblance to my mother, I often wondered how I was related to my parents. We didn't share the same opinions on religion, sex, the environment or politics. As a teenager, if I challenged their household rules and decisions, they preferred to mute my voice instead of letting me engage in grown-up debates.

Sunday mornings:

"But I don't like going to church. I don't understand why I have to go. Dad and the boys *never* go. Why do I have to?" I protested, pointing out the double standard that always irked me.

"You're *going*, and that's final. No more arguing. Get in the car."

The odd Friday evening:

"But you haven't given me a good enough reason. *Why* can't I go to the dance tonight? All my friends are allowed to go."

"Because we said so. Now, that's enough. You're not going, you hear?"

I heard my parents loud and clear. On some level I knew they were just trying to keep me on the straight and narrow path, especially after the night my sister came home stinking drunk when I was 11. Dad went ballistic, assuming the worst had happened to Sue when two of her friends, both boys, brought her home. I can still hear his enraged voice yelling at Mom, "Check to see if she was raped!"

Eventually, I learned to keep my thoughts to myself. Instead, I quietly imagined the day I would no longer be living in their household. My parents often quashed my attempts to question the status quo and challenge their decision making, never allowing me to become a confident, critical thinker – that identity could only be nurtured once I was away from home. But even then, I shied away from debates to avoid conflict.

I took a few sips of water and looked out the window. Sitting across from Thomas, I became that muted girl at the family dinner table again. My body became hot and flustered. Eloquent rebuttals formed in my head, but I remained speechless, fearful I might choke on my words. I knew my inability to effectively argue would only make Thomas's argument stronger.

"There have been lots of successful female leaders in the world," I began, scrambling to come up with my next serve.

"All right, go ahead...Name some of them then," he countered.

Blood rushed up to my face like Old Faithful, my insecurity mounting with each passing second. I felt like I was letting the entire female population down by only coming up with a handful of examples: Queen Elizabeth, Marie Curie, Oprah Winfrey. The Icelandic president whose name escaped me. Kim Campbell, Canada's only female prime minister, who had been in power for four short months and only by default. I believed my list to be thin and thought it best to remain tight-lipped instead of giving Thomas the satisfaction of thinking he was right.

"Well, your comments simplify a complex topic," I argued, unable to complete my thoughts, desperate to change the subject.

Thomas's stance that world leaders had mostly been men was an indisputable fact. However, his belief that women were weaker and inherently inferior infuriated me. He didn't take into account social or cultural politics, the history and oppression of women and minorities, or alternate definitions of success, power and leadership.

I thought of Mom as she went from her job as a caregiver for disabled children to fulfilling her maternal duties as a mother of four, volunteering as a companion for seniors, and then returning to the role of caregiver after Dad and Russ got ill. It was rare for her to *ever* put her own needs first. No holidays. No days off. She never complained or acted bitterly about the responsibilities she took on as a mother and wife. She certainly didn't let her *emotions* take over.

Here I was in Africa, travelling on my own terms, while she was stuck at home caring for grown men too weak to care for themselves. She exemplified great strength and a rare form of leadership. The kind society often doesn't recognize or value. I didn't know any men brave or strong enough in character to endure what she had.

In the end I felt helpless. Trying to articulate any valid points in order to change Thomas's opinion was an uphill battle I wasn't prepared to take on. I changed the topic to climbing to avoid further tension. Throughout my life I have learned repeatedly that avoidance is an ineffective way to deal with my problems. And yet, sometimes, it's the only way I cope with difficult situations.

THE NEXT MORNING, after some bouldering, Thomas and I headed over to the Flying Is Fun crag to get in some single-pitch climbs before his friends arrived.

The climbing calluses on my fingers and palms from training indoors during the winter had softened since arriving in Africa, but my grip strength and muscle memory were still intact. My rubber soles stuck to the wall's tiny nubbins and low-profile edges with little effort. I was happy to show off my technical skills and be on a more level playing field with Thomas *above* ground. It was a thrill for me to lead-climb a few routes up the shorter quartzite rock face.

Thomas's friends showed up at noon. With only one rope among the six of us, it was difficult to get in lots of routes. We did more socializing than climbing, but it was still wonderful to be outside and enjoy the camaraderie of fellow adventurers. I didn't come to Africa expecting to do lots of climbing: Waterval Boven was an added bonus.

With little shade, my yet-to-be-tanned skin sizzled in the unforgiving sun until thick clouds arrived to veil the humid sky. We were taken off guard when a thunderstorm rolled in. A brief downpour forced us to scurry back to the camp like a pack of drowned rock rats. But not all was lost. By the time we got back, the rain had lightened to a refreshing mist, and then the clouds thinned. We spent the rest of the muggy afternoon having fun swimming in the campsite's outdoor pool.

The uncomfortable conversation between Thomas and me never came up again. After spending a few days with him, I assumed his more conservative South African upbringing and experiences as a privileged white male contributed to his way of thinking. All I could do was accept the fact that I couldn't alter his opinion overnight.

Despite our tense debate, I had fun with Thomas and was grateful he'd gifted me my first real adventures in Africa. After we returned to Joburg, I was more than ready to hit the road on my own.

Four

A DARK-SKINNED MAN with exquisite cheekbones rushed to open the passenger door for me. "You must be Lisa." His charismatic smile shone brightly and made me feel welcome. "I'm Vincent. I'll be driving you to the Drakensberg." I could have listened to Vincent talk for hours. I didn't hear British or Afrikaner dialects in his accent. He enunciated every word beautifully, giving each syllable equal importance.

Vincent stood half a foot taller than me, but his long, tapered forearms weren't any thicker than mine. I moved toward the open door. "I'll get that for you," he said in a friendly tone. He lifted my pack off my shoulder with little effort despite his thin build.

"Thank you, Vincent. I'm so happy you could fit me in with such short notice." I squeezed myself into the last remaining seat of the Kombi's compact quarters.

I had no idea getting to the Drakensberg mountains would be so difficult. There were no public buses going to the Royal Natal National Park. Taking the train to Ladysmith meant a 1:00 a.m. arrival, and I would have had to figure out the last hundred kilometres on my own. Hitchhiking wasn't an option given the high crime rate.

My hope was restored after I called the Rockey Street hostel from Thomas's. The Walkabout-Bus, a carpool service catering to backpackers, drove to the park every few days. "There's one spot left, but the Kombi leaves at ten this morning," the hostel host had told me.

"Can you get here in an hour?" Thomas said he could drive me. "Yes, I'll be there...please don't let anyone take it."

Fearful I'd be stuck in Joburg if I missed this ride, I frantically packed up my belongings. Thomas assured me camping in the park was safe, so I stuffed his spare tent into my pack.

I was the only lone traveller among the five passengers. The seating was so tight my knees knocked up against the woman next to me each time the bus hit a bump. Dressed in an ankle-length, flowy skirt and hiking boots, I thought she looked like a modern hippie. Considering our intimate quarters, I thought it would be strange if I didn't introduce myself.

"Nice to meet you, Lisa. I'm Rowen. This is my boyfriend, Simon," she replied warmly.

Rowen's long, golden locks were pulled back in a low ponytail. A few loose strands grazed her cherub cheeks. I assumed she was an Aussie or Kiwi, but I didn't want to get it wrong. Simon threw me a friendly hello, his hawk-like features softened by a relaxed grin.

"So what are you doing in the Drakensberg?" he asked, his brown eyes squinting.

"I'm camping for a couple of nights. And definitely going to do some hiking," I replied.

"Oh, camping sounds fun," Rowen remarked with a hint of envy. "We're not set up to camp. The cabins are pretty pricey, so we're just going for the day, maybe one night. Then we're heading to the coast to spend a few days in Durban. I'm not sure if we'll have time to hike, but we'll definitely check out some of the waterfalls."

"You're camping by yourself?" Simon asked.

"Yeah, I've done a fair bit of camping and hiking back home, so I'm not really worried." Simon cocked one brow and nodded. I couldn't tell if he approved of my plan or not.

"How long will you be travelling in South Africa?" Rowen asked.

"Probably a month or so. Depends on how long I stay in Cape Town. I'm heading there after the Garden Route. You?"

"We're from Australia and halfway through our gap year. We'll be in Africa for another three weeks."

Rowen and Simon looked a couple of years younger than me. I could tell by their friendly banter and laid-back manners we'd get along. Despite my desire to travel solo, I was happy to share this ride with them.

Talking to people I didn't know hadn't always come easy for me. Unless I was among close friends, I'd always been too self-conscious and introverted to put myself out there. It wasn't until my late teens that I adopted my mom's ability not to worry about what people think. Whether it was walking along the dyke, shopping at the grocery store or just passing someone on our street, Mom always made talking to strangers look so easy.

My most memorable moment of her in her element was during our 1985 family trip to Europe. Our travels began in London, and I was completely smitten with the city. Along with my sister, I pretended to be British, perfecting my best English dialect while donning a T-shirt with "I Love London" written five times across my chest in bright green and blue uppercase lettering.

Mom, Sue and I were crossing Westminster Bridge toward Big Ben on foot. Walking briskly toward us was a short male figure clad in traditional British parliamentary attire. The man really looked out of place. And then things got stranger when Mom, without an inkling of hesitation, strolled right up to him and said, "Hi Mike!" like they were old friends.

Our jaws dropped when we realized she was talking to Michael J. Fox. He just happened to be in England filming a *Family Ties* episode that summer. Sue and I were ecstatic to see a celebrity we adored, but we were mortified Mom had stopped to talk to him to explain we lived next door to his sister.

Mike's friendly reception toward Mom was genuine. He looked so young and healthy back then – it was hard to believe he would be diagnosed with Parkinson's a year after Dad's diagnosis. I have no idea why Sue and I were so embarrassed by Mom's easygoing nature. This experience showed me wonderful things can happen if I'm willing to put myself out there rather than worrying about how I appear to others.

A few hours into the 400-kilometre drive, it became evident we were travelling through unpopulated territory. I was pumped to leave the city behind and have my first adventure on my own. Drakensberg, South Africa's largest mountain range, sounded like the perfect destination for my solo journey. Dragon Mountain, called Quathlamba – the Battlement of the Spears – in Zulu, borders the tiny country of Lesotho, an enclave within South Africa. While reading about this magical mountain range, I became enchanted by the descriptions of its hiking trails, unique rock features and abundant waterfalls. I couldn't wait to spend a few days there.

I stared out the window of the Walkabout-Bus. The farmland seemed to have dried up and few cars passed by. Three men were walking along the highway shoulder. A few others sat on a makeshift wooden bench and appeared to be waiting – for what, I wasn't sure.

A few kilometres later, a small herd of goats grazed in an unfenced field. I marvelled at a woman carrying a baby on her back, effortlessly balancing a large rectangular jug on her head. Two young children trailed behind her. The smaller child dragged a long stick that kicked up dust. The other carried a sack of fruit resembling papayas. The sight of the fruit made my stomach grumble and my mouth water. In my rush to leave, I hadn't packed a lunch.

During the drive, my mind began to wander to the idea of being in the wild alone. After some quiet contemplation, I thought it might be more fun to have some company while camping and hiking in an unfamiliar mountain range. I doubt Simon and Rowen had any idea they had become targets for my clever scheme to invite them to join me. Since I knew they were planning on a single day trip in the park, I thought I'd use this as my opening.

I turned to Rowen and delivered my pitch: "You know, my South African friend told me one day isn't long enough to see the Drakensberg. I'm happy to share my tent if you and Simon want to spend a few days in the park."

As soon as the words left my mouth, I prepared myself for rejection, half expecting the Aussies to politely decline. *C'mon, Lisa. You think they want to go camping with someone they just met?*

Rowen turned to Simon. "Hmm, that could be fun. What do you think?"

"Yeah, maybe," he said with a grin, leaning out of his seat toward the driver. "Vincent, is it possible for the two of us to catch a lift to Durban in a few days?" Simon asked, sounding hopeful.

To my delight, Vincent replied, "I'm sure the other driver can fit you in. I can make the arrangements. No problem, my friend."

I beamed when Rowen and Simon accepted my impromptu invitation with, "Sure, we'd love to!" From that moment, our camaraderie grew as we compared guidebook descriptions and talked about what we wanted to do and see over the next few days.

An hour later, it felt like a dream when we entered Royal Natal National Park, home of the Drakensberg. As soon as the Kombi passed through the park entrance, I was seduced by the Amphitheatre. From the vast valley floor, the spectacular eight-kilometre ridge rises up to a height of 1200 metres, its gentle concave slope bookended by dramatic cliffs shaped like irregular blocks.

Extending for 200 kilometres, the Drakensberg dwarfs the likes of El Capitan in Yosemite in terms of height and total area. But it wasn't just its sheer scale that impressed me. My first glimpse of its exquisite beauty was nothing short of postcard-perfect. The afternoon sun illuminated the Amphitheatre cliffs, revealing glistening hues of magenta, fuchsia and copper that contrasted with the tawny brown earth and olive-green vegetation.

Simon, Rowen and I waved goodbye to Vincent. We were walking across the grassy field toward the campsite when Rowen stopped and called out, "Look at those baboons over there!"

I looked in the direction she was pointing. Two baboons were sitting on the field, side by side, less than 20 metres away. My heart sped up at the sight of them: this was my first encounter with African wildlife.

We set down our packs to watch them. The smaller one was fixated on something in its fur and paid no attention to our gawking. The second baboon scratched its armpit and threw us a cursory glance. To my untrained eye, they appeared docile, as though they had just woken up from a nap. There were no sudden movements, no high-pitched screams or displays of dagger-sharp teeth. I was expecting something more riveting, mildly intimidating perhaps. But they had no interest in us as far as I could tell.

As we continued to the campsite, some curious guinea hens and chicks followed us and unlike the baboons didn't hesitate to get close. Their presence amused me: the second we inched toward them, they scurried off then slowly wandered back.

I dumped the contents of the tent bag onto the ground and began setting up our bare-bones campsite. After I put the poles in place, I made a terrible realization: Thomas's spare tent was the width of a twin bed. I had *no* idea how the three of us were going to fit.

Simon walked over to help me peg out the tent. His taut, tan biceps popped out of his oversized brown tank top, giving the appearance that he was no longer a boy but not yet fully a man. I felt my cheeks flush. It never occurred to me our sleeping arrangements would be so intimate. I threw in my mattress pad and sleeping bag, trying to mask my embarrassment.

"I guess it's going to be a bit tight," I joked, praying he didn't think I was looking for a threesome.

Rowen walked over with their sleeping bags. "Well, if it's too cramped, Simon can always sleep outside," she quipped.

"No way," Simon shouted back, failing to hide his smile. "Those bloody baboons might come 'round."

"Or the guinea fowl," I said with a laugh.

With our campsite ready, we walked over to the postage-sized corner store. I purchased some provisions, a trail map, and a card featuring a photograph of the Drakensberg for my mom's birthday.

Back at camp, we studied the map and made a plan to hike to the Gorge the next morning. The return trip was 22 kilometres, with just over 500 metres elevation and an estimated hiking time of five and a half hours.

With a long day ahead of us, we decided to get an early night's sleep. I invited the Aussies to settle into the tent before I crawled in. It was so narrow I had to wedge the lower half of my body between Rowen and Simon's legs with my feet facing their heads.

"Hope you gave your feet a good wash," Simon joked.

This tight positioning created a comical scene that gave the three of us a good chuckle. By then I was convinced they didn't think I had ulterior motives. It wasn't long until we were snuggled into our sleeping bags like one big human tessellation.

AFTER A BREAKFAST of instant coffee, stale bread and Gouda, we filled our water bottles and set out for the hike. The beginning of the trail to Tugela Gorge was pleasantly flat, allowing us to keep our feet steady and our gazes upward. We delighted in unhampered views of the nearby rolling hills and the jagged buttresses, crumbling crevices and steep rock faces that make up the Amphitheatre. Off in the distance Tugela Falls beckoned us, but we had no plans to hike that far.

Tufts of wild, straw-coloured grass tickled our legs until the smoother dirt trail was filled with rocks, boulders and clusters of green Erica shrubs. The geographical formations of the pockmarked cliffs flanking the trail were fascinating swirls and layers of brown, black and tan rock sediment. It looked as though nature's hand had stopped blending partway through.

The wide valley floor was blanketed in lush green vegetation, thanks to the February rains. The trail followed a gradual rocky slope with modest elevation gain, demanding little from our calves and quads. We only saw a handful of hikers and enjoyed the solitude of the trail. Rowen suffered from back pain caused by an old car accident, so our pace was more social than speedy.

I found the trail easy, but within the first hour, the oppressive 30-degree heat and stifling humidity sucked our energy dry. Our bodies turned into sweaty slugs. It was a relief to have the colder waters of the Tugela River close at hand. We made several stops to dip in our wrists and arms and rinse the sweat from our foreheads.

While snaking along the wide rubbly trail, we hopped across large polished rocks and crossed chilly pools of water. When we came face to face with a water-streaked rock wall, looks of astonishment washed over our faces. The wall was about 12 metres high, leaning at an 80-degree angle. Bolted to the rock face was a chain-link ladder with narrow cylindrical metal slats spaced one foot apart for steps. Reaching the base of the ladder required us to wade mid-calf through rushing, frigid water.

"Wow, cool. That looks sporty," I commented, looking over my shoulder at the Aussies.

Rowen stared at the rock wall without smiling. Her gaze moved toward the top of the chain ladder and I could tell she didn't share my enthusiasm.

"I'm not sure about this…That's a long way up," she said.

As a rock climber, I routinely had to put my trust in steel anchors drilled into rock. Even though the ladder's construction looked a tad precarious to me, I kept my thoughts to myself. I didn't want to make Rowen feel more nervous than she already was.

"It should be fine," I reassured her. "I'm happy to climb up first and test it out."

I stepped into the freezing water wearing my Teva sandals. My feet instantly felt numb, making me scurry up to the base of the ladder. I climbed up steadily, gripping each rung tightly to avoid slipping or falling into the shallow pool below. Once I reached the top of the rock, Simon followed. We tried coaxing Rowen to climb up after him, but to no avail.

"Are you sure?" I asked. "I can climb back down and talk you through it."

"I might make it partway up, but I'm getting vertigo just looking at it. I don't think I could make it back down. You guys go on ahead without me," she called up to us. "Honestly, I'm fine to stay down here."

"Okay," I shouted back. "Be back soon. We won't go that far."

After walking across a flat section surrounded by exotic trees and plants, Simon and I scrambled up a steep narrow path for about a hundred metres. We were puzzled when the trail ended abruptly. I had hoped our slight elevation gain would reward us with a better view of Tugela Falls – the second-highest waterfall in the world – but there was no clear path ahead. We weren't about to go on a make-your-own trail adventure and knew it was unwise to stray too far without Rowen.

"Doesn't look like there's much up here," I said. "Let's head back down for a swim and have some lunch."

Simon and I rejoined Rowen and continued up the Gorge through a narrow, tunnel-like passage made up of boulders, rock walls and freezing flowing pools. The surrounding rock formations were a geological spectacle. The Gorge resembled a high-ceilinged cave with large sections blasted out that let in pockets of sunlight. The upper parts of the steep, tan, sandstone walls looked like they had been brushed with soot then splattered with imperfect white circles of varying sizes.

"This is unreal!" Simon hollered, his voice drowned by the sound of rushing water. "I can't believe we have this place all to ourselves." He stripped off his tank top while standing at the edge of a larger pool.

I had been overheating all day and was *dying* to plunge my sweaty body into one of the inviting pools. I changed into my swimsuit, stood at the water's edge and braced myself for the cold.

"Don't just stand there, Lisa!" Simon shouted. "Five, four, three, two, one!"

I hesitated for two more seconds then rushed in with a squeal. I bashed my big toe against a raised rock feature and lost my footing. I stumbled into the water sideways, up to my shoulders. My chest froze and I gasped in shock. I didn't expect the pool to be so deep or so cold. I dashed out unsteadily like a dunk tank victim, my body covered with goosebumps.

"Well, that definitely cooled me off," I yelled, shivering. "The water is *freezing*."

The Aussies laughed. Unlike Rowen, who stayed close to the edge only to dip her feet in, Simon went in full force, submerging his entire body into the pool. He came up for air. Instead of looking stunned, a huge grin spread across his face. He let out a resounding whoop that echoed across the rock wall, then braved the piercing water for several minutes longer. Simon swam in the waist-deep water over to the bottom of a cascading waterfall. With a smirk on his face, he stood underneath it like he was taking a tepid shower. I have no idea how he endured the icy waters for so long.

Minutes later, Simon emerged from the pool. He hovered over Rowen and shook the water from his dark brown mop top onto her back and shoulders like a Portuguese water dog.

"Simon! Get out of here!" she protested, giving a playful jab to his thigh.

Over a lunch of bread, cheese and trail mix, I was curious to find out more about the Aussies' journey.

"So you mentioned you're partway through your gap year," I said. "What places have you visited so far?"

"We spent almost two months in Asia. After Africa, we'll head over to Europe. We should be in North America by July. Flying home at the end of August."

Asia. Africa. Europe. North America. Despite my varied travels, I couldn't help feeling envious: Simon and Rowen seemed so free.

"That's a long time to be away from home...I'm jealous," I admitted.

"Yeah, it's been fantastic all right. Australia is so far from, well... pretty much everywhere," Simon explained. "Lots of Aussies take a gap year. It's just easier to do all the travelling in one go."

This rite of passage seemed like a brilliant plan, albeit an expensive one. A chance to see the world, maybe home in on what they wanted to do before the commitment of school, work or family got in the way. Then again, I knew being away from home didn't guarantee having one's whole life figured out.

I'd been trying to figure out my own path for the last year. After I'd completed my degree, friends and family had encouraged me to go into education. "You would make a great Japanese teacher!" they had all said with conviction.

I wasn't sure if this was the right calling. I didn't want to pursue a career just because it might be easy or practical. Nor did I want to alter my future path again because of my family. I knew one thing for certain: if I did decide to become a teacher, I wanted to have more life experiences under my belt. I really hoped that before I returned home my mind would be made up.

Rowen turned to me and said, "We should be in Vancouver by the end of July. We'd love to see you once we get there."

"Yes, definitely," I said excitedly. "I love playing tour guide."

We lingered at the pools a bit longer before starting the hike back to camp. The thin, wispy clouds that had been hugging the Drakensberg swelled up and spread across the sky, offering us some much-needed protection from the blistering sun. My energy bounced back under the cooler temperatures.

With only a few kilometres of the return trip remaining, we arrived at a faint fork in the trail that none of us had noticed when we started out in the morning. Our mouths were parched and our water bottles near empty. We were ravenous and eager to get back for dinner, so we opted to take the detour, assuming it was a shortcut back to camp.

The detour took us past the Thandele hut turnoff. Though there weren't any hikers or lodgers around, we assumed we were on the right track. Minutes later, we bushwhacked like baboons for 45 minutes before intersecting a well-trodden trail going uphill in the opposite direction. My patience waned: it seemed like we were meandering away from the campsite area.

"We've been walking forever. Don't you think we should turn around and retrace our steps?" I asked, hoping they'd sense my frustration.

"Yeah, you're probably right," Simon agreed. "But we've already gone this far. Let's just go a bit further."

I was annoyed and exhausted. My arches ached, and the straps of my daypack chafed my shoulders. My skepticism increased with each step, but I kept my thoughts to myself. A few minutes later, Rowen let out a cheer. "Look! Isn't this the trail leading back to the campsite?"

She was right. But our "shortcut" had added one hour and a few extra kilometres to the already long hike. But we were so happy to be back on track we just shrugged off our error in stride.

Back at camp, our dinner required nothing more than my Swiss Army knife can opener and three forks: our sun-warmed tins of spaghetti were the perfect temperature for consuming. In anticipation of getting up early the next day to do more hiking, the three of us settled into bed before nine. With our bellies full and our bodies tired, we fell asleep to the gentle sounds of inquisitive guinea fowl pacing outside the cozy tent.

FOR OUR SECOND DAY we took it easy. Instead of another long hike, we opted to walk to a couple of waterfalls, starting with the Cascades, which was only five kilometres return.

We reached the Cascades within half an hour. Instead of one distinct waterfall plummeting from high above, the spectacular falls crashed over tiers of rocky steps and boulders, the frigid waters cascading from one level to the next like a stretched-out staircase designed for giants.

The water summoned me the second we arrived. Wearing my swimsuit under my shorts and tank top, I stripped down and headed straight into the falls. My back and shoulders had gotten badly sunburned while climbing in Waterval Boven. The heat and sweat from our long hike to the Gorge made my back erupt into a dozen heat blisters the size of dimes and nickels. The falls soothed my bubble-wrap skin in an instant. Like the icy cave waters from the day before, the Cascades were shockingly cold, but a comforting relief.

Simon, Rowen and I spent the next hour going in and out of the falls, taking cover underneath some of the low rock roofs before warming up our chilled bodies in the sun. We repeated this routine over and over again, finding a balance between the extreme temperatures of air and water.

This was our last day in the park. Determined to see more of the area, we hiked another two kilometres to Tiger Falls. This smaller waterfall wasn't as convenient for cooling off, however, and the late morning sun was scorching. We headed back to the Cascades to further perfect our cooling-off-warming-up ritual.

At noon, we set out to find the Bushman (San) rock paintings we had heard so much about. Though we were able to locate the only visible trail sign, the poorly marked path didn't lead us anywhere promising. After a lot of uphill sweating and fruitless searching, Rowen voiced her frustration.

"Good god. How hard is it to mark a trail properly?"

I shared her sentiment. It really seemed like someone had sent us on a wild guinea fowl chase. Given the late hour, I decided it wasn't worth missing my afternoon ride back to Johannesburg. Rowen and Simon were catching a lift in the opposite direction a few hours after me. We gave up searching for the rock paintings and returned to the campground to disassemble our tent for two.

An hour later, we were packed up and exchanging addresses and phone numbers. "Make sure you get in touch when you get to Vancouver, okay?" I could have easily spent a few more days with the Aussies and felt a twinge of disappointment that our time together was already up. I had arrived at a place where I wasn't worrying about my family back home. I'm sure this had a lot to do with their company.

Simon gave me a quick hug then Rowen leaned in. "We'll definitely call you. I promise. See you in July."

Rowen's words comforted me. Her confident tone made me believe I *would* see them again. At the same time, thinking about what my life would be like in six months made me feel uneasy. I didn't want to think about home so early in my journey.

Rowen gave me one final embrace before I hurried to the park entrance. I waited nervously for nearly two hours before the Walk-about-Bus finally appeared to take me back to Joburg.

I RETURNED TO THOMAS'S HOUSE eager to leave Johannesburg for good and travel along the Garden Route toward Cape Town. For my last day, I was determined to give Joburg one last chance to make an impression.

My final exploration on foot included a visit to the expansive Bruma flea market, a popular place for local shoppers and tourists alike. From inside a moving car, Thomas's neighbourhood had appeared relaxed and safe, but a closer inspection told a different story. En route to the market, I saw many homes with razor wires attached to their fences. It was alarming to see properties with shards of glass built into their concrete perimeter walls, as a means to deter intruders – back home there was no way this would have been legal.

I was shocked that the residents revealed their fear in plain sight. I'd always kept my deep-rooted fears hidden away: tiny razor wires and shards of glass surrounding my insides.

Despite observing these extreme security measures, I didn't feel scared. That same morning I had run laps around the gravelly trail at a nearby park, enjoying the sight of wading ducks in the tree-lined pond, not once worrying about my safety.

While travelling the two kilometres to Bruma market, however, I felt self-conscious as soon as I turned onto the busy main road. It seemed like I was the only white person walking about, and I only saw one other woman. I politely nodded and said hello to the few male pedestrians I passed, but it felt like they were eyeing me suspiciously.

I'd been the only Caucasian at the high school I attended in Japan: I knew what it felt like to be a foreigner, to have people stare out of curiosity. But this experience as an outsider in Johannesburg was different. I lost count of how many times drivers and their passengers turned their heads like stunned ostriches through their closed car windows while I walked freely, breathing in the petrol fumes, drinking soda directly from a can. Instead of friendly curiosity, I sensed judgment. *Why is that silly woman walking? Doesn't she have a car? Doesn't she know it's not safe to walk around here? And why isn't she using a straw?*

It made me realize how fortunate I was to live and grow up in a part of the world where these concerns had never been on my radar.

THAT EVENING I hopped onto the overnight southbound bus to Port Elizabeth (present-day Gqeberha). With the trip covering more than 1000 kilometres, I thought the most logical way to pass 14 hours was to spend half of it sleeping.

I took my seat on the bus, revelling in the fact I had *officially* begun the leg of my trip where I'd be relying solely on myself, my guidebook and the kindness of locals and fellow travellers. Birds of elation fluttered in my stomach: I couldn't wait to discover what my travels would bring in the months to come.

By 11:00, my eyes were heavy with sleep. Despite the late hour, the bus driver played action movies back to back at full volume. Screeching cars, random explosions and heated yelling matches crackled through the worn-out speakers of the little TV mounted at the front of the bus.

I squirmed in my seat, wishing I had brought some earplugs or, better yet, my Discman.

Music has always been an essential part of my life. The decision to leave my portable player behind stemmed from a desire to remove barriers in meeting people and tune into whatever the locals were listening to. Not to mention the inconvenience of lugging around a bunch of CDs and packs of AA batteries.

The seat next to me was vacant. Wide awake and with no one to talk to, I peered out the window. There was nothing to look at but the dark night sky. I blocked out the flickering glare of the TV with a T-shirt draped over my eyes. I was determined to get some sleep, but the incessant noise was impossible to ignore. I gave up after midnight.

With little to distract me, my mind wandered. My gaze moved to the large sign above the driver: "Port Elizabeth." Given our destination – the coastal city where my tour of the Garden Route would begin – Peter Gabriel's song "Biko," performed by Ladysmith Black Mambazo, popped into my head.

Prior to this bus trip, I had never given much thought to where Steve Biko, the anti-apartheid activist, had spent his final moments before his death in September 1977. I had sung along to this upbeat version of "Biko," and Peter Gabriel's sombre original, countless times. It took this uneventful bus ride to the city of Port Elizabeth – where Biko was brought to jail, put into shackles, interrogated and severely beaten – for me to fully contemplate the power of the opening lyrics and their link to South Africa's oppressive history.

In the early 1990s, Peter Gabriel's music introduced me to several African musicians he collaborated with at the WOMAD festival. My love of African music grew with each new artist I discovered. My coveted *Wakafrika* album, along with the music of Angélique Kidjo, Geoffrey Oryema, Youssou N'Dour and Salif Keita, captured my imagination. Their upbeat and sometimes sobering sounds and catchy lyrics made my desire to travel to the continent even stronger. Now, sitting on the bus, I desperately wanted my *Wakafrika* CD to pass the time.

In addition to African music, a couple of romantic relationships played a small role in my decision to travel to Africa, though I was loath to admit it. A South African student stole my heart in my first year of university. I was seated amid a sea of 200 students. The banal sociology lecture had failed to capture my interest, and listening to the bald, aging professor's drivel made me wonder if I even belonged there.

The South African student seemed like the only one in the class capable of engaging in intellectual discourse. His articulate, outspoken manner made an immediate impression on me, yet I was equally intimidated by his intelligence and confidence. After a few weeks, we started hanging out as friends. Even though I was attracted to him from the start, I was too insecure to make a move.

When we first met, Ian had just arrived in Canada. I'd only been home from Japan a few months and hadn't fully shed the more reserved identity I'd adopted while living there. His stories of South Africa intrigued me: listening to him describe wildlife in Kruger National Park and the African bush expanded my curiosity about his homeland. Compared to him, I felt dull and unworldly.

FOUR

After a few months, our friendship turned romantic, but I could never fully shake off my insecurities around him. Before university, I had only briefly dated a friend from high school. My tendency to shy away from speaking my mind, in addition to my lack of experience in matters of love and sex, compounded my feelings of inadequacy. Unintentionally, Ian made me feel intellectually inferior. On top of it all, I was trying to grapple with Dad's and Russ's illnesses. Emotionally, I had few coping skills, and Ian wasn't someone I could open up to.

This was my first major relationship, and I fell hard. I was young and impressionable and placed him on a pedestal simply for having grown up somewhere I dreamed of visiting. Months later, when he left to attend a university on the other side of the country, I was heartbroken.

After this first dose of heartache, I moved on, gained perspective and discovered I could never reveal my true self when shrouded in insecurity.

Now that I was in South Africa, I made a new discovery. *Yes*, the country was incredibly beautiful. But all those years it had only seemed so exotic because I had always seen it through someone else's eyes, as if it could never be mine to experience.

Sitting on the bus to Port Elizabeth, I felt proud of the big journey I was embarking upon. I was in Africa on my own terms, ready to take on the unknowns that awaited me. Nothing – and no one – was going to get in my way.

Five

I ARRIVED IN PORT ELIZABETH at seven in the morning, feeling like someone had just released me from a sleep deprivation experiment. The brightness of the sky stung my dry eyes. My armpits were sticky. I craved a shower, some toothpaste and a fresh pair of underwear.

I hauled my zombie ass over to the front steps of the Greyhound bus station, sat on my oversized pack and waited for the Walkabout-Bus to show up. I was counting on it to take me west along the coast via South Africa's picturesque Garden Route.

The sun rose above the horizon. Its first light warmed my bare shoulders and forearms, reminding me the day was just getting started, even though all I wanted was a dark room with a bed. Five painful hours of tedium passed. I was convinced the Walkabout-Bus had abandoned me.

My bum had become a numb mass by the time the Kombi squealed up to the station. My frustration faded when I recognized the apologetic driver was Vincent, the same man who had driven the Aussies and me to the Drakensberg. I was so tired I let chivalrous Vincent grab my pack from the ground without protest.

Already seated in the Walkabout-Bus were three women from the UK who barely looked 20. I got into the Kombi and a quiet couple followed in behind me. The women were having a great time, laughing and chatting. I struggled to keep my eyelids open and failed to match their enthusiasm. I found it impossible to sleep but was too exhausted to socialize. A few minutes into resting my eyes, my ears perked up when one of the women began recapping a recent incident she'd heard about to the couple.

"Did you hear about the two American blokes and the woman travelling in a car together last week? Bloody awful. Two men pulled up to them on the highway and robbed them at knifepoint. They attacked the woman too."

My eyes widened as I looked in their direction. I was shocked. So far nothing I had seen had made me worry about my safety.

I'd always thought of myself as a pretty wise 24-year-old. Not to mention that, when I was 12, I discovered that despite my limited life experience I had adequate self-defence skills.

There had been no warning or explanation the morning I arrived at school and found myself without a single friend. My last thread of pre-teen self-worth unravelled when my former best friend convinced the other Grade 7 girls to shun me. For a solid week I dreaded lunchtime. I thought it was better to hide in the classroom with Carrie, the other friendless girl in school, rather than go outside and face more rejection or ridicule.

During one lonely lunch hour, the school psychopath from our class – an unpredictable tyrant who would be charged with murder a decade later – arrived on the scene. I knew trouble was brewing the second we saw his grim face at the door. His dark, crazy eyes scanned the classroom before he stormed in, picked up a chair and hurled it in our direction. Carrie and I bolted, darting behind a table. The chair crashed and bounced across the floor. His rampage was just getting started.

An untapped fury took hold of me. When he moved toward us, smirking, I lunged toward him and connected my right fist with his face. Blood flowed from his nose. His expression instantly went from smug to stunned. Carrie and I fled down the hall to find the principal.

Crazy eyes never bothered us again.

No, I wasn't worried about being on my own in Africa. I could take care of myself. I liked to think that one glance at my broad shoulders and climber biceps would make most predators – human or animal –

think twice before messing with me. Still, hearing this revelation in the Kombi made me realize that perhaps I shouldn't be too relaxed while travelling solo.

Forty-five minutes later, Vincent pulled off in Jeffrey's Bay, a little surfing village. The couple exited the Walkabout-Bus and two women arrived to replace them. A soft-spoken woman around my age settled into the empty seat next to me. She smiled shyly and, in an accent I couldn't place, introduced herself as Anna.

Anna's dark eyes exuded friendship and acceptance. Her facial features reminded me of a ballerina or a flamenco dancer: soft *and* strong. Her straight, hickory, chin-length hair contrasted with her solid wrestler's build.

Anna was from Greece and travelling with a Dane named Clara, whose tall, lean physique and ruddy complexion made her appear giraffe-like. Unlike the kindness in Anna's gaze, I detected a hardness in Clara's eyes. She was rummaging through her daypack when Anna introduced us. Clara shot me a glance that appeared more of a sneer than a smile. She acknowledged me with a quick "Hey." Then she dug out a compact mirror and began running a comb through her limp blonde hair, studying her face from all angles with a scowl.

"Oh, Jesus. Look at my skin," Clara remarked in perfect English. "This air is making such a fucking mess of my face."

I glanced in her direction. She looked a little flushed and sweaty from the heat, but otherwise I thought she looked just fine.

"You look beautiful, Clara. I can't see what you're talking about," Anna reassured her.

Anna radiated a gentle, down-to-earth nature: I liked her immediately. I had a hard time warming up to Clara though. Her fixation on her appearance made me think she was prone to bringing negative attention to herself. I thought Anna must have been quite accepting of others' shortcomings to travel with someone like Clara. Or maybe, in my exhausted state, I didn't have the patience to be more tolerant.

Once we arrived in Knysna, Vincent dropped us off at the Overlander's Lodge, a pale-yellow house topped with a green roof. An enthusiastic host emerged from the front door seconds after our arrival. "Hello. Welcome to Overlander. My name's John. Follow me. I'll show you the dorms out back."

Colourful patterned tiles framed a few of the windowpanes. A collection of potted tropical plants was scattered across the property. John led us through the communal lounge, a cozy living room with mismatched furniture. We passed through a brightly lit kitchen where the cooking staff were busy chopping up vegetables. We walked out the back door onto a spacious paved patio. The large backyard wedged between the main house and the two-story dorm was covered in a patchwork of brown and green grass. A few lodgers sat under the shade of large trees, while some lay on beach towels soaking up the late afternoon sun.

Anna, Clara and I set down our backpacks in our dorm room. John turned to us before leaving. "Tomorrow there's a canoeing trip on the Knysna River. We still have a few spots open if you want to join in. Trust me, it'll be a *real* blast. You ladies interested?"

He spoke in such an excited manner that it was hard to say no. Anna, Clara and I looked at each other and agreed with a resounding, "Yes!"

WE AWOKE TO WARM TEMPERATURES and sunny skies – perfect conditions for our river adventure. After we enjoyed our breakfast of oatmeal and fruit on the patio, two guides picked us up in an overlander truck. They introduced us to the eight women who were joining us on the trip. The women ranged from their early 20s to mid-30s. Everyone looked easygoing and outdoorsy in their sandals, shorts and tank tops. After a short drive, our group of 11 arrived at the river to prepare for our four-hour excursion.

Although the Knysna River carries enough water to feed into the Indian Ocean, our guide assured us the section where we would start paddling was no deeper than our shoulders and didn't require any advanced canoeing skills. The river was lined with densely overgrown vegetation, and it felt magical to paddle through large clusters of blooming lily pads. The absence of rapids and the slower water flow made it easy for our group to bond from the get-go.

After a few gentle bends, the river narrowed and became more shallow. While dipping my forearms deep into the warm water, I became confused by the change in the river's colour. I hadn't seen anything like this before in nature. The diluted, copper-red hue was alarming and fascinating and reminded me of the smooth, nutty-flavoured *rooibos* (red bush) tisane I drank at my cousin's.

"Is it just me, or does it look like we're paddling in a bloodbath?" I asked no one in particular.

One of the guides turned his boat around to explain. "That red colour comes from all the protea flower petals and leaves that have fallen into the water. They contain high levels of tannin. The river has dropped a fair bit during these drier summer months, so the effect is more pronounced than usual."

Just then I heard a big splash. One of the women had jumped out of her canoe, fully clothed, into the water. Her squeals of delight invited us all to follow suit. An hour earlier, most of us had been strangers. Now we were laughing and frolicking in the warm red river like modern-day nymphs.

After our dip, we paddled further and stopped at a sandy stretch along the river's edge for lunch. I felt completely at ease with these fellow adventurers. A few hours later, our friendship grew over some post-paddle toasts of Castle lagers. None of us wanted the fun to end. Five boisterous women from the canoe group joined us back at the hostel. Along with the other lodgers, including some attractive men, we celebrated with a good, old-fashioned South African *braai* (barbecue) prepared by John and the kitchen chefs.

By the end of the night, our bellies bulged from the feast of grilled meats and vegetable kebabs. Nearly everyone was giddy from copious amounts of red wine and beer. Our collective stamina died off just after midnight. It didn't take long before I witnessed travellers from around the world become friends and lovers. I raised my eyebrows and threw Anna a knowing smile when she snuck off into the darkness with John trailing behind her.

After we'd gone to bed, a blustery storm blew in. I had been asleep for a few hours when the high-pitched beeping of someone's alarm clock woke me up. I peeked at my travel-size clock and cringed: it was 3:00 a.m. Through the dorm window, the outside floodlight flickered off and on several times, making me realize all the commotion had been the power going out.

Dazed, hung-over bodies staggered out of the dorm rooms the next morning. After my interrupted sleep, I was glad I'd only consumed two lagers and a few sips of wine the night before. Groggy-eyed, I walked across the lawn to the kitchen to get my morning coffee. I felt something underfoot and chuckled to myself upon stepping on someone's black bra. Its origins were unclear, but I assumed it was from the collection of undergarments, T-shirts and shorts the wind had launched across the property from the clothesline. Then again, maybe a couple in the throes of passion had left it behind.

AFTER ENJOYING KNYSNA'S SMALL-TOWN CHARM for a few days, Anna, Clara and I left the Overlander Lodge. We were continuing west, making our way to Cape Town with a few stops along the way.

Several minutes after the Walkabout-Bus pulled away from the hostel, panic set in: I had left my precious guidebook and prescription sunglasses on a table in the hostel lounge.

"Oh, dammit! How could I be so stupid? Can we go back to the hostel?" I asked the driver as a wave of unease settled into my chest.

The driver met my eyes in the rear-view mirror. "I'm so sorry, miss. If we turn around, you will not make it in time for the train to George."

My heart sank. With three months of travel remaining, I didn't want to be without my trusted bible. The driver must have seen the disappointment on my face.

"Miss, don't worry. I promise, I will contact the other driver and get him to pick up your things. He's driving back to Johannesburg tomorrow. He can drop them off at the Rockey Street hostel. Don't worry. You will get your belongings back," he said.

Despite his sincere smile, I still felt like a child who had left behind a beloved stuffie.

THE SLOW-MOVING STEAM TRAIN pulled up to the platform, hissing out a piercing sigh from its smokestack to announce its grand appearance. Misty whorls of steam and smoke engulfed the black locomotive, creating an air of mystique. At any moment I expected a horse-drawn carriage to arrive in front of the green-roofed, yellow-gabled station to deliver a handful of white-suited colonialists.

Anna, Clara and I boarded the Outeniqua Choo Tjoe steam train and settled into our seats. Once the train pulled out of George station, I couldn't contain my excitement and remain an idle passenger stuck behind glass. I left the train car and rushed to the outdoor viewing platform of the caboose to drink up the gorgeous surroundings.

Gusts of cooler wind blew through my hair as the sun warmed my back. I took in vistas of scrubby cliffs, sandy beaches and an inviting lagoon. We crossed over the Kaaimans River where it feeds into the Indian Ocean via a multi-columned bridge resembling elephant legs. I marvelled at the engineering feat. How a structure that large and heavy could be supported by a wet sandy beach was astonishing.

The train continued west, hugging the steep, rocky terrain above crashing waves. Once we travelled inland, a few bends in the railway line allowed me to view the entire length of sleek, burnt-umber train cars gleaming proudly in the late-morning sun.

Immediately, the train ride to George made me think of my father. Over the years, Dad had cultivated a wide variety of hobbies. Stamp collecting. Reading Dick Tracy comics. Studying the great wars.

Nurturing his vegetable garden and prized dahlias. But his greatest interest had to be the locomotive steam engine.

I don't recall visiting any of Dad's work sites until I was about 7. All I knew was that he had put in long hours to earn himself the title of "First-Class Steam Engineer." Mike, Russ, Sue and I believed Dad worked as a train conductor, and of course we thought this was a pretty cool profession.

After dropping out of high school to support his mother, Dad was determined to make up for his educational sacrifice. Mom had always boasted about Dad's strong work ethic and how hard he had studied to reach his steam engineer status. When he wasn't engrossed in one of his mechanical engineering textbooks, Dad spent countless hours building and fine-tuning his model railroad. His obsession spanned decades and only reinforced my childhood misconception about his profession.

Dad's massive train model was no small endeavour – it covered *all* four walls of our downstairs rec room, complete with a drop-down bridge at the doorway, built to accommodate the out-of-tune piano I loved playing. He even went so far as to use one of the bookshelves to house one of his hand-painted waterfalls.

As I got older, the rec room's tacky wood panelling and unrefined decor embarrassed me: there was no way I would ever escort a boyfriend into *that* room. But no one could argue the space lacked character. Despite the swirled brown carpet, a hodgepodge of old furniture and the mauve-taupe, speckle-painted fireplace – my failed attempt to modernize my parents' home – the "train room" oozed a quirky charm.

British Columbia-inspired landscapes, replicas of quaint little towns featuring miniature pedestrians strolling along quiet, tree-lined streets, vintage cars, mom-and-pop shops, neighbourhood parks, lumberyards and a pulp and paper mill – where Dad *actually* worked – created an alternate universe for him. After he became ill and could no longer travel with ease, this idyllic little world became a place where Dad could lose himself. Somewhere to escape to and become young again.

I loved all the details Dad put into his model work. As a child, the lit-up trains captivated me as they navigated around handcrafted mountains, passed through tunnels and crossed bridges over wide rivers and steep canyons. Now that I was travelling on the Outeniqua Choo Tjoe train, I felt like a passenger on one of Dad's steam trains. Never could I have imagined such an extraordinary setting as the one I saw from the caboose.

Dad had asked me why on earth I wanted to travel to Africa. And while I might have been in Africa to see elephants and giraffes, I was certain the Outeniqua Choo Tjoe steam train would have piqued Dad's interest the most.

THE THREE-HOUR TRAIN RIDE from Knysna to George covered 67 kilometres along the Garden Route. George, named after King George III, appeared lifeless to us backpackers. This small town served as a brief pit stop for Anna, Clara and me while we waited to catch a bus inland to Oudtshoorn, the "Ostrich Capital of the World," which was 70 kilometres away.

Our paths crossed with two more Danes also en route to Oudtshoorn. We killed five hours together, eating at Wimpy's Burgers – a popular fast-food chain named after the Popeye character – and relaxing on pillowy blades of sun-warmed grass.

The bus showed up two hours late. Back home, I would have whined about waiting so long to catch a bus. But over time I grew accustomed to this minor inconvenience. There was little reason to get worked up or complain about things that were out of my control. I began to view such delays as normal and even expected. Later, it would give me perspective and patience upon returning to Canada.

The dilapidated bus that finally showed up fell well short of North American standards of safety and comfort. The tattered vinyl seat covers were cracked and felt rough against the back of my knees. It quickly became evident that the bus's shocks were worn out, which resulted in a bumpy ride as soon as we departed. On board, I noticed the passengers were predominantly "coloured" people. Distinct from Blacks, whites, or citizens of East Asian (Indian) descent, "Coloureds" have a mixed-race ancestry.

The first time hearing this term, I was taken aback, assuming it to be racist, and I didn't feel comfortable saying it out loud. The word "coloured" dates back to the apartheid era and the government's efforts to categorize races. Historically, Coloureds were not considered equal to whites but did have more privilege than Blacks. The whole concept of ranking someone's worth on the basis of their skin colour seemed outrageous to me, not to mention the idea of an African being "Black" did not even come into play until the white man arrived on the continent.

It was a relief to see we were the only tourists on the bus. As a backpacker – on the move and frequenting hostels catering to foreigners – I knew it wouldn't be easy to find opportunities to interact with South Africans. I desperately craved social interactions with locals.

My intrigue grew when I detected some of the passengers speaking a language I couldn't place. I turned around and smiled at the two women sitting behind me, hoping to make a connection despite my inability to understand their language.

"Excuse me...what language are you speaking? It sounds very beautiful," I said.

They smiled back shyly. The younger-looking woman whispered something to her companion that made them giggle. She replied back, "Xhosa. We speak Xhosa." One of South Africa's 11 official languages, Xhosa is recognizable by its distinctive clicking consonant sounds. Despite my knack for learning languages, I found the sounds difficult to mimic but loved listening to them.

I was so happy to have the chance to connect with these women. This small gesture of mine was all it took to develop a rapport with the friendly passengers during our two-hour ride. Waves of laughter and hollers of surprise filled the bus when our driver dodged or drove over a pothole. We gasped in unison each time he took a turn too aggressively. A few times the bus got harrowingly close to the edge of the barrier-free road that narrowed dangerously to a single lane above steep drop-offs. I held my breath, thinking we might not make it to Oudtshoorn in one piece. Each time we approached a tight switchback, I turned and smiled nervously at the women behind me, thinking that if this was the end, at least I was in good company.

As we neared Oudtshoorn, the driver made frequent stops to unload passengers. Each of them gave us a friendly nod and waved goodbye as they exited the bus. For several minutes, I watched the sunset transform into magnificent hues of mango and melon. When I turned around and saw that Anna, the Danes and I were the last remaining passengers, I felt regret that everyone else was gone.

The driver dropped us off at the Backpacker's Oasis. The hostel was clean, safe and quiet compared to the Overlander's livelier party atmosphere. After our adventurous, bumpy ride, I went to bed, reliving those comical and stressful moments on the bus until sleep took hold of me.

THE SMALL TOWN OF OUDTSHOORN sits in the Klein (small) Karoo region of South Africa. Compared to the lush and humid Garden Route, this area consists mostly of desert and was consequently much hotter and drier. Anna, Clara, the Danes and I woke up early to go bike touring in the nearby mountains. The hostel owner made all the arrangements for our bicycle rental. Because of the heat and the steep grade, we accepted his offer to drive us 50 kilometres away from town to Die Top (The Top) of the Swartberg Pass to begin our descent. I was so happy to be able to travel by bike and stop at various sites along the way.

The view from Die Top boasted bright-ochre rock formations and scrubby vegetation. The almost car-free twisty road had countless hairpin turns cutting through a desiccant landscape of desert grasses, blooming succulents, oversized cactus plants and acacia trees. A cooler wind pounded us for the first half-hour of the descent, forcing us to pedal furiously downhill to keep our speeds up. Unrelenting winds aside, it was a tremendous treat to have the road to ourselves and the freedom to pull off wherever we wanted.

En route to the world-famous Cango Caves, we rode past a one-story schoolhouse set back from the paved road. As soon as I saw a group of children peek out of the windows and front entrance, I turned around and pulled my bike over. The Danes wanted to head straight to the caves, but Anna joined me at the side of the road and agreed to visit the school.

The children's smiling faces were glued to ours as we approached the entrance. A woman walked outside and called out warmly, "Hello. Welcome, welcome! Please come in."

She introduced herself as the headmaster and led Anna and me into the small classroom. A teacher with dark wavy hair and glasses was sitting on the floor, leading a group of students in some kind of a word game. The headmaster explained, "Many of the school children here are *San*, but they all speak Afrikaans. They are studying English too and would love to practise with you."

A group of students sat on the floor next to piles of books and notepads, while others worked at wooden desks. They talked quietly among themselves, observing Anna and me with curious smiles. There was a beautiful diversity among their facial features and skin tones. With their arresting light-bluish-green and pale-hazel eyes, I thought some of the children looked like they could be from the Middle East or South America.

The children ranged in age between 5 and 10 years old. Most of them were wearing colourful sweaters, jerseys, pants and long skirts, despite the warm temperature. Some were barefoot, while others wore socks and shiny dress shoes. Anna and I appeared underdressed in tank tops, shorts and sandals.

The classroom was sparsely furnished and cramped by Canadian standards, but it radiated warmth and a love of learning – in my books, a teacher's dream class. All of the kids were engrossed in their studies. That was until I sat down on a child-size chair next to a row of small wooden desks. The students looked up at me expectantly. I didn't know how much English they understood, so I spoke slowly in a clear voice.

"Hello. My name is Lisa. I come from Canada. What is your name?"

The children burst out laughing. One of the girls sitting next to me grabbed my hand then gave it a little squeeze. Another leaned in and patted my arm and said hello. Their smiles warmed my heart. *How wonderful it would be to teach children like this*, I thought.

Half an hour later, a chorus of cheerful goodbyes and waving hands sent us on our way. Anna and I raced over to the Cango Caves to make it in time for the 90-minute tour. The guide had already begun his rehearsed commentary by the time we arrived:

"And then, in 1780, a local farmer came across this first massive chamber. The farmer, faint candlestick in hand, had no idea how astounding his discovery would be, nor could he have understood the full extent of what lay underground beneath him. It took another 12 years before the second chamber was discovered."

While passing through the first chamber, I looked up, in awe of the surreal setting. Dripping, mineral-rich rainwater created striking stalactite formations that hung eerily from the 15-metre-high chamber ceilings. These limestone caves comprised breathtaking abstract sculptures in shades of cream, beige, yellow and orange that needed to be seen in person to be fully appreciated. The largest chamber was the perfect setting to shoot a sci-fi film: enormous, gravity-defying, rust-stained icicles, and ceilings looking like they were made out of petrified cobwebs that had taken on the texture of gigantic seashells.

This was nothing like my spelunking experience with Thomas. Compared to the cramped cave at Mamelodi, Cango Caves was a stadium. It was hard to believe the system of underground passages spanned more than four kilometres – almost the same length as the expansive Amphitheatre in the Drakensberg. I was impressed to learn that only a quarter of the caves were accessible to the public, and that one of the chambers had been converted into a concert hall for a brief stint.

With so many visitors coming through Cango, some of the narrower passages had become smoother than sanded wood. When our guide asked if anyone wanted to slide down, I jumped at the chance.

While shimmying my body through one of the polished openings, I recalled my first visit to Nara, Japan, home to Todaiji Temple, the world's largest wooden structure. The temple houses *Daibutsu*, a 15-metre bronze statue of Buddha. Visitors of the leaner, more flexible variety can attempt to crawl through a hollowed-out log representing the diameter of Great Buddha's nostril. I was up for this challenge, especially since a successful passage meant enlightenment would be in store for my next life. It was a great relief when my 18-year-old Canadian frame passed symbolically through the nostril with minimal struggle. Of course, back then I had no idea what struggles lay ahead for my family in my current life.

Anna glided down the passage right after me with a wide grin. "Want to go again?" she asked. I nodded. We ran and slid down a second time, like excited kids playing at a playground that was neither indoors or outdoors.

Satisfied with our cave exploration, we hopped back on our bikes and rode toward an ostrich farm. We were halfway there, pedalling along a straight stretch of road, when I saw an odd cluster in the middle of the road moving away from us, 100 metres away.

As we got closer, the mysterious mass revealed itself: a flock of 40 ostriches was being herded by four men clad in blue jumpsuits and holding orange flags. Further down the road, at a T-junction, was a large white chapel with a prominent steeple.

"Looks like they're being ushered to church today against their will," I joked to Anna. "I know how they feel."

Minutes later, we arrived at the Cango Ostrich Show Farm. A white man in his 40s wearing a cream-coloured polo shirt and beige shorts led the tour. With his relaxed manner, he looked like a veteran guide, yet his delivery was far from stale.

"All right, then. Who's up for a challenge? You think you have what it takes to crack this ostrich egg?" he asked our small crowd, looking quite serious.

My hand shot up with the eagerness of a teacher's pet. I walked over feeling cocky, determined to break it on the first try. I balanced my feet on an egg measuring close to 20 centimetres. I moved my legs up and down. Nothing happened. I willed all of my 128 pounds onto the shell from my thighs to the soles of my feet. Still nothing. I jumped up a bit, convinced an extra *oomph* would do the trick. That didn't work either, and that's when everyone, including myself, laughed at the result. Try as I might, the stubborn shell proved impossible to break.

Two more eager competitors followed my attempts. Both of them failed. Our guide didn't seem the least bit surprised. "Ostrich shells are ten times thicker than chicken eggs," he explained, holding the large egg in his hands. "Most of them can withstand the weight of a female ostrich, which is typically around a hundred kilos."

I had eaten ostrich meat a week earlier in the form of a *potjie-kos* (stew). Oddly, both its flavour and texture resembled red meat. During the farm tour, I learned that the volume of one average-sized ostrich egg can equal a dozen chicken eggs and could be easily made into an omelette large enough to feed a few hungry cyclists.

Although the farm existed for breeding purposes, visitors could also try their hand at ostrich riding. Anna and I were both willing participants, and she volunteered to be the first victim in what seemed to have all the makings of an African comedy of errors.

Using a long hooked stick, two slick jockeys caught the ostrich by its neck in one swift move. One of them placed a bag over its head. The bird froze. Our guide kept a running commentary while the jockey prepped Anna. "Ostriches have a killer forward kick. Covering its head stops it from running away and will prevent you from getting injured," he assured us.

From the sidelines, Anna's awkward attempt to mount the bird made me chuckle. It looked nothing like riding a horse, where riders can at least sit on a saddle, use stirrups, hold on to reins and trot at a slower speed. It took almost a minute for Anna to get a firm grip of its wings and find her balance before the jockey removed the bag. The ostrich took off, and all traces of Anna's smile vanished. She hung on for dear life while the jockey sprinted alongside her. Her facial expression was equal parts concentration, surprise and panic. I laughed so hard I almost peed my pants.

With her 30-second lap complete, Anna dismounted the ostrich and walked back to me, beaming. After her laughter subsided, she must have seen hesitance in my eyes. "That was so much fun!" she giggled. "Lisa, it's your turn now. You *have* to do it."

I approached the blinded bird and looked down at its reptilian, two-toed feet. An image of it kicking me to death popped into my head, but I wasn't about to chicken out. My hands grazed the ostrich's feathers, which were as soft and flowy as down.

I turned to the jockey and asked, "Are you sure I'm not going to hurt it?" He shook his head. *Damnit.* There was no getting out of this one.

I raised my right leg over the ostrich's back and pulled myself up, feeling as graceful as a bowlegged elderly woman mounting a mechanical bull. I awkwardly gripped its wings, which were sturdy like handlebars. The jockey picked up on my reluctance.

"No need to worry. You're not hurting it," he insisted. "Ostriches… they are very, very strong."

Despite the jockey's attempts to convince me I *wasn't* causing the bird any pain, I felt cruel clutching onto its wings tightly. I struggled to stay upright. The backs of my thighs slid clumsily down its firm rump. Once I balanced myself, the jockey removed the bag from the ostrich's head. It bolted madly. The sudden jerking motion felt like a bumper car was hitting me. My body shifted sideways. I thought at any moment I'd find myself with the wind knocked out of me, lying on my back in a pile of dust.

Despite my inelegance, I completed one short lap without falling on my ass. Whether or not I made a complete fool of myself is still up for debate. I'm certain the jockeys and spectators got a kick out of watching incompetent amateurs like Anna and me.

THE NEXT MORNING I said goodbye to Anna and the Danes. I wanted to keep travelling with Anna to Cape Town, but I had promised to pay my mom's eldest sister – Rika's mom – a visit after Oudtshoorn. I was so happy when Anna said she couldn't wait for us to meet up again in Cape Town and instructed me to find her at Hip Hop Hostel.

Tante Atje picked me up from the hostel to drive me 110 kilometres inland to her home in the small town of Prince Albert. My aunt had been too ill to travel to the Netherlands for the big family reunion, so this was my first time meeting her. When she stepped out of her car, I was struck by how much this broad-shouldered woman resembled my mom. Tante Atje's short, wavy, brown hair had faded to white-gold and silver and her tan skin had fared well against the African sun. She wore beige nylons with sandals and a flower-patterned pink and purple dress that fell past her knees, something Mom rarely wore because of her ugly veins. Atje was taller, slimmer and older-looking than Mom, but had the same unmistakable features of their Feitsma gene pool: short fine hair, light-blue eyes, high cheekbones, strong jawline. As she walked over to open the car door for me, I noticed she also had been cursed with varicose veins.

As a child, I'd always been fascinated by the idea of my South African aunt. This fascination stemmed partly because she lived in a faraway continent, but mostly because she had been born with 11 fingers. Aside from this distinguishing trait, I knew very little about Tante Atje.

In the 1950s, Atje left the Netherlands to take a job caring for the disabled son of a couple who worked at the Dutch consulate in South Africa. She met her husband there, and together they had two children. Tragically, her husband – Rika's father – died in a car crash, leaving my aunt to raise her toddler son and young daughter alone until she remarried years later.

Atje and my mom had only seen each other twice since leaving Holland. They kept in touch with the occasional phone call and exchanged letters and postcards. As a child, I studied the foreign postmarks from Zuid Afrika with inquisitive eyes. I was curious to find out if my aunt shared any similarities with Mom aside from their shared experience of leaving their homeland, working as caregivers and enduring family tragedy.

To reach Prince Albert from Oudtshoorn, Tante Atje drove through the twisty Swartberg Pass. She cautiously navigated countless tight switchbacks on the desolate, gravelly road, which would have been a road cyclist's dream had it been smoothly paved. I glanced over at my aunt's hands as she clutched the steering wheel. I detected the faded scar where the extra digit once was, but I didn't dare ask her about it.

Atje made idle chit-chat, inquiring about my time in the Drakensberg and my impressions of Johannesburg while staying at Rika's. When she seemed satisfied with my responses, she naturally asked about my family back in Canada.

"I can't believe how much you look like Wiesje," my aunt noted. "You have the same bone structure."

"Yeah, a lot of people tell me that," I replied, accepting the implied compliment.

"Tell me: How is your mother holding up? And your dad and Russ…how are they doing?"

It wasn't easy to summarize the last few years to someone I'd just met, even if my aunt was family. "Well, they haven't been doing very well…Both of them have declined quite a bit in the last year. My mom is doing okay, I guess, all things considered," I said, skirting around any details that might create uncomfortable tension for the rest of our drive.

I told her how Dad often took too many meds in hopes of negating his Parkinson's symptoms, and how this messed with his mental state, making him paranoid and agitated. I told her how Russ's muscles were getting stiffer by the month. He was 28, single, unable to drive or carry on working, and living with my parents. He relied on his walker to get around and had become completely dependent on others. I left out certain details, like how the simple task of using the toilet had become a humiliating feat, impossible without assistance.

"It must be so hard on your mom. I can't imagine," my aunt continued.

Silence.

Of course, it was hard on my mom. And yet she never showed it. Martyrdom and complaining were so far removed from her DNA. She always seemed upbeat and positive, despite their dire prognoses.

Mom was the first person who'd seen something unusual with Dad. They were out for a walk one day when she noticed one of his arms didn't move in sync with his gait. Instead, it hung straight down and limp.

She broke the news to me during my first semester at university. The two of us were passing each other in the entryway at the base of the staircase. Mom avoided eye contact. I could tell something was wrong. Fighting back tears, her voice sounded unsteady.

"I have something to tell you. Dad has Parkinson's disease."

I had climbed up and slid down those well-worn carpeted stairs too many times to count. Almost 19, I was no longer a child. I stood frozen on the landing, unable to go up or down. My fingers gripped the base of the black, vine-motif bannister. Instead of offering support, the vines seemed to be closing in on me.

I had never noticed anything abnormal about Dad's physical health. Mom's words stunned me – nothing had prepared me for this bomb and I was at a loss for words. My family never shared our feelings: I had learned to keep my emotions bottled up as a child. Whenever tragedy unfolded in an episode of *Little House on the Prairie*, Dad always mocked those "crybabies" as I raced to the bathroom and buried my tear-streaked face in a towel with the tap running.

It was rare for Mom to reveal a vulnerable side as well. Even when her own mother died, she seemed to suppress her sadness and grief in my presence, and never went home for the funeral.

With no words to comfort her, I felt like a useless daughter. So many emotions and questions about Dad's diagnosis had ricocheted around in my head. Instead, I had stayed silent, afraid to hear the answers.

Now that I was on the other side of the globe, I imagined what had gone through Mom's mind during her voyage from her homeland to Canada. Was she scared? Thrilled? Brave? Did she feel guilty for leaving her family and friends behind?

I'm sure, like me, Mom had big dreams and hopes about her future. I doubt anything in her life – not even her childhood experiences with war – could have prepared her for how her life turned out. To this day, I'll never understand why fate can be so grievous to some people. Mom was trapped. There was little I, or anyone else, could do. The only way I knew how to help was to be there, acting as a silent support. Making my weekly visits to make sure everything was okay.

And now I wasn't there.

Off in the distance, dry, barren mountains reeled me in. To me these wondrous geological formations looked like a long patchwork of African elephant ears. After we exhausted the small talk, the rest of the two-hour car ride to Prince Albert was quiet and peaceful. I was in awe of the impressive scenery of the Swartberg Pass but kept my focus on the road ahead to avoid motion-induced nausea. This pleasant drive with Atje contrasted greatly with many of the road trips I had taken as a child.

My family often headed south during spring and summer vacations. We travelled to the Oregon coast and California in my parents' red station wagon, which we affectionately called the Chuck E. Wagon. Mike would lie in the very back of the car without wearing a seatbelt. I sat next to Sue and Russ, staring off in the distance, trying to curb my motion sickness.

Tense moments in the car defined most of our family road trips. Dad routinely drove to a chorus of back-seat drivers and annoying bickering. Of course, there were stretches of peace and quiet, but etched in my mind are the nail-biting close calls when Dad missed his exit while frantically shouting, "Will you all just pipe down?" At the last second, he would make an erratic right turn to pull off the highway, the Chuck E. Wagon missing concrete medians and gas-food-lodging signs by mere inches. Once Dad located the nearest

Motel 6, the novelty of the coin-operated vibrating beds made us forget about the tension in the car.

I sat quietly next to my aunt. My peripheral vision pulled my attention away from the distant mountains, toward some subtle movement closer to the road. A curvy-horned animal that looked like an antelope was grazing in the distance. Its smooth tawny back and cream-coloured belly shimmered in the sun like crème caramel.

"Isn't that the animal on the one-rand coin?" I asked my aunt, feeling proud to recognize it in the wild. Its spindly legs looked too thin to support its wide girth as it darted away.

"Ja, that's the springbok, our national animal. It's rare to see them around here. You should see them when they pronk. It's quite something." She contorted her left hand awkwardly like a marionette master while keeping her right hand on the steering wheel. "They round their back like so, then leap up with all four legs in the air. They're very graceful *and* acrobatic."

Atje's animated manner of talking made her look like an excited young girl. Her voice and the sparkle in her eyes reminded me of Mom. Being by her side made me feel less guilty about being away. There was a certain comfort in my aunt's presence. In a strange way, spending time with her felt like I was still fulfilling my daughterly duty.

As Atje and I neared Prince Albert, the road straightened, allowing my mild nausea to pass. I gazed out the window and looked in awe at the transformation of the rocky landscape all around us. Towering walls of synclines and anticlines jutted out dramatically from the red dusty earth. My aunt eagerly pointed out the Wall of Fire and pulled the car over. At an astounding 700 metres, the spectacular rock face needed no introduction. Its fiery orange-ochre hues and gorgeous swirled and twisted textures gave the startling illusion the wall was ablaze. I took out my camera, even though I knew photographs couldn't possibly do it justice.

Before heading to her home, Tante Atje gave me a quick tour around Prince Albert. Nestled in a semi-desert valley, the little town was devoid of traffic lights, and, despite its grid formation, I didn't see any stop signs.

While driving around, my first thought was, *Wow, this place is really white*. But I wasn't referring to Prince Albert's 9,500 diverse residents. The town's unexpected architectural styles – delightful Victorian and Cape Dutch white-painted buildings – were Prince Albert's rightful claim to fame. Row upon row of pristinely maintained homes showing off delicate, rounded gables lined the quiet residential streets. Too meek to yell, the houses seemed to murmur, *Look at us. Ja, we came from Amsterdam.*

I found the style of the houses to be very attractive, but the sea of pure white and curvy clean lines seemed out of place given the wild African topography. It felt like I had been inserted into a *Twilight Zone* episode: I couldn't quite place where I had arrived or what year it was.

By bicycle, it would have taken me 15 minutes to ride around the centre of Prince Albert. An hour, tops, if I cycled along every street and stopped to admire the gables and colourful verandahs.

Atje lived with her husband on a rural property next to a horse stable. I was happy to finally meet my mom's eldest sister, but I hadn't travelled over 16,000 kilometres to hang out in this sleepy town. Despite its humble charm, my hunch told me Prince Albert couldn't keep me entertained for long. Tante Atje seemed so pleased I had come all this way to visit: I didn't have the heart to tell her I'd only be staying a couple of days.

THE NEXT DAY, Tante Atje brought me to the local grocery store. The common sight of white women shopping with "Coloured" domestics seemed strange and dated to me. I grew up with Mom as our sole caregiver. It had been rare for anyone else to watch us. She seemed to manage just fine looking after four kids and keeping a household without any outside help, even after Russ and Dad became ill. In South Africa, what might have seemed peculiar or racist to outsiders was accepted as the status quo by many – regardless of skin colour.

I wondered why it didn't appear to be racist to the locals. I certainly didn't see any Blacks or Coloureds accompanied by white maids. Seeing these domestic workers in a subservient role made me think of scenes with Miss Millie from one of my favourite films, *The Color Purple*. I felt uncomfortable and, because of my Dutch ancestry, borderline guilty.

I could only assume years of apartheid had made it an acceptable dynamic and that big social changes would take years, if not decades, to occur. Of course, I was an outsider looking through a small lens. It was easy for me to assume this was a case of whites keeping Blacks down.

That afternoon, my aunt and uncle drove us along rolling hills through a seductive landscape of vineyards and olive groves before taking me to see a fig farm run by one of their old acquaintances. I was intrigued: this would be my first time seeing figs in their natural state.

From the car I headed straight to the first fig tree I saw while my aunt and uncle walked over to greet farmer Jan. After a closer inspection, I reached up to a branch to pick what looked to be a ripe fig covered in a whitish powder. I was startled when Jan rushed to my side and scolded me in his strong Afrikaner accent.

"*Ag*! Don't touch dose vhite vigs. See that milky coating? It's toxic, *ja*. It vill make your throat itchy and veel like a burn." He selected a handful of ripe figs for me to sample without any of the white coating. "Here, try dese ones. Dey should taste real *lekker, ja*."

I bit into the fig. It was moist and gooey, and still warm from the sun. Parts of it stuck to my palate, and tiny seeds coated my tongue. While deciding whether I liked the fruit's sweet, nutty texture, I was surprised to learn that South African figs had been labelled as originating from California so they could be exported during apartheid-induced sanctions. According to Jan, this sneaky measure worked for South African wine as well.

On my last day in Prince Albert, my aunt beamed with pride as she escorted me through the front doors of the little library where she worked part-time. I was glad to have spent time with her, but I was growing restless. I waited until after we exited the library and were back on the street to let her know my plans.

"Tante Atje, I've really enjoyed spending time with you. But I've decided I'm going catch the early bus to Cape Town first thing tomorrow morning."

My aunt turned to me, surprise and disappointment erasing all traces of her smile. "Oh, no, but you just got here. There's so much I want to show you. Can't you stay a few more days?"

My guilty conscience surfaced, but my yearning to be in Cape Town was too strong to give in. "I'm really sorry...I want to keep travelling with my friend Anna. We get along really well, and she's waiting for me in Cape Town. She's going home to Greece next week. I don't want to miss her."

Tante Atje looked displeased. I felt bad, but I wasn't going to let guilt hijack my plans.

I LOADED MY BACKPACK into Tante Atje's car at 4:30 the next morning. With no light pollution, the stars and the moon shone brightly. We drove in groggy silence to the bus depot. I hugged my aunt farewell, promised to write then boarded the near-empty bus.

Minutes later, the bus slowly pulled away, leaving my aunt behind, standing next to her car. She smiled and waved at me until I was out of sight. Just like my mom would have.

I looked out the window, east toward the horizon. The fading darkness of dusk was met with a warm glow and the promise of a new day. My mind was hazy from the early rising, but my body tingled with an unwavering excitement: Cape Town was waiting.

Six

JUST MY LUCK: Hip Hop Hostel was completely full by the time I arrived, and I didn't see Anna there. I headed over to Long Street Backpackers. Its inconvenient location, absence of lodgers, and sterile, barrack-like environment left me feeling dejected – right away I understood why it was the less popular option. As I unpacked my belongings onto the bed of the compact sleeping quarters, a twinge of loneliness crushed my initial enthusiasm about arriving in Cape Town.

An hour later, I returned to Hip Hop, walked through the entrance of the hostel and entered the main living room. It was standing room only, and there was no sign of my Greek friend.

I went outside to the pool deck. Under a cloudless sky, rows of backpackers were reclining poolside on lounge chairs. Two slender, bikini-clad women dangled their calves in the inviting water, taking deep drags of cigarettes as if their lives depended on it. Half a dozen people were spread out on beach towels, baking in the late morning sun. They looked like they had passed out from the heat or the booze – likely a combination of both. At the far end of the pool, a group of five was laughing like hyenas, guzzling down beers and slurping cocktails. It wasn't even noon.

I scanned the pool area one more time in search of Anna and recognized Clara among the sea of partiers. I walked over to her. She peered at me through oversized sunglasses, then lowered them to the tip of her shiny nose. Her eyelids were darker than usual, and droopy. Her fair complexion was much pinker than the last time I'd seen her in Oudtshoorn.

"Lisa, is that you?" she asked in a gravelly voice. "Oh, my god. I'm *sooo* hungover. I drank way too much last night."

Clara boasted about her excessive inebriation as though it was a coveted contest worth winning. I became irritated. It's not as though I didn't like having a good time. I loved going out to dance and drink in moderation. But I hadn't travelled all the way to Africa to party all night and waste the days away. After a few minutes at the overcrowded Hip Hop, I felt much better about staying at the lifeless hostel.

Shortly after my arrival, Anna showed up, carrying a small bag of groceries. Her face lit up when she saw me sitting in the hostel lounge.

"Lisa, you made it! It's so good to see you. I'm heading to the waterfront in a bit. Do you want to go to Green Point market with me?"

"Yes, definitely...Let's get out of here," I said, thankful to escape the party scene.

It was a relief when Clara stayed behind to malinger.

Anna and I strolled down to Cape Town's modern waterfront. The smell of the ocean, nautical-themed buildings and seafood restaurants reminded me of summertime back home.

We walked straight to the large flea market known for selling a wide variety of new and used crafts, clothing and jewellery. I meandered up and down each row, scanning every stall, unsure what I was looking for.

I stopped at a jewellery stand to check out some necklaces, when a tiny silver pendant in the shape of the African continent caught my discerning eye. The pendant was thin and slightly smaller than my thumbnail. Its line cuttings took the shape of a human figure and animals, including one of my favourites, the giraffe.

Anna looked over my shoulder to admire the pendant. "Oh, it's so pretty. I love it. I would like to buy the same one too...if you don't mind."

"Of course, I don't mind," I said.

Back home, I avoided giving in to impulse purchases, but I couldn't resist the pendant's simple allure and its 6.5-rand (two-dollar) price tag was a bargain too good to pass up. After purchasing our matching pendants, we put them on right away. This modest keepsake carried more value for me than fine jewellery. One look at it now and I am transported back to the lovely day I shared with my friend Anna.

THE NEXT MORNING Anna and I left to explore the Cape Peninsula on a trip organized by Adrian, one of the cooks who worked at Hip Hop. Since it was only a 65-kilometre drive between Cape Town and the Cape Peninsula Reserve, our group of seven had the luxury of driving short distances and taking little breaks along the way.

Our first stop was Camps Bay Beach, home to fine white sand and turquoise waters. All morning, low-lying clouds clung to the nearby hills. It felt like a stroke of serendipity when the sun peeked out and blue skies opened up to reveal clear views of Cape Town's crown jewel: Table Mountain.

I slid off my sandals and ambled along the beach, relishing the sensation of soft sand squishing between my toes. Our visit before nine meant we had the pristine beach to ourselves, save for a pair of waddling albatrosses fighting over some crustaceous remains. The scenery thrilled me. No matter which direction I faced, the beauty of the ocean and mountains overwhelmed me. The mostly flat rooftop of Table Mountain and the jagged, granite folds and peaks of the Twelve Apostles mountain range were as impressive if not more so than the Drakensberg.

Carefully crafted photographs tend to obscure reality, idealizing places by what they *don't* reveal. From the inviting waters to the nearby peaks begging to be climbed, everything I saw at Camps Bay exceeded the perfect photos I had seen. As we piled back into Adrian's van, I felt a wave of regret that our time there was up. How wonderful it would have been to stay there the whole day.

By the time we reached the fishing port town of Hout Bay, Adrian was fully immersed in his tour guide role. As the van rounded a corner, the landscape opened up into gentle, rolling hills. Adrian pointed out a structure in the distance. "Can you see it? It's less than half a kilometre away and looks like a castle." My eyes scoured the bucolic, hilly landscape. The castle was impossible to miss – the palatial structure stood out like my ass on that ostrich.

This was Lichtenstein Castle, originally built as a family home by its wealthy German owner. As we got closer, it became apparent that the castle's style was Gothic. Its tall, medieval tower conjured up images from a fairy tale, making me feel like I had time-travelled to another era. There weren't any houses nearby. As impressive as it was, I thought that the castle, similar to the Dutch Cape homes in Prince Albert, didn't fit into its rugged environment.

We all laughed in agreement when, a moment later, one of the Brits remarked, "That would make an *absolutely* posh hostel!" Little did we know that two years later, the castle would be abandoned and converted into a guest house.

Adrian followed the road until we reached the most highly anticipated stop of the day: Cape Point in the Cape of Good Hope Nature Reserve, the southwesternmost point in Africa.

Blustery winds pummelled us as we took turns posing on the Cape of Good Hope wooden signboard. Our arrival here meant I would have my first real opportunity to view African animals in the wild, and I was giddy with anticipation.

It felt like a dream when a lone mountain zebra and dozens of springbok gathered nearby, seemingly indifferent to our undivided attention. Off in the distance, I saw a herd of zebras. Their sea of black and white created a dizzying abstract pattern and, according to Adrian, the array of stripes serves an important function: the visual effect confuses potential predators and keeps them at bay.

The seven of us stood there in reverent silence, lost in our own thoughts and impressions. Observing these graceful animals roam freely in the wild rocky reserve seemed too good to be true when, half an hour earlier, we'd been ambling along a gorgeous sandy beach.

In the midst of this grand moment, a cool gust of wind carried an acrid stench, spoiling the pristine air around us. Our short-lived serenity was interrupted by the suffocating stink of diesel and petrol fumes. A drove of overlander trucks and tour buses had pulled into the nearby parking lot. Masses of tourists spilled out of the vehicles, quickly transforming the tranquil environment into a place we wanted to escape. Adrian was quick to pick up on our collective sigh of disappointment.

"Let's get out of here. We can go to the other side of the peninsula, where there are usually few tourists," he proposed reassuringly.

We jumped back in the van and drove less than a few kilometres to Cape Point National Park. There we were met by unobstructed views of steep, uneven granite cliffs above Diaz Beach's pale-blue-green waters. Gale-force winds spewed foamy whitecap spray onto the white shoreline. The picture-perfect composition was spectacular, but the untamed waters made it too treacherous for swimming.

Adrian drove a little further before leading us along a short path to the ocean. In a matter of minutes, we escaped the offensive odors and annoying crowds. A desolate, unspoiled beach on the east side of the Cape of Good Hope stood before us with no one else in sight.

Anna and I walked along the belly of an upturned, abandoned, wooden ship with some of its boards missing. The skeletal remains of the boat extended to the water's edge. Its advanced state of disrepair made it just as integral to the fine creamy sand as the bed of sea grass and succulent plants that had taken root. The shoreline was peppered with blackened seaweed and large rocks blanketed in ochre-coloured lichen. I was impressed by a pair of red-orange blooming fynbos, looking like miniature tulips leaning against each other for support. Somehow they stood upright and unscathed despite the fierce winds. Had they been rooted alone I doubt they would have survived.

I gazed toward the horizon and breathed in the fresh, salty air. A feeling of calm and freedom embraced me. How many times had I imagined being in this part of the world?

With Mom's family sprinkled across four continents, the globe in my family's living room wasn't some random dust magnet. As a child,

I loved spinning planet Earth as fast as I could. When it came to a stop, my fingers sprinted along the 49th parallel from the west coast of Canada and hurdled over lines of longitude across the Atlantic to the North Sea for a stop in the Netherlands. From there I long-jumped past the equator to South Africa, feeling curious about my relatives, and confused about why the ocean was called the Indian, not the African.

The trip took barely a minute, but during that brief time, my head was full of wonder. I had no idea that holding the globe in my little hands, imagining myself travelling to Africa one day, was a small act of courage in the making.

I can't believe I'm actually here. I ceremoniously dipped my feet into the unexpectedly cold waters where the Indian Ocean meets the Atlantic. *I'm really here.*

Adrian had driven us as far south as possible. After lingering at the beach, it was time to turn around and continue north up the quiet road along the east coast of the peninsula. Captivating ocean views and friendly chatter in the van kept us occupied. Forty minutes later, Adrian announced, "We're almost in Simon's Town. Anyone game for swimming with penguins?"

I was surprised to learn that penguins live in South Africa. Since the Cape Peninsula is so close to the Indian Ocean, I assumed the ocean temperatures would be too warm for them. However, the water was 15 degrees Celsius – chilly even by my Canadian standards – and the African penguins in Simon's Town were accustomed to these cooler waters.

We exited the van and walked toward a colony of 30 penguins that had congregated on the nearby beach. A few of us were standing side by side, admiring them from a respectful distance, when I noticed a cute penguin couple cuddling upright nearby, in a large hole in the sand. I giggled awkwardly after realizing we were witnessing a mating ritual in real time.

Adrian walked over and laughed. "Most penguin couples are monogamous," he explained. "Many of them stay with the same mate for ten years. Sometimes even longer."

Between the ages of 17 and 24, seven boyfriends and one fling had defined my love life. Most of my relationships had lasted only a few months: eight months had been the longest. The relationships usually ended because I didn't want to get too close, or they moved away to pursue their goals. Considering a typical African penguin lives around 20 years, I found their long-term commitment impressive.

The penguins seemed unperturbed by our presence. When Adrian said, "It's fine if you want to take a dip just to the right of where that group is swimming," I quickly changed into my swimsuit and waded in. It was shockingly cool, but I kept going, whinging quietly until I was in rib-deep, with my arms up out of the water like I was under arrest.

I held my breath and dunked my body past my shoulders. My chattering teeth grinned widely as I looked toward the penguins floating ten metres to my left. I'd been in South Africa almost a month, and already I'd learned there was no way for me to predict what would happen next. Unlike in my family circumstances back home, I loved not knowing what was around the corner.

On the way back to Cape Town, Adrian stopped off at a seaside pub in the quaint town of Valsbaai for a late lunch. It was delightful to sit together at the outdoor patio with the waves crashing at our feet. Just one day before, we'd barely known each other. Now we were dining together as friends.

Over a jug of beer, an Irish traveller in our group told me about a couple he met at the hostel. They had planned to rent a car and drive north to Namibia and were looking for more people to share the costs of the trip.

Dream-like images of the Namibian sand dunes captivated my imagination, putting this country at the top of my list of places to visit in Africa. However, its barren, uninhabited landscape and the great distances between major towns and cities made travelling there as a backpacker difficult: I was hopeful this was my chance to make it happen.

We returned to Hip Hop in anticipation of chef Adrian's sweet-and-sour chicken stir-fry. Over a communal dinner, I introduced myself to Rachel and her boyfriend, Marcus. The Kiwis could have passed as siblings with their light-brown hair, button noses and tan skin. They had already secured a rental car and were leaving for Namibia as soon as they found three more passengers. Right then and there, I secured my spot and made it my mission to recruit two more adventurers.

AFTER BREAKFAST I returned to Hip Hop to see Anna. She told me a bed had opened up there so I took it. With the Namibia road trip looming, I only had three days remaining in Cape Town and was tired of going back and forth.

While chatting with Anna, I recognized a Canadian woman from the hostel in Oudtshoorn. Phyllis was seated on the living room floor, reading a book and taking sips of tea. She was petite but muscular. Her flawless skin was darkened from the sun, like maple syrup. Her long chestnut hair was wrapped in a bold-patterned fabric, creating a stylish result few foreign women could pull off.

Phyllis's yogi-like demeanour exemplified a humble confidence and an acceptance of others. I sensed an instant kinship as soon as we began chatting. Back home in Winnipeg, she worked as a drama and English teacher. She was on a one-year sabbatical to teach in Malawi and do some travelling. I told her about the trip to Namibia and was thrilled when she agreed to join us.

Phyllis introduced me to her Aussie friend Karen, who was also set on travelling with us. Gold-coloured, John Lennon-style glasses framed Karen's dazzling blue eyes. Her light-blonde, short, bed-head hair suggested a no-nonsense personality. I was glad my hunches proved to be right.

I knew driving to Namibia with like-minded people would be a rare and extraordinary opportunity. Yet I had envisioned myself spending another week in Cape Town to explore its surrounding areas. I felt torn knowing I wouldn't have time to visit the local climbing areas or wineries I had heard so much about. I decided this compromise would be worth it once I reached the Namib Desert.

Later that morning, Anna and I set out to explore Cape Town together one last time. She was returning to Greece the next day, so we shared the same sense of urgency as we tried to make the most of our final moments in South Africa.

We bused downtown to visit Cape Town Castle. Built in 1666, it served as a modern-day museum for the military. Although it housed some eye-catching antiques, the stuffy bastion monument failed to keep our attention. We ended up traipsing along Adderley Street, the main drag of the business district in Cape Town, without a map or destination in mind.

I was beginning to regret our decision to explore this busy, white-collar part of the city. That was until Anna and I stumbled across Café Africaine. The diner was run by two lesbians, making it seem an unlikely establishment given its conservative location.

Café Africaine's culinary creations smelled too good to pass up. Anna and I walked in and settled into one of the cozy booths, ordered sandwiches and took in the kitschy decor. The midday sun illuminated the diner's walls, cluttered with bold, expressive paintings of varying styles and questionable quality. The restaurant's diverse clientele and funky atmosphere gave me the same comfort I'd experienced during my dinner in Yeoville with Thomas. I'm glad Anna found this little gem for it left me with a positive impression of an otherwise dull excursion.

One final item on my to-do list was to spend a few hours at one of Cape Town's gorgeous beaches. I had hoped to return to the stunning Camps Bay beach, but it was too far given my time constraints. Someone from the hostel recommended Clifton 3 Beach as a great alternative.

Five of us naively boarded a metered taxi instead of a local minibus taxi. This oversight resulted in us paying a small fortune. Black taxis, despite their tendency to cram in more passengers and disregard traffic regulations, were much cheaper and generally a safe alternative.

Our sour mood sweetened as soon as we gathered on the sandy beach and laid down our towels. The afternoon sun warmed my skin to the perfect temperature. Clear views of the conical Lion's Head and majestic Table Mountain wowed us. With the exception of Anna, I was surrounded by people I barely knew. And yet I didn't hesitate to slide my bathing suit down to my waist to go topless. Among strangers, lying on the beach with my pasty 34Bs out in the open, I felt happy and free.

Nobody would have guessed this act of confidence didn't come easy for me. My relationship with my body had never been smooth sailing, but one that had evolved out of a series of awkward moments and embarrassing events.

The day I discovered my body could bring me unwanted attention, I was around 11, having a carefree day at the waterslides with my sister and our cousin. The three of us had just plunged down a steep chute and were relaxing in tractor-tire-size inner tubes, our arms and legs splayed out like starfish. We were moving at a slower pace in a wider, shallow pool when I noticed a boy around my age a few metres over. He was grinning at me like the Cheshire cat, his eyes as wide as 45s. I closed my eyes to enjoy the sun's warmth on my face. Seconds later, my sister's urgent voice startled me.

"Lisa! Cover up your chest!"

I looked down in horror: moments earlier the force of the water must have shifted the flimsy triangular pieces of my bikini top sideways, exposing my sand-dollar breasts for all to see. I glanced at the boy. He was really smiling now. For the rest of the day, I wore Sue's baggy, knee-length T-shirt. It would be another decade before I dared to don a bikini again, and even then I wore it with a layer of insecurity.

Like most suburban kids, I hadn't been completely naive in matters of sex. Around age 9 or 10, an older neighbour friend and I had snuck a few peeks of her brother's *Playboy* in their dark, dusty crawl space minutes after we messed around with a Ouija board. The carnal images in the magazine freaked me out far more than our failed attempts to communicate with the dead.

I grew up feeling self-conscious and guarded about my body without ever really understanding why. As a young child, I referred to the general vicinity of my vagina as my "front bum." As humorous as it sounds, I am still baffled as to why my mom never corrected this gross anatomical inaccuracy.

When I was around 8, I sprinted home from our neighbour's after watching a dramatic episode of *Dallas*. After learning Miss Ellie had breast cancer and had to have her breast removed, I was completely traumatized. The concept of a mastectomy sounded horrific to me. For months I couldn't get the grim image of Miss Ellie getting her nipples cut by scissors out of my head.

On the subjects of sex and nudity, my parents were prudish. The Christian dating handbook in our home had never been required reading for me. Yet its presence served as a warning: holding hands leads to sex, and sex out of marriage was sinful. There was no way I *ever* wanted to bring a boy home.

Typical mother-daughter discussions never happened for me, making girl-specific rites of passage silent, embarrassing times. I never shared personal matters with Mom. She never brought them up either, except the one time before I headed off to outdoor camp in Grade 6. Before I boarded the school bus, she handed me a brown paper bag containing three sanitary napkins the size of small diapers. "Just in case you get your period," she said. *Thanks, Mom.*

A year later, I wanted to disappear into oblivion when she asked me why I'd discarded my blood-stained underwear into the bottom of a large bin filled with grass clippings. *Uh, geez, I dunno. Maybe because I never wanted you to find them?*

When I needed a bra, I snuck one of Sue's well-worn ones to avoid the humiliation of asking Mom to take me "brassiere" shopping.

Like getting my period and my first bra, nudity and sex had always seemed taboo to me. Fortunately, in Grade 8, a killer combo of aerobics and Madonna's *Like a Virgin* album loosened my reserved tendencies a few notches. Then, in the summer of 1985, my attitude shifted further during our European family vacation.

Mom, Dad, Sue and I spent a glorious day on the little island of Ameland, swimming in the chilly North Sea with our Dutch relatives. This was the first time I witnessed casual topless sunbathing for all body shapes and sizes. To my surprise, my parents seemed unaffected by this common practice.

That morning I was wandering along the beach on my own when I stumbled across a pair of nudists. Like someone at an accident scene, I couldn't tear my eyes away, yet my presence unfazed them. The obese couple was lying on a beach blanket, large sagging breasts and plump, dimpled buttocks out in the open for all to see. The man and woman were reading a newspaper and snacking on melon, cheese and crackers like they were in the privacy of their own home. They looked so at ease in their unapologetic carnality.

My initial shock was replaced with envy: I longed to be half as confident about my 13-year-old body. In spite of my teenage insecurities, this exposure to shameless displays of flesh was forever imprinted in my malleable memory and helped break down some of my inhibitions.

Going topless at Clifton beach felt like a major screw-you to all the insecurities and reservations I'd held on to for so many years. I sat up, leaned back on my elbows and gazed up at the beauty of the mountains before glancing down at my breasts. I smiled confidently, convinced they had already turned a shade darker from the African sun.

TO CELEBRATE ANNA'S LAST NIGHT, we feasted on delicious seafood at one of the waterfront restaurants before attending a screening of *The Serengeti* at the IMAX theatre. Seeing the larger-than-life landscapes and the wildebeest migration on the big screen reinforced my desire to travel to Tanzania and Kenya to see it first-hand. My excitement grew as I daydreamed about my arrival in East Africa in a few months.

Phyllis and Karen joined us after the film. We hit the De Waterkant district in search of Angel's, a gay nightclub known to be a happening dance destination. While strolling along a dark, quiet road, we saw a lone dark-haired prostitute standing under a flickering street light. Few cars passed by, yet she seemed like a regular fixture to the neighbourhood. I stopped to ask her for directions.

She blew cigarette smoke away from us while tugging on the straps of her tight lace dress. "Oh, honey…Angel's closed down months ago. If you keep going along this street, you should find a few clubs that will be open just now."

I thanked her, then paused to think for a second. "Just now" was one of those confusing South African expressions that didn't mean *now* but rather *possibly later.*

Determined to have a celebratory night out dancing, we took the woman's advice. A few blocks over, the hypnotic music of a club spilled out into the street, enticing us to the dance floor. After we danced to a few catchy songs, the talented DJ's shift ended. A live cover band showed up to replace him. We waited around for them to set up, but their mediocre talents failed to deliver and our enthusiasm waned. With Anna's early departure, we called it a night. The next morning, after showering, I returned to the dorm and noticed Anna's pack was gone. It was just before eight. Clara was still lying in bed.

"Where's Anna?" I asked apprehensively.

Half-asleep, Clara turned onto her side to face me, rubbing her eyes. "Her cab showed up a bit early…She left about five minutes ago. She told me to tell you goodbye and said she'll write to you when you get back home."

I couldn't believe Anna was gone. I felt a pang of disappointment and sadness that I never got a chance to say a proper goodbye. I would miss Anna's good company and easygoing nature. Just as my time with Rowen and Simon in the Drakensberg had shown, I had to accept that my backpacking friendships were temporary. All I could do was take comfort knowing Anna and I shared some special memories and that we had promised to keep in touch.

I knew I would keep my promise. I was certain she would too.

WITH ONE DAY REMAINING, time passed like the grains of an hour-glass. After preparing for Namibia, I squeezed in another topless sunbathing session at the beach before my visit to Table Mountain. Having viewed the mountain range from various vantage points within the city, it had always been my plan to tackle the vigorous hike and stay to watch the sunset. Now I wouldn't have time.

The views from the cable-car ride were stunning, making the compromise worthwhile. On the ride up, I ran into Karen and a few other familiar faces from the hostel. Once we reached the top, though, I wanted to spend my time there alone.

I was searching for a spot to take in the sunset when Clara appeared. I was impressed she had managed to get off her hung-over ass to see some sights beyond the hostel compound. Maybe I had judged her too harshly. Perhaps she was working on some of her own issues in Africa. I said hello but didn't invite her to join me. With Anna gone, I didn't feel obliged to hang out.

I secured the perfect viewpoint to savour my last moments of solitude. The sun hovered above the horizon. Brilliant lavender, streaked with pale yellow and amber, lit up the sky, the colours changing against the billowy clouds with each passing minute.

Up on the mountain, I felt a surge of emotions: my time in South Africa was coming to an end. So far my backpacking experiences had been fairly Western in scope, yet the first leg of my journey had been marked by spectacular landscapes and connections with wonderful people. Despite the twinge of regret I felt about leaving earlier than planned, I relished my last Cape sunset. Greater adventures were on the horizon, and the dunes of Namibia were calling.

Seven

PHYLLIS, KAREN, RACHEL, MARCUS AND I crammed ourselves and our mountain of backpacks into our compact rental car – a white VW Rabbit. From Cape Town, it would take us a full day to cover the 700-kilometre drive to the Namibian border control. We hit the road at dawn.

We pulled up to the crossing lineup 11 hours later. Two customs officers were taking their sweet time inspecting every nook and cranny of the car in front of us. Though we had nothing to hide, I felt nervous. I had heard stories about border officials in East Africa asking for bribes and using their positions of authority to intimidate nonresidents. An image of the officers tearing apart our car and dumping out the contents of all our packs popped into my head, and my palms turned sweaty.

A tall, beefy officer shot us a dismissive glance. He impatiently waved us over while talking with a co-worker who was having a smoke. Marcus pulled up to the booth so slowly the Rabbit sputtered and almost stalled. The officer walked up to the driver's side and peered in.

"Open the hood of the car," he demanded.

To our relief, the inspection involved nothing beyond a quick peek at the serial number.

Then a second border official showed up. He poked his head into the front and rear passenger windows and revealed a gap-toothed smile.

"Good day. Please tell me, what are your citizenships?"

The man grew visibly excited when Phyllis and I replied, "Canadian." He treated us like celebrities, admiring our passports while paying no attention to Karen and the Kiwis. He returned Phyllis's passport, then studied mine.

"Miss Louis…Louisa, you are from Vancouver? Oh, you are *so* lucky to live in such a beautiful place," he exclaimed, his smile stretching wide across to meet his plump cheeks.

Karen turned to me and raised her blonde eyebrows. "Louisa? Who the hell is Louisa?" she cackled.

I rolled my eyes. "It's my legal name. My mom gave me one name, but for some reason called me another. I've been called Lisa from birth, so *please* don't start now."

I never had an attachment to my birth name. Even though it embarrassed me when I was little, I much preferred my nickname Bird, which Mike, Russ and Sue used from the time I was 2 until my late teens. No one *ever* called me Louisa, except for Mom a handful of times when she got really angry. I can still picture her serious expression, shaking a wooden spoon and shouting, *Louisa Kim Duncan!*

Mom never followed through on her archaic threats. I could outrun her, and eventually Russ broke that spoon in half over his thigh, which gave us all a good laugh, Mom included.

The smiling officer got a dreamy look in his eyes as he handed back my passport. "Oh, on the television I saw this program about Canadian landscapes. One day I want to visit Canada."

Just as I had dreamed of visiting the dunes of the Namib Desert, this man hoped to see the Rocky Mountains. His enthusiasm for our homeland was infectious. It reminded me it isn't always necessary to travel across the world to experience something exotic. Often it is right outside the door, waiting to be noticed with a new set of eyes.

Once we crossed into Namibia, the changes in the landscape became more pronounced. A barren, desert-like topography overtook the palette of wild grasses and rich greens. The terrain turned into a gritty blend of concrete grey sand and pebbly earth, with few signs of life. But it wasn't the visual transformation that stood out the most. For me, it was the stifling arid heat that made such a strong first impression.

I don't do well in extreme temperatures, hot or cold. Anything beyond the upper 20s makes me sluggish and irritable. It was 40 degrees Celsius. Being packed into the tiny Rabbit with four other people and no air conditioning was insufferable – on par with being trapped in a sauna. *Are we there yet?* took on a whole different meaning.

I'd experienced extreme cold just four months earlier while visiting friends in Montreal. I thought my bones would freeze and break off into shards of ice as I walked outside in minus-20 conditions in the evening, seeking shelter in ATM machine booths to reduce the painful ache of cold until I reached my destination. The unbearable Namibian heat was the exact opposite, yet the effect was very much the same. It felt as though it could melt me to the bone, liquefying my body until my remains seeped out of the cracks of the Rabbit's doors like a melting Salvador Dali clock.

Aside from the riparian vegetation flanking the banks of the winding Orange River, the landscape lacked diversity. The odd camel and mud home added some much-needed novelty to the long, hot drive. In the middle of the uninhabited landscape sat a lone, thatched-roof, rectangular structure topped with a white cross. A beat-up corrugated metal sheet functioned as the main door. With no houses in sight, I'm not sure how the church summoned any followers.

Three hours after sunset, we arrived at Ai-Ais, a mineral hot spring located on the Fish River. After studying our road map back in Cape Town, we had all agreed this popular holiday resort sounded like a logical place to stop for the night. The prospect of staying at a hot spring conjured up romantic images for all of us. We couldn't wait to escape the car to finally arrive at our destination.

With our 800-kilometre journey complete, we were thrilled to see an outdoor pool at Ai-Ais. We raced out of the Rabbit and catapulted ourselves into the pool, fully clothed, expecting the cool waters to wash away our lethargy.

Our combined gasps and shrieks bounced loudly across the pool deck. Upon entering the bath-like water, we bolted out of the pool as though a crocodile attack were imminent.

Karen was the last to cannonball in. Her head shot up like she was a mongoose leaping out of a pot of boiling water, her shocked expression reminding me of Edvard Munch's *Skrik* painting. I would have laughed hysterically if I hadn't been shrouded in disappointment.

"What the *hell*?" she cried out. "Is this some kind of joke? I don't fucking believe this!"

It was 11:00 p.m. The air temperature was 37 degrees Celsius. The pool's water was set to 38, one degree warmer than a healthy person's temperature. Our bodies were not expecting this absurd joke. Somehow we had all overlooked one important description in our guidebooks: *Ai-Ais* translates to "fire-fire."

Hot springs. In the middle of the desert. *What* were we thinking.

However, after learning the science behind this unusual cooling-down method, it kind of made sense, assuming there were no cool water reserves to be found.

Once a German colony, Namibia had many people who vacationed at Ai-Ais. In order to escape the intense heat, visitors took several dips into the hot mineral pool. Upon exiting the water, the outside temperature felt cooler. In theory it worked. But only if we were willing to go in and out of the pool. Over and over and over again.

Don't they know it's far more enjoyable to travel to the Drakensberg and cool down under the likes of Tiger Falls? And what the hell do they do here in the daytime?

I couldn't understand why anyone would willingly choose this peculiar holiday destination. I could understand going there during the cooler months, but spending time there in the middle of the Namibian summer seemed ludicrous.

The unforgiving heat ensured everyone stayed up past midnight. It was strange to see a poolside so active late at night. After our long, exhausting drive and disappointing dip, we set up our camp. Falling asleep proved exasperating. Phyllis's tent was too hot for the three of us. Instead, I tried sleeping alone on a bench not far from the pool.

I placed my Therm-a-Rest on the bench, laid down a cotton T-shirt then placed a dampened hand towel across my chest and shoulders, in hopes it would keep me cool. I tossed and turned, but it was impossible to get comfortable. Despite the calmness of the clear night sky, it was noisy with all the chatty pool-goers. A few street lamps lining the paved path ensured it never got entirely dark. A group of English-speaking vacationers strolled by me, making idle comments. "Oh, look at the girl passed out on the bench. She must be drunk."

I wanted to shout, *I'm not drunk, you morons! Just utterly exhausted, grumpy and desperate to get some sleep if you would all just shut the fuck up!*

I shook my head in frustration and threw them my best Bertha scowl, though I doubt they could see my face in the shadows.

By 1:00 a.m. I'd abandoned the bench. I curled up in the fetal position in the Rabbit, where I had a much quieter, albeit restless, night. The next morning I woke up feeling completely exhausted. I never expected my first night in Namibia to be so memorable – for all the wrong reasons.

BECAUSE OF OUR LATE-NIGHT ARRIVAL and early-morning departure, no staff had been around to collect our campsite fees at Ai-Ais. We arrived at Fish River Canyon at seven the next morning. While taking in the views, we laughed when a park operator stopped to ask, "Excuse me, have you seen a white VW vehicle? They never paid for their campsite at the hot springs."

Even without modern technology, word of mouth proved an effective communication.

At 161 kilometres long, just over half a kilometre deep and 27 kilometres wide, Fish River Canyon is Africa's largest canyon and the world's fifth largest, right behind the Grand Canyon. Beyond its grand dimensions, we had no idea what to expect. Fish River's raw beauty and grand scale impressed the five of us, but there was no time to linger: we still had to drive another 700 kilometres to reach Windhoek, Namibia's capital.

Since our entire journey would cover over 3000 kilometres, and we only had the rental car for just over a week, the five of us agreed to share the driving. So far I hadn't stepped up. Marcus's eyes met mine in the rear-view mirror, "Lisa, you mind taking the next shift?"

"Sure, no problem," I replied, masking my reticence. In South Africa and Namibia, drivers drive on the left-hand side of the road. My very first car had been a manual, but I had doubts about my ability to shift using my left hand with ease.

This would be my second attempt driving a right-hand-drive vehicle. The first time had been six years earlier in Japan. The eccentric English teacher from the high school I attended took me on an excursion. Despite our 40-year age gap, we had forged an unlikely friendship. Takeuchi-sensei's long, pointed nose, thick eyelashes and purple-tinted hair made him look atypically Japanese. His peculiar accent was an endearing blend of British and Australian dialects, resulting from his addiction to English-language cassette tapes he listened to at full volume on his car stereo. I grew to love his goofy, high-pitched rendition of "Horse's ass anyway! Ha ha ha!" as he sped down the highway, gripping the steering wheel with his signature tan gloves like a NASCAR driver.

That afternoon, Takeuchi-sensei pulled into a random parking lot without warning and suggested I drive his car. I was 18 and held a valid Canadian driver's licence, but I was well aware that high school students were forbidden to drive in Japan. I accepted his unusual proposition reluctantly and drove figure eights at 20 kilometres an hour as a precaution.

I found the Rabbit no easier to drive than Takeuchi's Toyota. Stress messed with my confidence the instant I got behind the wheel. It was awkward shifting with my left hand. I struggled to get the car up to the 100-kilometre-an-hour speed limit. Fifteen minutes in, I looked in the rear-view mirror: a trail of three tailgaters was lined up behind the Rabbit.

I didn't want to put my travel companions in harm's way and refused to give in to intimidation. Half an hour after the cars passed us, Karen and the Kiwis sensed my discomfort and offered to take over my driving duties. Secretly, I was relieved – for the rest of our trip, I stared out the wide-open windows, my hair blowing wildly in the hot desert air.

This driving experience in Namibia took me back to my family trip to Europe when I was 13. My Dutch aunt, uncle and cousins boarded a Paris-bound train in Amsterdam, while my parents, my sister and I travelled in my uncle's car through Belgium before meeting them in France.

While driving along the freeway, Dad became the recipient of blasting horns and foreign profanities yelled in his direction. Tensions ran high as he failed to keep pace with the crazy high speeds typical of European expressways. By the third day, Sue and I were in the habit of ducking low in our seats, dying of embarrassment over Dad's cautious Canadian driving habits. "Just drive faster!" we urged him in impatient, whiny tones, while arrogant French drivers made it nearly impossible for him to move into the slower lane.

Sue and I avoided eye contact with the irate drivers who shook their fists at what they assumed was an incompetent Dutchie. After several stressful minutes, there was an opening and Dad escaped the death lane.

I had no idea that one day I'd find myself in a similar predicament. Perhaps my brief driving stint in Namibia was a little payback for the insensitive way Sue and I behaved toward Dad.

ALTHOUGH NOTHING LIKE PARIS, Windhoek made it seem like we had been magically transported to a lost European city. Namibia had been colonized by Germany for almost three decades until 1915, which explained why most of its urban architecture looked European and many of the country's town and city names were German. The name *Windhoek* (windy corner), however, was derived from Afrikaans. South Africa also took its colonial turn ruling Southwest Africa for more than seven decades, imposing its apartheid system until the country gained independence in 1990.

Windhoek, located smack dab in the middle of the country, was mostly a stopover on our long-distance journey. The Skeleton Coast and world-famous Sossusvlei, known for its dramatic, red-orange dunes, were high-priority destinations – there was no time to waste in the capital.

We didn't arrive at the Cardboard Box Hostel until 8:00 p.m. After pitching our tent and wolfing down a plate of canned beans and bread, it was time for my monthly postcard-writing session.

It wasn't easy to sum up the highlights and surprising discoveries I made during my travels. I crammed as many words as I could fit onto each postcard, hoping friends, family and my soon-to-be ex would appreciate my frank descriptions of the Drakensberg, my ostrich ride with Anna and the recent visit to Ai-Ais.

AT SUNRISE we drove west toward the coastal villages of Swakopmund and Walvis Bay. Now that Phyllis, Karen, Rachel, Marcus and I were about to arrive at an undisturbed seal colony on Namibia's Skeleton Coast, I daydreamed about what we might see. I assumed our visit would be a once-in-a-lifetime wildlife experience that would make my friends back home ooze with envy. Anticipation filled the Rabbit with the prospect of escaping the hot car's sticky vinyl seats to take in the rare sight of the Cape Cross Seal Colony. We were just as excited as we'd been moments before plunging into the pool at Ai-Ais.

Apparently, we hadn't learned our lesson.

As soon as the car entered the gravel parking lot, a nauseating stench assaulted us through the open windows. The seal colony *did* in fact have hundreds of seals swimming in the Atlantic waters and lounging on its shores. Their silvery brown coats glistened and gleamed in the sunlight. Everything we saw indicated its population was healthy and thriving.

The unexpected odour of rotting flesh held our noses hostage and confused our senses. I gagged twice before covering my mouth and nose with the top of my T-shirt in an attempt to squelch the uncontrollable urge to puke. I assumed we were walking away from the revolting smell only to discover it was becoming more pungent with each step we took. As we walked along the pebbly beach, the source of the smell became evident.

To our horror, countless rotting seal corpses littered the shoreline: the pitiable pinnipeds didn't stand a chance against the pounding waves. After drowning, their lifeless bodies were left to decompose along the stretch of beach. We didn't see any skeletal remains. "Corpse Coast" would have been a more accurate name to describe the graphic scene at Skeleton Coast.

The five of us said nothing, though we shared a mutual understanding. Queasy, we rushed back to the Rabbit, closed the windows tightly and got the hell out of there.

We escaped and drove ten kilometres south along the Atlantic coastline. Our senses found redemption in the fresh-smelling port town of Walvis Bay. While setting up camp, there was a heated, awkward exchange between Rachel and Nigel – it was their second argument since leaving Cape Town. This time there were tears in Rachel's eyes when she left to be on her own. I didn't know what the fight was about, but it made me appreciate my decision to backpack alone instead of having to deal with the tension that can build when travelling with the same companion.

Karen and I strolled over to the nearby cricket club and got our hands on some Windhoek beer. By dinnertime, our appetites had returned to normal, and the friction between Rachel and Nigel was smoothed over. After a few lagers, we walked into town to have supper at Crazy Mama's restaurant.

It was in this unassuming German-inspired town of bratwurst and beer that I discovered my love for Amarula Cream liqueur. While savouring this dessert-like elixir on ice, I decided it tasted even better than Bailey's Irish Cream. Over drinks, the five of us joked about our foul experience at the beach. Only a group of backpackers would travel such a distance to see rotting seals "on the rocks."

THE NEXT MORNING the Rabbit was hopping with excitement: our dune exploration of the Namib Desert was imminent. The long, hot drive into Namib-Naukluft National Park covered 350 kilometres. To break up our pilgrimage to Sossusvlei, we planned on making stops along the way. Less than 15 kilometres out of Walvis Bay, we made a requisite visit to Dune 7. With a height of over 380 metres, it ranks as the highest dune in Namibia.

We were all eager to have our first taste of sand trekking. Phyllis and I began climbing the dune without shoes, preferring the feeling of sand between our toes. The steep ascent started out fine, but halfway up, the burning heat from the sand intensified and scorched the soles of our bare feet. Each step became so painful we had to descend the dune at full speed. After retrieving our sandals from the car, we restarted the climb. The sand surfing down was fun and effortless, so there was little reason to complain about our rookie oversight.

Prior to Namibia, my experiences with sand dunes had been small-scale. As a young child, I made several trips to the man-made Steveston dunes, which could be reached by bicycle via the dyke three and a half kilometres from my home. Until their removal, the dunes had been an iconic destination for Richmond residents and a popular hangout for partying teens. After I overheard stories about drunken youth almost dying there, my mind filled with fear as I pictured billions of grains of sand burying my body.

I made dozens of visits to the Steveston dunes with my family. The massive mounds of sand towered above my three-and-half-foot stature. Climbing partway up the dunes as a child made me feel brave and adventurous. I never imagined that one day I would be in Africa, confidently climbing up some of the most spectacular dunes in the world.

We jumped back in the car to escape the scorching wrath of the late-morning sun. While driving in Namibia, it was rare to meet locals or other travellers with the exception of a few overland tour groups at gas stations. In the tiny settlement of Solitaire, aptly named for its remote location, we were delighted to find a food mart that sold freshly baked bread. Given the heavy German presence in Namibia, it wasn't that surprising to find this treat. We bought two large loaves anyway, since so far, fresh bread was a rare find in the desert.

The food mart was a popular pit stop for people travelling in overland trucks. Others had ridden motorcycles all the way from Europe via Spain and West Africa. I felt a twinge of inadequacy upon meeting them – to me, their journeys exemplified what it meant to be truly brave and adventurous.

A few hours later, Marcus pulled into a small junction off the highway. We snacked on the delicious soft bread and sliced cheese under the shade of some leafy camel thorn trees next to a chain-link fence. In a nearby dirt lot, five bright-eyed, barefoot children playing soccer kept looking in our direction with big smiles. I walked over to greet them. They were kicking a small ball covered with tattered tape. Like the schoolchildren Anna and I met near Cango Caves, these kids didn't seem to have a lot, but they looked happy.

The oldest girl, with long, skinny legs, looked to be around 8 or 9. Her slender, cheerful face was framed by chestnut hair like a lion's mane. I found it hard to look away from her luminous hazel eyes. She kicked the ball toward Marcus and me, initiating a simple game of scrimmage. In spite of us not sharing a common language, this young girl's small gesture transformed an otherwise uneventful stop in the road into a special moment.

Kicking the ball around with this girl made me reflect on my own childhood. It was far from humble compared to these kids, but my parents made sure my siblings and I were brought up to be grateful for what we had and not judge a person by what they did or did not have.

Mom was 6 years old when the Second World War broke out. Her wartime stories about German soldiers taking over the local schools in the Netherlands and widespread food shortages left a big impact on me. I was impressed by the upbeat manner in which she recapped these events, as if they were of little consequence.

Dad grew up in Vancouver and had his own set of challenges as a teenager after his parents divorced in the 1940s. His mom had little money and they were short on food, often relying on their father for handouts. It wasn't until I was much older that I understood how Dad had suffered the shame and stigma of being poor.

Seeing these kids in Namibia playing happily reminded me how fortunate I was to learn early on that true happiness stems from life's simple pleasures and nature's treasures.

Later that afternoon, we parked the Rabbit in what seemed like the middle of nowhere to photograph some barren acacia trees. The stark black hue of the dead trees was striking against the near-empty sandscape, epitomizing what many people envision when they think of the Namib Desert. Since I was taking slide photos, trying to construct a close-to-perfect desert composition without wasting precious film required a critical eye and a pinch of patience.

After snapping a few shots, I detected something off in the distance, heading in our direction, stirring up dust. Against the backdrop of the clear blue Namibian sky, a figure riding a recumbent trike appeared. As he got closer, my eyes focused on the strained face of a weathered, dishevelled-looking man who looked to be a few years older than Russ.

I didn't see another bike, car or person in sight. The man's only companion was the wind whipping around his untamed, sun-bleached hair. Beyond a quick glance and faint nod, he barely acknowledged us. Given the fact that he looked like he hadn't seen another soul for days, I assumed he would have jumped at the chance to socialize.

"Hey there. Where you headed?" Karen called out in her usual friendly, bellowing voice, impossible for him to ignore.

He slowed down his trike enough to answer but kept pedalling slowly against the wind.

"North," he said stoically in a German accent.

The man stopped long enough to tell us he'd been cycling cross-country for the past few weeks. It felt as though we had interrupted him in the midst of a spiritual awakening. He uttered a diminutive goodbye and pedalled away, his tattered German flag flapping violently in the wind.

"Remarkable, don't you think," Karen said after he left. "Now *that's* what I call solitude."

"Yeah, and such an unusual ride," Marcus replied. "I guess for such long distances in the wind, it'd be more comfortable."

After the man was gone, I kept picturing his fatigued, dusty face. I wondered what in his life had brought him to this part of the world, travelling by such unconventional means, all on his own. The powerful image of him remained etched in my mind like the wrinkles around his eyes. I admired his courage and extreme solitary nature. I too was in Africa alone, but so far I'd enjoyed some sort of companionship.

The sight of this man in the desert stood out for other reasons. Nothing about him indicated he was physically disabled, but seeing him ride the recumbent bike made me think of Russ.

"My brother has a trike like that," I blurted out. "He has MS, so he can't ride a regular bike anymore." I hadn't talked about family with any of my backpacker friends. It felt awkward to share this out loud. I was thankful that only Marcus and Rachel were within earshot.

Marcus said something like, "Oh, man. Sorry to hear that." Then we all got back in the car and drove away.

My family was shocked and confused the day Russ's leg went numb and he could barely walk home. It took the neurologists several months to rule out other causes. We were still processing the news of Dad's disease when they confirmed my brother's MS diagnosis.

Russ had been a relatively fit 23-year-old. He had played baseball and hockey and had been climbing the ranks of karate. He worked a physical job, and loved cars. His illness seemed to pop out of nowhere.

In retrospect, his medical history wasn't perfect. At age 15, he developed a painful bone infection in his hip, forcing him to stay in bed for weeks. But his health troubles began long before then.

When Russ was almost a year old, he'd gotten a bad cold and had been napping. My parents hadn't noticed when he woke up and got out of bed. He crawled into the living room where a steamer had been plugged in to help alleviate his chest congestion. Russ must have pulled up on the cord, causing the steamer to topple over onto his tiny body. My parents and brother Mike, who was 4 at the time, were in the kitchen when they heard the screams. The scalding water severely burned Russ, leaving disfiguring scars on his arm, shoulder and back.

My parents and Mike were deeply traumatized. This horrific accident burdened them with guilt for decades. Now, years later, it's hard not to wonder if the burns and bone infection were somehow connected to MS, as if one or both had triggered the disease.

Doctors confirmed Russ had primary progressive, the worst form of the disease. This meant he would only get worse, his body unable to bounce back from attacks. So far his decline had been steady. Each time he lost some mobility, it was gone for good, like rows of knitting unravelled. The disease didn't appear obvious to others at first: because he was unsteady on his feet and his speech was slurred, people often assumed he was drunk.

There was one afternoon I've always remembered with disbelief. A couple of years after his diagnosis, I was home for an afternoon visit. Russ and I went out for a bike ride in the neighbourhood. I sensed him lagging behind and looked over my shoulder: he was nearly 50 metres away and no longer pedalling his bicycle but still upright. Then his momentum came to an abrupt halt and he lost his balance. His stiff body collided with the pavement with a jarring bounce.

I'm sure I rushed to his side – I must have. Yet I can't recall helping him up or going back home together. All I was left with were grief and trauma and the image of him hitting the ground, over and over like a slow-motion film sequence set on repeat. The gravity of his disease hit home the instant he hit the ground. His symptoms were no longer hidden in obscurity. This fall crushed any hopes that the disease might retreat. There was no denying it then: he was getting worse.

For my family, bike riding had been as habitual as brushing our teeth. But biking became impossible for Dad and Russ. The summer before I left for Africa, Russ discovered a new way to get around: a sleek, cobalt-blue, recumbent trike. He could often be found pedalling his new ride on the dyke with Breeze in tow, the trike granting him some freedom for a few more years. A few months later, Dad bought the exact same model in bright red and could be seen ripping around street corners at full speed.

I didn't go travelling to avoid family responsibilities, but even in the middle of Namibia it was hard to forget the tragedy unfolding back home. Once again, the familiar pull of guilt crept into my conscience while my able body roamed freely in the desert.

WE ARRIVED AT SOSSUSVLEI CAMPSITE at 4:00 p.m. and wasted no time getting our camp ready. Our evening plan was to drive to the dunes in time to catch the sunset. Since the Rabbit didn't have off-road capabilities, we had to leave the car behind, walk five kilometres in and then trek five kilometres out again.

None of us were forward-thinking enough to pack a headlamp or flashlight in preparation for our dusk endeavour. I suppose we were counting on our superior navigation skills to complete the return trip. In retrospect, lights wouldn't have helped us in the desert. There were no landmarks or discernible features to guide us, nor did we have a clear path to follow. As soon as we set out, our footsteps in the sand disappeared as if we had never been there. Karen was tired and stayed behind with the car, so at least one person knew about our intended destination if we lost our way.

Minutes into our trek we spotted a gemsbok, a type of African antelope also known as an oryx. Its unmistakable straight, long,

V-shaped horns, sandy-coloured body and black-and-white striped head and legs were striking against the backdrop of the fading orange mountains of sand. None of us expected to encounter a gemsbok at night *or* during the day: this rare sighting was a pleasant surprise. In hindsight, we should have been more cautious. With their dagger-like horns, gemsbok can turn aggressive and are known to kill animals as large as lions. This beauty must have sensed we weren't the least bit threatening. Like the baboons in the Drakensberg, the gemsbok barely gave us a second glance.

After walking roughly four kilometres on the flat, we began climbing up the dune as the sun dropped below the horizon. Trekking up the steep sand was a slog compared to hiking, but it was exhilarating to be in such a remote environment unaltered by humans. My calf muscles burned as we pushed upward, but I didn't care: I was grateful for my unfailing body. Each time we thought we were about to summit, the ridge snaked along with no end in sight. The dune kept us humble, reminding us to enjoy the moment instead of trying to get higher and higher.

Growing up on the west coast of BC, I was accustomed to dynamic seaside sunsets. Forest-green mountains morph into unexpected deep purples and blues. The sky comes alive with pinks and yellows reflecting back onto the ocean. Here in the Namib Desert, the sunset was stunningly simple: the monochromatic dunes became silhouettes of deep orange and rich brown against the darkening indigo sky.

Phyllis, Marcus, Rachel and I sat down to take in the surrounding beauty. There wasn't a cloud in sight. I gazed up at the shimmering crescent moon hanging in the sky. Witnessing one of the world's most spectacular sandscapes at sunset was a true privilege. The absolute silence and lack of artificial light made me marvel at the night sky with greater appreciation. The vast ocean of flickering stars made me wish I had paid better attention during my astronomy class at university.

As much as we wanted to linger, we had to get moving. The light from the descending sun vanished much more quickly than we'd anticipated. The absence of urban lights or ocean reflection was turning the sky into a dark pool.

The descent was thrilling, but once we hit the flats again, the thrill turned into a race against time. Running in the sand was no easy feat. We were on edge, unsure whether our chosen path would lead us back to the car. We quickened our pace and took turns reassuring one another that we were on the right track, even though there were no tracks to follow.

Despite our short-sightedness, we made it back to the car under the guidance of the moon. It was a great relief to see a set of dim headlights. Then a familiar voice called out to us.

"Yoo-hoo! Over here, you guys." Karen was sitting on the hood of the Rabbit. "Thank god you made it. I was starting to get worried...I thought you might all be stuck out there for the night."

Back at camp, the night sky was calm and clear. With no fly on the tents, the five of us slept soundly under a blanket of twinkling stars. This time, reality hadn't let us down.

AT TEN THE NEXT MORNING we arrived at Dune 45, simply named for its distance in kilometres from the park's entrance at Sesriem. After our fun but tense trek in the dark, we were happy to tackle a much shorter and easier dune in the daylight.

Dune 45's name didn't do it justice – right away we understood why it is the most photographed dune in the world. With the exception of the blackened, leafless acacia trees, it was barren, but the emptiness made it easier to notice its subtle, unassuming beauty. The red-orange hues of the dunes were a natural complement to the cloudless, cerulean sky.

Dune 45 wasn't nearly as steep as Dune 7 and required less effort to climb. In photographs, it looks like there is one distinct conical peak. But as in our experience at Sossusvlei, the star dune went on forever, with several branches radiating from a central point.

The parallel between the journey to the top of the dune and the effort to conquer life's challenges wasn't lost on me. Often, just when we think we have overcome some obstacle or achieved a goal, another opportunity or setback presents itself. A new path begins if we choose to take it. All we can do is accept or adapt, follow the path set out in front of us, and trust that it will lead us where we need to go.

Our seven-hour journey south brought us to the coastal village of Luderitz. The long drive filled with picturesque dunescapes greatly contrasted with the rugged Atlantic harbour. Within an hour of arriving in Luderitz, I was walking alone through the town centre toward the ocean. The fresh salty air greeted me as if to say, *So sorry about the rotting stench the other day.*

Located on the edge of the Namib Desert, Luderitz's antiquated, German-inspired architecture – complete with bakeries, cafes, Lutheran churches and a schnitzel haus – made me feel like I had timewarped into a forgotten, enchanted European city. Light ochre and white facades and red-tiled roofs lined the streets. I was delighted to see that many of the shops featured the art nouveau architectural style. Oddly, the colonial buildings fit well against the backdrop of the Atlantic coast.

I perched myself on a large, pockmarked rock in the harbour to write in my journal. Mid-sentence, I looked up toward the cloudy horizon. I was taken by surprise when I saw a tall ship sail past the harbour's mouth. I had only ever seen a tall ship once before, a few years back near the old Steveston dunes. This sighting was an unexpected connection to home, and one that didn't make me feel guilty about being away. A few seconds sooner or later, I would have missed it altogether.

Over dinner Phyllis and I read about Kolmanskop (Coleman's hill) and knew we had to include a visit to this ghost town before our Namibian journey came to an end. From Luderitz, it was only ten kilometres away, so we planned on joining a tour the next day.

KOLMANSKOP WAS ESTABLISHED in 1909 after diamond deposits were discovered in the area. But after the First World War and the Depression, most people couldn't afford luxuries such as diamonds. Additionally, hundreds of kilometres to the south in Oranjemund, much larger diamond deposits were found. Once again, the white man's pursuit of wealth and power found its way to these tiny dots on the map.

Despite Kolmanskop's short-lived prosperity, there was ample evidence that a thriving community once existed: houses, a school, a hospital, a theatre, a casino were all still standing. The most surprising structure was the skittle alley where the five of us got to try our hand at skittles, a game similar to bowling that uses wooden pins and balls.

After the town was abandoned in 1956, sandstorms reclaimed the buildings. It was both eerie and fascinating to walk through the empty structures. Even though the town's buildings were old and at the mercy of the elements, the faded interiors were one of a kind. A mix of pastel paint and textured plaster created a weathered effect on the walls some people would pay good money for. In the staircases and main floors of the houses, sand had piled thigh-high in the corners of the rooms, preventing the doors from shutting. I tried to imagine what it would have been like for the hired help, who had the tedious and never-ending task of keeping the floors free of sand.

A few hours after our tour ended, Karen, Phyllis and I strolled into town for a bite to eat while Rachel and Marcus stayed behind at camp. Our 800-kilometre drive to Johannesburg meant an early departure from Luderitz the next morning. This was our last chance to explore the town.

Over a dinner of schnitzel and roasted potatoes, we discussed the unorthodox relationship we observed between the Kiwis. When I first met them in Cape Town, I assumed they were a couple, even though I didn't recall ever seeing them show public affection. I was surprised when Karen said, "You know they broke up months ago?" Phyllis and I shook our heads.

"Yeah. But they'd already bought their plane tickets and decided to go ahead with the trip as planned."

This revelation explained some of the tension we witnessed while travelling together. In my experience, usually one person suffers the emotional pain of the breakup. From what I observed, this person was Rachel. I thought the best thing would have been for her to travel without Marcus. Perhaps then she might have been able to move on instead of hoping he might change his mind. Of course, love makes people do irrational things. It was easy for me to judge when I knew nothing of their history.

While wandering around Luderitz after dinner, I learned more about Karen's background. She had been travelling for several months, including a month-long stint on the island of Cyprus, where she picked olives to support her travel addiction. It seemed once she'd had a taste of a gap year, she found a way to create a work-travel lifestyle.

I admired Karen's courage to uproot her life for so long, but I felt envy well up in me. Meeting people like her, who seemed to pick up and leave so easily, presumably with little consequence, made me feel insecure and anxious. Deep down, it bothered me. Before fear and obligation crept into my conscience, I'd always assumed I would be *that* person.

In Africa, I had found freedom and was learning it was possible to escape these crippling emotions. I just wondered how long I could make it last.

EIGHT DAYS AFTER ARRIVING IN NAMIBIA, we were back on South African soil, lounging at the grassy Kuruman campsite halfway between Luderitz and Johannesburg. Despite the intense dry heat and cramped quarters, I couldn't have asked for better company to share this 3500-kilometre road trip. My time in Namibia was short compared to the longer stints I would spend in other countries, but its impact was significant.

We returned the Rabbit in Joburg and bid farewell to Marcus and Rachel. Phyllis, Karen and I spent our last evening together lodging at Rockey Street Backpackers in Yeoville. To my delight, the trusted *Lonely Planet* bible and sunglasses I'd left behind in Knysna were waiting for me. I was happy about this reunion, especially since I was leaving for Zimbabwe. I ran my fingers across the guidebook's smooth cover featuring an elephant. I studied its wrinkled trunk and large tusks and a wave of elation raced through me. In a month or two, I would see elephants in the wild.

For our last night together, I took Phyllis and Karen to Iyavaya. I devoured a creamy chicken stew on a bed of couscous and a lentil, papaya, spinach and cheese baked salad like I was a restaurant regular. I liked the fact that the woman sitting in my seat was a wiser and more interesting version of herself.

Thomas and his friend accepted my invitation to join us for dinner. Our plates were empty by the time they arrived. Phyllis, Karen and I watched them shovel down their food like modern cavemen. Though the dinner and company were perfect, my second time feasting at Iyavaya couldn't match my first dining experience with Thomas.

I savoured everyone's company, knowing that once I left for Zimbabwe, I would be on my own again in a country I knew little about. After ascending some of the most incredible dunes on the planet, I was eager to take my desire for adventure to the next level.

Eight

WITH PHYLLIS AND KAREN GONE, I was itching to leave Rockey Street Backpackers. After a solid week of predictable company in Namibia, I couldn't wait to discover the next set of unknowns in Zimbabwe. Despite my eagerness to get there, starting the process of meeting new people all over again and figuring out a ride on my own made me a tad nervous.

I joined a group of backpackers in the hostel lounge. One of the guys overheard me asking about bus schedules and piped up. "We caught a lift from Zim to Joburg with a bloke named Doug three days ago. He stops here a few times a week…should be back any day. Just ask one of the staff."

After a bit more digging, I learned Doug was notorious for making the 1900-kilometre return trip within 24 hours, twice a week. He hailed from Bulawayo, Zimbabwe's second-largest city. My guidebook described Bulawayo as laid-back despite its former name, *Gu-Bulawayo* – "the killing place."

Doug made regular runs into South Africa in search of curios to sell at flea markets. It sounded like he may have been smuggling products illegally between the two countries. Even though fellow travellers vouched for him, I was reluctant to get a ride on my own.

I walked into the communal kitchen. A young guy was sitting at the table. His leg shook as he took a sip of Sparletta cream soda. The light stubble on his jawline resembled apricot fuzz. His dark blond crew cut and thick eyelashes made him look like he was barely the legal drinking age. For some reason I imagined him wearing an army fatigue, though I couldn't picture him engaged in war, or any sort of confrontation for that matter.

He looked away when my eyes met his. He was textbook handsome, but not my type. Too young. Too clean-cut. My judgmental side couldn't help asking, *What kind of backpacker wears a peach-coloured Ralph Lauren polo shirt?*

After probing this baby-faced Brit about his travel plans, I could tell Jake was a decent, albeit reserved, 19-year-old. Like me, he wanted to get to Zimbabwe. He wasn't much of a conversationalist, but I was wary of getting a lift with a complete stranger. I hoped to have Jake along for the ride and was relieved when he agreed. I asked the hostel staff to keep their eyes open for Doug while we awaited his arrival.

I woke up early the next morning in anticipation of leaving on the fly. Hours passed. Still no sign of Doug. By early afternoon, I decided I had better look into other transportation options – I didn't want to be stuck in Joburg another night.

I was chatting with a staff member about bus schedules when a ruddy-faced Rhodesian in his 40s rushed into the lounge: Doug.

Doug's eyes were volcanoes, his fleshy nose wallpapered with burst blood vessels. He looked like he hadn't slept in days, but he moved like a jackrabbit. His short ginger hair, damp with perspiration, needed a wash. The short-sleeved, floral cotton shirt he was wearing was wrinkled and had armpit sweat stains. His belly bulge threatened to send a few buttons flying. Spider-veined calves popped out of his baggy shorts like columns of play dough.

Our introduction was brief and businesslike. "Be ready to leave in two hours," he told us. After a shower, wardrobe change and catnap, Doug appeared more presentable when he sauntered back into the hostel lounge. Jake and I were sitting on the sofa with our backpacks resting at our feet, looking like obedient schoolchildren waiting outside the headmaster's office.

"Meet me outside in five," he instructed us. We did as we were told and loaded up our packs into the back seat of his BMW. The beat-up, rusted sedan sat low to the ground and matched his exhausted exterior to a T.

I was anxious about the time: the Beitbridge border was over 500 kilometres away and closed at 10:30 p.m. I took my seat in the back of the car and glanced at the clock in the dash. It was after 3:30.

Doug had already driven ten hours and was surviving on minimal sleep. I've never been able to doze off as a passenger. After all the close calls during family road trips down south on the I-5, I developed a preoccupation with my own self-preservation and the safety of others. The second the BMW pulled away, my vigilant back-seat driver instincts kicked in, ensuring Doug didn't veer off the road.

For reasons I didn't understand, Doug didn't follow the obvious signs leading to the highway. Instead he began driving along an unlit rural road. Five kilometres in, I was inclined to interrogate him with a point-blank, "Um, is there a reason *why* you aren't taking the main highway?" Instead, I remained close-lipped. I didn't think it was my place to question him so early in the ride.

Doug must have noticed the look of unease on my face in the rear-view mirror. Minutes in, he casually mentioned, "My rear light is burnt out. This road has less traffic." I could only assume this route made him less of a target for police. With a trunk full of suspect goods, I'm sure Doug didn't want to bring attention to his Bimmer's malfunctioning tail light.

A less plausible explanation, but one that crossed my mind, was that Doug was a serial killer. In this scenario, he preyed upon trusting backpackers before dumping their bodies in the desolate countryside. Jake had looked so unassuming when I first met him. Maybe he had been part of Doug's scheme all along.

Gu-Bulawayo.

After sunset, Doug pulled the car over onto a wide gravel shoulder with no explanation. I looked outside. An expanse of deep purple had swallowed up the magenta sky. A few of the brightest stars were shimmering. We were somewhere in the middle of the countryside. I saw no houses. No street lights.

Doug put the car in park and killed the engine. He opened the door and walked around to the boot of the car. I turned around and peered out the window. I saw a flash of Doug's hunched-over back move up and down, side to side. He was rummaging through the trunk in search of something. For what, I had no clue.

I sat on edge in the back seat. My jaw muscles were clenched like a vise while I second-guessed my decision to get a ride with Doug. Here I was, travelling with a complete stranger in a suspicious car, on a dark, desolate road. Aside from Jake and a few random backpackers, *nobody* knew of my whereabouts. Fear and paranoia began to wrestle with my usually calm mind, filling my head with irrational thoughts.

I was completely aware this scene had all the makings of a low-budget horror film. If this had been an actual B movie, stressed-out theatregoers would have been yelling at the big screen while the camera zoomed in on my rigid body, shaking hands and eyes bulging with fear. "Run! Get out of the car now, you idiot! Why is she still sitting there? My god, that woman is stupid."

In the moment, I failed to find the humour in this ridiculous scenario and couldn't calm myself down. I chewed the skin around my fingernails. The erratic pounding in my chest was met with a queasy feeling that travelled up to my throat from my stomach. I didn't say a word to Jake, who was seated in the front seat, but my voice of reason was screaming, *What the hell is Doug doing back there?*

I hadn't felt this scared in a car since I was 6 years old, riding in my family's red Chuck E. Wagon. We were coming home from a visit to my grandparents. Dad was in a foul mood for some reason. It was past my bedtime. My whining must have tried his last bit of patience.

Without warning, Dad turned around from the driver seat and shouted sternly, "Quiet down!"

Seconds later, I felt the back of his hand clock me across the face. My nose gushed blood all over my beloved stuffed animal. For the rest of the drive home, I sobbed quietly, feeling the sting while trying to make sense of his violent reaction. Removing the bloodstains proved impossible – Dumbo the elephant never looked or felt the same again.

As far as I could remember, this was the first and only time Dad ever hit me. From that day on, I was sure to be on my best behaviour when sitting in the back seat of a car.

Despite being filled with fear, I was ready to defend myself against Doug if needed. I reached into my daypack. My trembling index finger rested on the trigger of the pepper spray I'd brought with me from home. Canada Post had issued me this compact canister to defend myself against aggressive dogs during my stint as a letter carrier. I brought it to Africa in case I encountered threatening wildlife. Never could I have predicted my first time using it might be to ward off a potentially aggressive male *Homo sapien* from Zimbabwe.

Doug slammed the car boot shut. I jumped in my seat and held my breath. I was paralyzed by fear and uncertainty but managed to hide the pepper spray behind my right calf.

A jolt of panic ripped through my chest when the rear passenger door creaked open. I looked over. Doug was unfolding a chequered woolen blanket. He turned to me and said, "I'm completely knackered. I'm going to have a kip in the back seat. Jake can drive for a while, yeah? Lisa, you sit up front and keep him company. Don't need us driving off the road now, do we?"

My erratic heartbeat returned to normal. I felt so foolish for thinking the worst of Doug. The absurdity of the situation made me smile. I wasn't going to die after all. At least, not at the hands of driver Doug.

Even though I had more driving experience than Jake, I was not the least bit offended by Doug's request. After all, Jake was British and accustomed to right-hand drive. I might have just put us in danger had I been in the driver's seat.

Jake took the wheel but struggled to get the car up to 50 kilometres an hour. After the harrowing moments in the back seat, the car ride became more surreal. A thick mist settled into the cool night air. It didn't take long before our journey into the dark void involved dodging and running over a variety of small animals, from hares to frogs. When we got to a bend in the road, my foot slammed down on an imaginary brake pedal. "Watch it!" I yelled out as Jake narrowly missed striking two donkeys.

Later he swerved to avoid hitting a pack of jackals while navigating the foggy road. My heart sank when we witnessed a lifeless leopard lying on the side of the road as it took its final breaths: its sleek, muscular magnificence had been pummelled by 3,000 pounds of fast-moving steel just minutes earlier.

The entire night felt like a bizarre dream bordering on a nightmare. I had no idea what would appear with each turn in the road. Jake and I could see only a few metres ahead of the car. We were red-eyed, afraid to blink. The possibility of colliding with an animal or driving off into the abyss kept us wide awake and on high alert while Doug snored away in the back seat.

After a two-hour slumber, Doug resumed his driving duties. He picked up speed. My stomach tensed into a crampy, knotted mess when he announced he was trying to get us across the border in time to pick up some cash from an undisclosed location.

Doug rolled up to the border crossing. A surly, thick-necked customs officer asserted his authority by making us sit there for no apparent reason. His nostrils flared like an incensed rhino's when he poked his head into the back seat. The officer's bloodshot eyes barely acknowledged my presence. "Wait here," he told Doug before disappearing into a small office building and closing the door behind him. I was getting antsy. Any more delays and I feared we would be forced to sleep in the car until morning.

Ten minutes passed before a different guard appeared. With a flick of his fingers and a nod of his head, he motioned us to cross into Zimbabwe. No questions asked.

Doug drove a few kilometres to what appeared to be an abandoned mechanic shop to get his money. The building was dark. No one was around to make the money exchange. We were too late, *thank god*. I exhaled a deep sigh of relief. He then stopped at a nearby corner store for a caffeine fix – Bulawayo was still over 300 kilometres away.

Hours later, I stared into the darkness like a zombie on Ritalin when Doug pulled into a long driveway. A lone floodlight illuminated a patch of his spacious property. Towering plants and broad-leafed tropical trees cast forbidding shadows onto the corner of a tasteful, two-story home.

It was three o'clock in the morning. Jake was slouched over, fast asleep in the front seat. In case there was any doubt, Doug said, "Yeah, don't worry. You both can stay here tonight. I'll drive you to the hostel tomorrow."

Given the late hour, sleeping at his home seemed like the most logical part of our journey. By then, I was mostly convinced he wasn't a machete murderer. Doug led Jake and me into the house and upstairs to separate guest bedrooms. I crawled into the comfy double bed, relishing the clean, crisp duvet against my skin until sleep took hold of me.

My body crashed for seven hours. I felt lazy sleeping in until after ten in the morning. I approached the top of the staircase. Wafts of Earl Grey tea floated up to greet me. I heard the cheerful babbling of a child and the clinking of a spoon in a teacup. I descended the stairs, trying to convince myself I *wasn't* an imposter but an invited guest.

I saw no sign of Jake or Doug – they must have been asleep still. I prayed Doug had explained my presence to his wife. Given his unorthodox occupation, though, I assumed having overnight guests was a regular occurrence for them.

I walked into the living room. Robert Mugabe's farcical inauguration was playing on the muted box television. Only the corrupt were celebrating his re-election, proclaiming his victory with over 90 per cent of the vote.

Doug's toddler daughter and nanny were sitting on an area rug, playing with some wooden blocks. His wife, dressed in a silk robe and slippers, was sipping tea at the dining table. She looked up from her newspaper when I walked in.

"Morning. You must be Lisa. Did you sleep okay?"

"Yes, thank you for letting me stay the night. The bed was very comfortable."

She nodded and threw me a knowing smile that seemed to say, *Thank you for getting my husband home alive.*

I was delighted when she offered me an instant coffee, a soft-boiled egg and buttered toast. Fear and stress must have burned a thousand calories. I was starving.

I didn't want to appear ungrateful, but after breakfast I wanted to leave. Jake and I stuck around the house for three hours, waiting for Doug to drive us to the hostel. When I asked him about getting a lift, he replied, "Oh, I was planning on driving you two there later this afternoon on our way to a wedding."

I was annoyed that he'd waited so long to tell us this, especially since we could have made other arrangements.

Doug pulled out a pad of paper and completed some unnecessary and tedious calculations. He determined Jake and I owed him 70 rand for gas. With our debt settled, we walked a kilometre to the closest bus stop: I wasn't about to waste my first day in Zimbabwe hanging out at Doug's.

Jake and I each paid a whopping $1.20 Zim dollars (12 cents) to ride the fully packed bus. Our large packs and fairer complexions made us stand out. I felt curious faces studying us as we searched for a vacant seat. Jake took the seat next to an older man holding a live chicken in a bag on his lap. Across the aisle, a woman holding a stack of patterned woven bowls shared her seat with a cardboard box. As the bus sped off, I stood in the aisle, hoping someone might offer me a seat. No one did.

The bus hit a bump. The weight of my back propelled me sideways. I lost my footing and grabbed the edge of a seat to steady myself. I turned to face forward and saw an unoccupied seat for one at the front of the bus. I tripped and practically fell into the seat, only to realize it had no legroom. For some reason the floor was almost the same height as the seat.

It took my brain two long seconds to register the hot poker sensation. I jolted up and cried out in pain. The overheating engine housed beneath me scalded my calf like a branded farm animal. No wonder the seat had been empty. Passengers stared in my direction as if to say, *What the hell is wrong with that* mutorwa? I stood in the aisle for the rest of the short ride.

After checking into the Shaka's Spear hostel, Jake and I left immediately to explore Bulawayo with a Dutchie named Burt, who invited us on his way out. My excitement was replaced with displeasure when I saw streets littered with plastic and trash. We walked around for half an hour, but our search for a decent pub or restaurant was fruitless. All we found were Westernized establishments and greasy food chains. I was so disappointed. I wasn't sure what I imagined for my first day in Zimbabwe, but KFC and Wimpy's Burgers were definitely not what I had in mind.

I returned to the hostel with Jake and Burt, feeling defeated. We walked into the adjoining pub and ordered a round of Bohlinger's. Aside from a few people playing pool, the room was empty. "Stand Back" was playing loudly in the background. The song's melodic, catchy synthesizer sounds and Stevie Nicks's sexy, raspy voice made me forget about our disappointing experience in the city.

We sat down at a table with our beers. My head moved to the beat of the song as I looked around to see where the music was coming from. I grew excited when I spotted the jukebox in the corner. The last time I remember plunking a dime into a jukebox, I was 10 and timid, attending the end-of-season wrap-up party for my softball team. Back then, I felt so cool after selecting my favourite hit, "Bette Davis Eyes." When Kim Carnes started singing, it had been so gratifying to see the reaction of my older teammates as they hummed and sang along.

After another hosteller finished making his selection, I walked over like a kid with a quarter in a candy store. My fingers grazed the lit-up buttons of the modern jukebox. I took my time – thanks to the invention of CDs, there were *hundreds* of songs to choose from.

I studied each spinning spool of song titles like it was the most important decision of my day. I searched and searched but to no avail: Whitney Houston. Sting. Journey. None of my favourite African musicians had made the cut.

I chose carefully, sat back down and took a sip of my beer, feeling like a smug DJ. I loved the anticipation of not knowing exactly when my songs would crank out of the speakers for all to hear. *Will mine be next? Will mine be next?*

Minutes later, my heart sped up when the opening chords of "Constant Craving" echoed across the room. In my mind, k.d. lang was singing just for me.

Hearing her voice felt like a religious experience. I smiled and reminisced about when I saw her live. After the concert, I snuck into the private party with my friend. We chatted to a guy standing a few feet over from where k.d. was receiving a shoulder massage. My friend and I dashed out of there when it became obvious we were the only ones without VIP passes.

After "Constant Craving," Massive Attack's "Unfinished Sympathy" queued up. The deep bass tempo triggered a dose of dopamine to my neurons. The vocalist's spellbinding voice, drenched in emotion, transported me straight to musical heaven. My body begged me to get up and dance. Instead, I remained seated, my shoulders swaying, fingers and feet tapping to the soulful beat.

I had hoped to get a taste of Zimbabwe. For now, I had to settle for some of my favourite tunes and a cold Bohlingher's. I was okay with that.

THE NEXT DAY I arrived at the train station to book my ticket to Vic Falls. I thought I must have misunderstood the ticket clerk when she told me the overnight trip would take 12 hours: the falls were only 400 kilometres away. Then again, the 60-kilometre train trip to George had taken three.

I was about to leave Shaka's Spear after dinner when Jake showed up with his backpack and announced he was catching the night train too. I was fine having him come along with me to the station, but I had no intentions on travelling together. Despite the unusual circumstances we found ourselves in, nothing resembling affection or a bond had developed between us. Our arrangement had been one of convenience, forged out of necessity. I preferred to keep moving on my own. After arriving at the station, I wished Jake well to avoid any confusion.

I boarded the train before 7:00 p.m. Two women around my age were already settled into my assigned women-only sleeping car. Miriam and Grace introduced themselves. They were from Zambia and had been speaking their native Bemba. They switched to fluent English as soon as I sat down.

During the first hour, a shyness filled our intimate quarters. But by the time we were ready for bed, the three of us discovered we had more in common than expected. A natural connection grew while we discussed careers and our shared love of travel. And it didn't take long for the conversation to turn more personal, when Miriam brought up the topics of love, relationships and marriage.

Miriam announced she was single, sounding proud of her status. Grace had a serious boyfriend who was away a lot for work. Miriam turned to me with a coy grin. "Tell me…Do you have a man back home?"

My smile turned into a grimace. I took a moment to think of a suitable response without going into detail. "I did when I left Canada… but not anymore," I replied, somewhat truthfully.

I had barely thought about my soon-to-be ex. I had written Ryan, but it had only taken a few weeks apart for me to confirm what I already knew: I had no intentions of being with him when I returned to Canada. Initiating a breakup via a letter or long-distance phone call would have been awkward. I didn't want to deal with that in Africa. Or anywhere else. So I did what I did best – shirked my responsibility, choosing avoidance over honesty.

Miriam playfully twisted her long plaits into a spiralled bun the size of a soup bowl. I looked at her admiringly. I would *never* be able pull off a hairstyle like that without looking ridiculous. She cocked one eyebrow and leaned in closer, eager to hear some juicy details. "Oh? And *why* are you not together anymore?"

I wasn't prepared to spew out the complicated reasons why I dated someone knowing there was an expiry date. Or why I never bothered to break up with him before I left for Africa. "He just wasn't a good fit for me. And it wasn't love."

"Oh, yes. *Love*. It can be very complicated, don't you think?" she said with a chuckle.

"Yes, it certainly can be," I replied with a smile, but unwilling to share any more.

"Yes, but does it have to be?" Grace asked. Then she moved to her bed to do some studying.

Miriam got up and started going through her small suitcase. She put on some face cream, then pulled out a book, leaving me with my thoughts about Ryan.

I cringed thinking about some of our more intimate moments together. Despite my conservative upbringing, by the time Ryan and I started dating, I had lost a lot of my sexual inhibitions. I convinced myself I was open-minded enough to accept his invitation to a fetish party – *once*. I thought it would be a fun social experiment, on par with dressing up in costume and attending a *Rocky Horror Picture Show* screening.

I was wrong.

I would have been far more comfortable playing a round of Scrabble at my Grandma's than sitting in a dark bar full of pleather-clad strangers. Wearing a sheer black top, I felt like a lone ostrich trying to blend in among a flock of flamingos.

Time and distance had made me realize it wasn't just my family situation or matters of love and sex that had been the issues with Ryan. My attraction to ambitious, intelligent men had left me by the wayside more than a few times. Six months before leaving for Africa, I had a brief romance with an aspiring photographer. Shortly after we started dating, he left to attend university on the other side of the country. This was the same university that had accepted me into its design program – the one I never went to because of family.

Of course, I was happy for him. I was happy he had this wonderful and exciting path ahead of him, with nothing and no one holding him back. But after his departure I felt the sting of being left behind, again. Since I had no educational or career prospects of my own to look forward to, my depressing family circumstances worsened my emotional state.

Settling down and getting married had never been on the radar for me. Nor was I naive enough to think my relationships would last forever. That didn't change the fact I felt deflated each time a boyfriend left to follow his dreams. I envied their freedom to do what they wanted, while obligation and guilt were making me stand still.

Now that I had been travelling for over a month, I had grown accustomed to putting my needs first. To finally be in a position to do what I wanted.

I suppose this time it was *my* turn to leave someone behind.

Miriam, Grace and I settled into bed just after ten. I was still wide awake when the train came to a startling halt. The sleeping quarters were dead quiet. Lying in an unmoving train in the dark was eerie, and it took me a while to fall asleep.

I had been asleep for an hour or two when someone started banging furiously on our door. Then a man's impatient voice yelled, "Tobias! Tobias! Let me in!" making my heart stop.

I bolted up in bed when he tried opening our locked door. I prayed this was a case of someone getting disoriented after leaving their train car to use the washroom. I felt some relief when Miriam whispered, "Ignore him. He's probably drunk and can't find his car number."

A few minutes of silence passed. I assumed the man had wandered off and wouldn't bother us again. Then the pounding on the door started up again, his urgent voice pleading over and over, "Tobias! Let me in! Tobias! Open the door!"

I was no longer scared. Instead, I was furious at the late-night intrusion. "Go away!" I shouted back. "There's no Tobias here!"

Silence followed. He never returned.

After tossing and turning, I fell into a deep sleep and started dreaming. In the dream, the train wasn't moving at all. I looked out the window and made a horrible discovery: our train car had been disconnected from the rest of the train. We were stranded in the middle of the tracks, hundreds of kilometres from our destination, in the dead of the night.

Things turned ugly when a mob of men began shouting violently. Angry fists pounded our door before someone started kicking it so hard I thought it might come off the hinges. My heart raced with panic. I contemplated escaping out the window, but we were in the countryside without a village or town in sight. There was nowhere to run: Miriam, Grace and I were trapped.

The loud yelling intensified. A rattling sound made me sick with fear. Then I saw the door handle moving up and down...

Knock, knock, knock. A firm tapping on the door woke me with a start. The familiar chugging of the moving train thrust me back to reality. A man's meek voice calmly spoke to us through the locked door: "Good morning. It is time to wake up. We will be arriving in Victoria Falls shortly."

I rubbed my eyes, looked at the time and uttered a quiet groan. It was 5:40 a.m. We weren't arriving for over an hour. Though I didn't appreciate this early wake-up call, I *was* relieved my nightmare was over.

Grace was already sitting up and putting on a bright-red, patterned, cotton dress and matching hair scarf. "I had to use the toilet last night," she said. "Luckily, I never saw that man when I got up to go."

Miriam stirred in her bed then turned to face me, her dark almond eyes heavy with sleep. "How was your night?" she asked, groggily.

"Awful," I grumbled. "After he left, I had a terrible nightmare. We were stuck on the tracks and some men were trying to get into our car. I think it must be from the anti-malaria pills I've been taking. The pharmacist warned me Lariam can cause violent dreams."

"That sounds horrible. Thank goodness none of that really happened," Miriam said as she got out of bed.

A few days earlier, I'd woken up feeling stressed after dreaming about the murder of a close friend and the suicide of a high school acquaintance. I'd always been a vivid dreamer and could often recall the details of my dreams. But they'd always been of the bizarre and humorous variety, never violent or disturbing.

Despite these Lariam-induced nightmares, I considered myself lucky. Malaria was rampant in the Victoria Falls area because of the exploding mosquito population. So many Africans went untreated and became ill or even died from this preventable disease. In the grand scheme of things, these nightmares were nothing more than a mild nuisance. .

The train pulled up to the station at seven. I followed Miriam and Grace onto the platform. They wished me well, and we went our separate ways. I walked a kilometre to the dormitory to discover check-in wasn't until noon. I stashed my backpack at the front desk and wandered into town, which appeared sleepy like me.

I found a little diner open for breakfast. After a quick coffee and a dry pastry, I began my exploration, pleased to be walking around the area first thing in the morning. The sun was heating up. The thick humid air coated my skin with a sticky layer. It was before eight, and already droplets of sweat trickled down my forehead and chest.

A wooden bulletin board advertising some local adventures offered by guiding companies captured my imagination. A two-day canoeing safari on the Zambezi River reeled me in. I rushed over to the tour office and made my booking for the next day. I had to pinch myself when the booking agent assured me, "Oh, *yes*. You will definitely see hippopotamus and crocodiles on the banks of the Zambezi!"

Later that morning, while writing postcards to my friends, I quipped that if I had the misfortune of being killed on the canoe trip by a hippo, they should find humour in my unusual death. In reality, getting close to a hippopotamus can be a serious life-or-death encounter. Hippos are often depicted as cute and harmless. But I learned that most animal attacks causing death in Africa were at the jaws of these ancient, amphibious creatures. Even though they are herbivores, hippos are very territorial. If threatened by the presence of a large object in their waters – say, a young woman in a canoe – they will attack with one swift deadly bite, severing anything, or anyone, in sight with their enormous chompers. Despite this knowledge, I was thrilled at the prospect of seeing one in the wild.

The first time I saw a photograph of Victoria Falls, I thought someone must have expertly spliced two photos together as a trick. How a flat, mile-long mass of water could just fall away and plunge a hundred metres into a misty abyss was baffling. I couldn't wait to see this phenomenon in person.

I heard the falls before I saw them. The steady roar of cascading water resonated more loudly with each step. I had no intention of rushing my visit, but the far-reaching spray found me quickly. Over 500 million litres of water plummet into the Zambezi Gorge every minute. Right away I understood why locals call it *Mosi-oa-Tunya* – the smoke that thunders.

Fed by the mighty Zambezi and extending across the Zambian border, Victoria Falls widens to an astounding 1700 metres. From the ground, it was impossible to fathom its immense scale. Naturally, I expected the area to be overrun with crowds. Yet, while strolling around, I only saw a handful of people there. Despite its reputation as a major tourist destination, I found nothing but peace and solitude.

There were multiple viewpoints accessible from a dozen footpaths: I wanted to try them all. It felt sublime to be enveloped by refreshing sprays of mist no matter which path I took. My fatigue and sweat were washed away after I allowed myself to get completely drenched. This hydrating, solitary experience was in stark contrast to the arid, dusty days in the hot Namib Desert, where I rarely spent any time on my own. I lingered at each viewpoint, enjoying my time alone. Everywhere I looked, there was an endless array of rainbows. Victoria Falls was a magical place, pure and simple. It was a thrill to be dwarfed by such a powerful force of nature.

After hours of exploring, I checked into the dormitory and met my short-term roommates: a mother and daughter from Japan who were excited to learn I had lived an hour away from their hometown.

Swarms of mosquitoes gathered outside our dorm room, trapping us inside with the doors and windows closed tightly. To pass the time in the stifling heat, I told them about my time in Namibia and they chatted with me about their safari in Botswana. It was reassuring to be so far from home yet have an instant connection with strangers.

AN OVERLANDER TRUCK picked me up early the next morning for my two-day Zambezi River adventure. Brian, a white Zimbabwean in his early 20s who spoke fluent Shona, introduced himself as the senior tour leader. Brian drove me to camp while two guides kept me entertained for the short ride.

I squeezed the overhead bar of the fast-moving truck as it bounced along the rutted-out dirt road. A pack of impala dashed across it. Despite Brian's speedy driving, the guides were able to point out a tortoise, a bull, a falcon and a small troop of baboons.

I arrived at the camp in time for breakfast. Four guys were sipping steaming cups of coffee and tea in the sun around an unlit campfire steps from the river. Fred and Craig – flatmates from South Africa – a Brit named Sion, and Damian the Aussie had spent the previous night at the camp. They turned in my direction with big smiles, looking relieved to see a single woman joining them on the trip. Even though I wasn't looking for romance, it felt flattering to turn a few heads.

After breakfast, the guides drove us to the banks of the Zambezi. The openness of the outdoor setting and the guys' willingness to accept me as the newcomer allowed us to chat and joke around with ease. En route, fleeting glimpses of more impala and baboons, a lone giraffe, a few antelope and some warthogs kept us occupied and attentive. One of the guides pointed out some lion tracks. Compared to the relative desolation of the barren Namib Desert, there was so much to take in: a lush forest, a variety of wildlife, the humid air and invigorating scents of earth propelled my senses into overdrive.

We began our river expedition in a section of the Zambezi too rough for a standard canoe. Sturdy, inflatable kayaks capable of handling the river's currents were the preferred mode of transportation. Once we started paddling, the sporty, unpredictable rapids pushed me out of my comfort zone and kept me on high alert. I was an inexperienced kayaker, and this was my first time paddling in rapids: it took all my muscle strength and concentration to avoid tipping over the boat.

The first moments on the Zambezi were riveting, but it wasn't until we reached a more shallow, calmer section of the river that I could relax. The guys and I carefully wedged our boats between some rocks and dipped our hands and forearms in the river to cool off. Sion and I exchanged mischievous looks before acting on a mutual understanding. We started splashing one another, slapping our paddles against the water like bratty adolescents. The other guys joined in until everyone was soaked. But nobody seemed to mind: we were having too much fun.

The five of us jumped out of our kayaks and sat with our bums and legs immersed in the shallow water, our feet sticking out toward the sky. Our guides watched from the sidelines, laughing. When I had gazed down at the Zambezi from the airplane window five weeks earlier, I never imagined I'd find myself in a playful scene like this.

Prior to my arrival at Vic Falls, I brushed up on some local history. I was interested to learn that Scottish missionary David Livingstone had spent months on the Zambezi. In the mid-1800s he tried to find a viable route from the Indian Ocean into Central Africa via "God's highway." He spent most of his days on the river, suffering the harsh effects of malaria. His efforts fell short when he realized the Zambezi was too treacherous to navigate. Even though I've always been critical of religious groups imposing their beliefs on others, I found Livingstone's attempts to improve the health of African villagers and abolish the slave trade commendable.

After some lunch and an hour-long siesta in the shade, we set out again, this time in larger Canadian canoes. The guys were three to a boat, but I – the only Canuck – got paired up with our Shona guide, Lucky. *Lisa and Lucky. Lucky Lisa.* I liked the sound of that. I took my pairing with Lucky as a good omen, considering we were romping around in well-known hippo and crocodile territory.

We were paddling the tamer rapids, enjoying the lush views of the grassy *dambo*, when Lucky stopped paddling. "Everyone, please stop…I just saw something moving…over there at the surface of the water."

Lucky's attention was focused on something further down the river, but I had no idea what he was looking at. My eyes searched desperately in the direction he was pointing.

"Look over there. Can you see them now?" Lucky asked.

I followed the tip of his pointed finger and gasped in amazement when I saw the two hippos. The tops of their heads and eyes were poking out of the water. I never would have detected them without Lucky's guidance.

We sat for a few minutes, observing the hippos. After they disappeared back into the water, Lucky announced, "Two days ago, one of the river guides died not far from here. His boat was struck by a hippo. The attack killed him."

I felt a lump in my throat. There we were, buzzing with anticipation, itching to see hippopotamuses up close. Lucky's words sank in like lead. For a short time after, a heightened sense of fear drowned our excitement, and thoughts of self-preservation washed away our fits of laughter. For the rest of the afternoon, whenever a head emerged out of the water off in the distance, one of us would yell "Hippoooo!" and we would all paddle in the opposite direction at full speed.

Despite the threat of a hippo or croc attack, we experienced more fun than fear. After parking our boats next to the riverbank, we switched back to the kayaks that one of the guides had shuttled over. Once we were back in the water, I noticed clusters of plum-sized, yellow fruit hanging off the low-lying branches of lush trees. I paddled over, reached up to pick a few and showed them to Lucky.

"Oh, that is the marula fruit," he said matter-of-factly, piquing my curiosity.

I was overjoyed to make this discovery on the Zambezi River: I was holding the source of the sweet, creamy Amarula liqueur I had learned to love in Namibia.

I grabbed a handful of marula. I bit into one. Its fleshy texture was mildly sweet, the flavour a bit like a tart pear. I heard a *plop plop* in the slow-moving water behind me. Then something hit my head and bounced off my shoulder. I looked behind me: Sion was chuckling to himself as if he had just told the most hilarious joke. "Sorry 'bout that. Didn't mean to hit you."

"C'mon, let's team up," I said with a naughty grin.

We stocked up and declared war on Brian, Lucky and the guys. This inaugural marula-throwing battle put us all into a state of uncontrollable laughter. Fred, Craig and Damian ganged up on Sion and pelted him with no mercy. Tears welled up in my eyes when he frantically paddled away like he was being chased by an angry hippo.

A bucket of chilled Bohlinger's waited for us back at camp. My mouth watered at the sight of them. Aside from the refreshing beers, the best part of our return was the ingenious outdoor shower set-up. The camp had two private showers constructed out of natural materials. Each stall was equipped with a pail filled with solar-heated water suspended from above.

I undressed and opened up the knob to start the shower flow. The sun-warmed water trickled down my body like gentle caresses. It was heavenly to be surrounded by fresh air, towering teak trees and a clear view of the sky. This normally indoor routine gave "creature comfort" a whole new meaning.

At sunset, Brian took us for a drive. We were all tipsy from the beer. The truck bumped along the rough road and threatened to send us into midair like a wild amusement ride. The wind cooled my face and whipped my hair around: I loved feeling alive and present.

Lucky got our full attention when he shouted, "Look!" as two giraffes galloped by before disappearing into the bush. A flock of thrushes scattered from the branches of an ebony tree. Though I was grateful for all these animal sightings, what I really wanted to see was an elephant. Lucky told me they had seen three separate herds the night before my arrival: I would have to be patient.

Back at camp, we feasted on wine and desserts and fell into bouts of hysteria until our bellies ached. After we shared dirty jokes around the campfire, sleepiness kicked in. I retired to the comforts of my spacious tent. The guys were two to a tent, but as the lone female, I had the pleasure of having one all to myself. The large canvas tent housed a double bed with crisp, cream-coloured sheets. This set-up was by far my most luxurious accommodation since the start of my backpacking trip, save for the sleepover at Doug's.

I WOKE AT SIX and sat at the river's edge to write. I watched the sun rise above the glistening river. Out in the wilderness, it felt decadent to feast on freshly baked biscuits smothered with butter and strawberry jam while sipping my morning cup of coffee.

We were about to depart for our final river excursion when Brian announced that five more travellers would be joining us. Within the hour, three French-speaking men from Burundi arrived at the camp. I couldn't stop staring at their outfits. They were wearing canary-yellow and bright-purple geometric-patterned shirts and matching pants. Their ensembles reminded me of loud ski apparel from the late 1980s.

The men were accompanied by a Dutch couple who were working in Harare as horticulturists. I greeted them with a cheerful hello and explained that my mom was from the Netherlands. The blank look on their faces seemed to say, *So what?* My friendly Canadian demeanour and shared Dutch heritage failed to impress them.

The spontaneous friendship that formed between me, the guys and the guides grew stronger during our second day on the river. The newcomers, however, didn't share our enthusiasm. When an explosive round of paddle-splashing erupted, I detected traces of irritation on their faces. It wasn't surprising when the five of them bolted while the rest of us engaged in more marula fruit warfare.

Once the battle subsided, Lucky and Brian led us to some flat rocks for a break in the sun away from the rapids. Malachite kingfishers showed off their vibrant indigo and orange hues while clusters of bright-yellow butterflies fluttered along the shores of the river. I spied a small crocodile perched like a statue on a fallen tree trunk, and my shoulder muscles tensed up when Sion pointed out a pair of hippos. A nervous energy ripped through my stomach. Lucky laughed and assured us we weren't in any danger. I relaxed a little but still maintained my hawk eye.

With only an hour of the river safari remaining, I treasured each minute with the guys. As with my time with Anna in South Africa and my week with the Namibia crew, I knew this separation would be another bittersweet farewell. In good company, my preoccupation with family had faded into the background. All I could do was appreciate these moments and embrace the friendships for what they were: fun but fleeting.

Brian drove me back to Vic Falls dormitory before dinner, but I left immediately to meet the guys at the local Explorer's Pub. At the pub, I ordered my second ever Amarula Cream liqueur and savoured its sweet yumminess. Somehow it tasted different – better, perhaps, now that I knew its origins more intimately.

As much as I wanted to spend more time with the guys, I was dog-tired from the river trip and couldn't summon the energy to stay up late. Sion and I made a plan to go biking the next day. This gave me something to look forward to before returning to my mosquito-coil-infested sauna for the night.

The hippo sightings were a perfect prompt for a Lariam-induced nightmare. Instead, I fell into a heavy sleep and didn't wake until morning.

I COULDN'T STOP LAUGHING TO MYSELF when I saw Sion waiting for me at the bicycle rental shop. His pasty British complexion had turned a painful shade of pink from his days on the river. He was dressed in a lilac T-shirt, a neon-yellow baseball cap and a black fanny pack. To complete the full effect, Sion wore electric blue, thick-framed sunglasses that wouldn't be a hot fashion commodity for another decade. I never asked him if he was embracing the tacky tourist stereotype. From what I could see, he was either oblivious or didn't care. I loved this about him.

We walked out of the shop with our rental bikes and pedalled along the paved road in the direction of neighbouring Zambia. If I hadn't known better and someone told me they had cycled across the Zambian border into Zambia, my reaction would have been, "Wow, that sounds so amazing!"

In reality, it was a flat, four-kilometre bike ride along asphalt. But that didn't mean Sion and I didn't have a fun time. Crossing the border was easy: with a quick stamp of our passports, we headed toward the undeveloped town of Vic Falls on the Zambian side, a stone's throw from the falls. We stopped at a spacious, stone-paved viewpoint to admire the falls with no one else around. An unobstructed view of a wide rainbow in front of the Victoria Falls bridge on the Zimbabwe side made this stop worthwhile. And it was a bonus that Sion and I were able to cool off in the mist without getting completely soaked.

A large curio shop was the obvious spot to park our bikes. As soon as Sion and I entered, we ran into Fred and Craig, who had driven their car across the border. The guys were in the midst of an intense haggling session, so we left them to negotiate and seal their deals.

At least 30 salesmen were standing in and around the shop. Sion and I were fresh meat: I felt their hungry eyes home in on us. Their determination to sell some souvenirs was palpable. Over and over, I was greeted with perfectly scripted spiels: "Good day, madam. What do you think about these lovely elephant earrings? You would look so beautiful wearing them. Oh, and I have a matching necklace. I can give you a good price for the set." Followed by, "How about this hand-carved wooden mask? It was made right here in Zambia. It's one of a kind. Made from mahogany by a good friend of mine."

The salesmen embarked upon some friendly competition with each other, trying to win me over with their suave sales pitches and debonair looks. Talk about sales pressure. But these men were just trying to make an honest living. And even a backpacker on a budget has some cash to spare.

"Thank you. I'm just going to look around first before buying anything," I replied in a friendly but firm tone. This kept them at bay a bit longer so I could browse in peace.

Walking the aisles of the curio shop reminded me of my favourite stores back home. By age 15, I made the wonderful discovery that there was life beyond soul-crushing shopping malls. I loved to explore the west side of Vancouver on my own. Riding the city bus to the nouveau-hippie neighbourhood of West 4th Avenue in Kitsilano only took 40 minutes. But for me the short journey felt like travelling, no passport required.

Kits was nothing like the suburban neighbourhood where I grew up. Trendy restaurants, art cafes, and one-of-a-kind clothing shops lined the street. Tastefully designed character homes were in close proximity to beautiful, sandy beaches boasting views of the North Shore Mountains. Walking along 4th Avenue for hours on end made me feel sophisticated. Cultured.

After an hour of meandering, one shop stood out among the rest. Something about its colourful awning and curvy lettering beckoned me. *Come on in, Lisa. I've been waiting for you.*

I stepped into Marimba and struggled to shut the poorly fitted door behind me. A choir of wind chimes alerted the barely present store clerk of my arrival. Immediately, I was transfixed by a plethora of wooden sculptures, expressive masks, patterned fabrics, foreign musical instruments and beaded jewellery that hailed from all over Africa. Like the snap of fingers, Marimba transported me somewhere magical and far away, even though I was 20 kilometres from home, standing in a space no larger than 30 square metres.

"Miss, have you found anything you desire?"

I snapped back to the present and looked up at the eager, smiling salesman. After showing him a few items that suited my tastes, the bargaining song and dance began. He offered me some reasonable reductions. I purchased a two-foot giraffe carving that lived in my backpack until I could ship it home. A hand-size, delicately carved, mahogany hippopotamus made its way into my heart. Whenever I look at that little hippo, it carries the warm memory of my time with the guys on the river, my bike ride with Sion and the charming salesmen.

Carrying our new purchases, Sion and I pedalled back toward Zimbabwe, somehow dodging the requisite border re-entry fee. On the way back, we stopped on the Victoria Falls bridge to observe a bungee jumper about to take flight. For 90 American dollars, adrenaline junkies could jump 111 metres off the bridge down toward the Zambezi River.

"What do you think? You want to try?" Sion asked. His tone could have been construed as serious, but it was hard to tell behind the sunglasses.

It was tempting, but I knew if I wanted to make it all the way to Kenya, I couldn't justify the cost of this short-lived thrill: one jump was worth a few weeks of travel.

"Nah. It's never been something I ever *really* wanted to do…and it's way too much money for my budget."

Sion and I stayed to watch a few brave souls take the plunge. I didn't feel like I was missing out and could definitely think of cheaper ways to crap my pants.

We continued biking along Zambezi Drive in search of wildlife. I got my hopes up when two park rangers waved to us. I asked them about elephant sightings.

"Oh, yes, just this morning we saw two young elephants walking with their mother only a kilometre from here. Just keep going that way. I'm certain you'll see them. But please, *do* be careful."

We searched for another 15 minutes. We didn't see any animals, big *or* small. I suspected the rangers were either overly optimistic or just told us what we wanted to hear. In retrospect, looking for large wildlife while riding a bicycle wasn't the smartest idea. Even with my cycling legs, there was no way I could out-pedal an irritated elephant.

Sion and I rushed back to the rental shop to return our bikes then walked over to the Pink Baobab Cafe to enjoy one final meal together.

"Here's to not getting chomped in half by a hippo!" I rejoiced as our bottles of Bohlinger's clinked together in a celebratory toast.

"And here's to surviving marula berry battles!" Sion replied as we laughed thinking about our high-spirited river antics.

Sion was heading home to England the next day. After dinner, we hugged farewell. Even though I didn't want to say another goodbye, I knew new friendships and bouts of solitude were around the corner. I was excited to discover what was in store for me as I explored the rest of Zimbabwe. Anticipation outweighed any feelings of loneliness.

While walking back to my dorm, I saw Fred and Craig. I was so happy when they offered to drive me back to Shaka's Spear on their way back to South Africa. Not only would I have their good company but catching a ride with them meant I could skip the 12-hour night train to Bulawayo.

Thankfully, the six-hour drive to Bulawayo with the guys was nothing like my ride with Doug. Not long after we departed, the guys opened up to me about their past relationships. Listening to their South African perspectives was an eye-opener. Fred and Craig both wanted girlfriends, but they said as soon as they met a woman, she would set limitations, expect them to pay for everything and discourage them from seeing their friends.

These restrictions sounded foreign and old-fashioned to me. My past relationships in Canada had been balanced and modern. The guys' experiences made me think about Thomas and his views of women. I was beginning to think that maybe both men and women in South Africa had a role to play in perpetuating certain gender stereotypes.

THE NEXT DAY A LOCAL GUIDE named Sebastian showed up at Shaka's Spear and took a small group of us to Matobo National Park, located 40 kilometres away. During this day trip, I had the pleasure of meeting Lynn and Cece, two Americans who had been stationed in the West African nation of Gabon as volunteers for the Peace Corps. I had seen both of them walking around Victoria Falls, and I recognized Lynn's arresting light-blue eyes from the hostel in Johannesburg. Although we had never spoken to each other, I was glad they remembered me too.

Living in Japan, I met my share of Americans. Many of them left me with a negative impression by disregarding social norms and standing out like squeaky wheels: obnoxious, drunk, frat boys; couples making out on train platforms, oblivious to the squirming Japanese around them; dubious cults that promoted a glass-encased paradise populated with blonde-haired, blue-eyed disciples and handed out pamphlets to dark-haired followers of Shinto and Buddhism.

After Lynn and Cece told me about their community work in Gabon, they seemed open-minded and respectful of local customs, culture and language. I was drawn to Lynn's down-to-earth, no-bullshit personality and admired her blunt but tactful manner of speaking. She was someone I could have easily been friends with back home. Cece exuded a positive energy that extended to the tips of her tight black curls. Her electric personality made her easy to be around. I was thankful that Lynn and Cece quickly punctured my narrow-minded preconception of Americans as ignorant travellers.

When we arrived at Matopo Hills, my eyes widened in amazement. The write-up in my guidebook didn't even come close to describing this geographical marvel. It looked as though supernatural forces had created rounded granite sculptures and stacked them without having to concede to the laws of gravity. The massive boulders stood as tall as small dinosaurs and were balanced so precariously they looked like they would tip over at any moment. When I got up close to admire them, I noticed they were blanketed with delicate, speckled patterns of lime-green, orange and blue-grey lichen.

Seeing these wondrous formations left me awestruck. Despite my forced Christian upbringing, I never turned to religion to explain life's mysteries. And yet the topic of religion fascinates me. I understand why so many people believe in a higher power, if only to answer the probing question: *Why on earth does any of this exist?*

According to Sebastian, there was no clear consensus among scientists to explain the mysteries of Matopo. One explanation was that 37,000 years earlier, there was a series of massive volcanic eruptions in the Matobo region. Other sources claimed that these spectacular works of natural art formed billions of years ago.

Despite Matobo's raw beauty and mystifying origins, it was hard to ignore Zimbabwe's colonial past while walking around the park. British businessman Cecil Rhodes, the founder of the De Beers diamond company, moved from South Africa to Rhodesia for health reasons in the late 1800s. Thanks to his lucrative diamond discovery in South Africa, he purchased huge chunks of land in both countries. Decades after his death in 1902, Matobo National Park was created to honour Rhodes's wishes. An area known as the World's View (Malindidzimu Hill) was one of Rhodes's favourite places to sit, and is home to his burial site.

As he was a colonialist who believed that the Anglo-Saxon race was supreme, Rhodes's presence was not without controversy. Matopo Hills had long been considered a sacred place for many Indigenous African tribes, who performed religious ceremonies there well before racist Rhodes arrived on the scene. Understandably, some statues of Rhodes were removed after Zimbabwe gained its independence in 1980.

Robert Mugabe, Zimbabwe's autocrat for decades who never hid his disdain for the white man, put more money into infrastructure and development near the capital, Harare, neglecting Bulawayo and places like Matobo. Because visitors to the park provide a steady cash flow, the removal of Rhodes's grave is unlikely. As far as I was concerned, his grave didn't add any value to the area nor did it enrich my experience. If anything, its presence was a blatant example of Rhodes's ethnocentric attitude.

Our informal tour of the area became more personal when Sebastian opened up about his childhood. "I grew up not far from Matobo. I used to play in an area about two kilometres from here with my friends."

His carefree exploration as a young boy had made him into a local expert. Sebastian led us into the nearby caves to view some Bushmen (San) rock paintings. Although some had faded, many were still visible with their red-ochre hues. We all gathered around Sebastian, who had squatted down to begin his lesson. Sebastian's dark moustache and medium-length spiral locks, along with the long wooden stick he held with casual authority, made him look like a modern professor. And an attractive one at that.

I studied the wall with an open mind and keen curiosity. The informal pattern of the rock paintings was predominantly made up of human figures equally spaced apart. Further down the wall there were more drawings of what appeared to be interlocking hands.

"There are thousands of similar rock paintings in Zimbabwe. They were created by the hunters and gatherers who lived here about 2,000 years ago. But the San painting you're looking at here is only about 500 years old. It's possible the style was influenced by Egyptian artists or even Chinese drawings."

Even with my art history background, I had no way of knowing if Sebastian's interpretation was fact or fiction. But his enthusiasm for the subject was admirable.

Sebastian brought us to lesser-known pockets of the park, maintaining that no scholars had ever set foot there, even though I found it hard to believe these places could remain secret. In one of these spots, Sebastian told us, "Not far from here, my friend and I found an old copper relic that was later donated to a museum. It happened at the end of the Rhodesian civil war, so we lied about where we found it." He laughed. "We were only 10 and had been warned repeatedly *not* to play in the park because of all the land mines buried there."

Not once in my childhood did I have to question the safety of my surroundings. Sebastian was only a few years older than me. I couldn't imagine what it would have been like to find out a classmate had been maimed or killed because of some innocent exploration in nature.

Listening to him casually reminisce about his precarious childhood reminded me of Mom and her childhood in the Netherlands during the Second World War. The schools in her town were occupied by the German military, forcing the children to stay home or find alternate places to learn. Mom told me about a soldier who pilfered the bicycle her brother used for his butcher delivery job. Food was scarce: Mom and her sister were proud when they hid potatoes from the German soldiers. She and her siblings were warned never to answer the door at night and to run upstairs if someone came knocking. Soldiers were known to arrive unannounced, looking for families hiding Jews.

Despite their serious and potentially dire experiences, Sebastian and my mom recollected their youth as a series of humorous anecdotes. For them, war was just a part of growing up.

Our group had fun bouldering on the small hills known as *kopjes* (little heads) and then Sebastian drove us through the game reserve, an area protected against poachers. He was in search of white and black rhinos, as this region was known to have healthy populations. It was cold, overcast and drizzly. The rhinos must have been taking shelter somewhere dry and warm because we didn't even spot one.

Our search for wildlife wasn't a complete bust. Cece saw two giraffes in the distance, while the rest of us saw warthog, impala and some peculiar-looking black birds I had never seen before. The birds stood slightly taller than Canadian geese and had bright-red, bulbous skin on the sides of their heads and necks. I learned from Sebastian these fascinating creatures were southern ground hornbills, a common species in Southern Africa.

Looking like a cross between a raven and a turkey vulture, these hornbills were ugly *and* beautiful. In addition to their bold red colour and bulging throat sac, the birds were very striking with their big beaks, human-like, long-lashed eyes and black wings that revealed white tips when they took flight. Anyone can recognize a giraffe or elephant. I was happy to identify this lesser-known African species.

CECE, LYNN AND I spent two more days together exploring Bulawayo. After we'd found nothing but cheap items at the flea market, our luck changed at one of the curio shops. It was fun bargaining with all the "mama" and "papa" merchants, who affectionately called us their friends. Their persistent sales tactics wore me down until I left with some brown-and-beige-patterned handwoven baskets.

After a feast of greasy Chinese food, we traipsed around the city in hopes of settling our bloated stomachs and ended up at the local movie theatre. *Disclosure*, featuring Michael Douglas and Demi Moore, had been replaced by two B films.

The plot and acting were abysmal. The white characters were portrayed as wealthy, corrupt, promiscuous liars. The exaggerated sex scenes made me squirm in my seat. I wanted to sink down and disappear through the floor. I prayed the locals in the theatre didn't think Westerners were anything like the unrealistic portrayals on the big screen.

EVEN THOUGH OUR TIME TOGETHER WAS SHORT, I felt lucky to have forged a friendship with them. Since arriving in Zimbabwe, I'd had the good fortune of spending time in exciting places and meeting interesting people. Despite this good run, I felt a twinge of sadness when Lynn and Cece left for Gabon: I was on my own again.

I left the comforts of Shaka's Spear and said goodbye to Bulawayo for good – I was heading east, roughly 300 kilometres, to visit the Great Zimbabwe ruins. As I loaded up my backpack in preparation for the next leg of my trip, the nail-biting drive with Jake and Doug felt like a distant memory, nothing more than a great story to tell. The unexpected connection with Miriam and Grace on the "nightmare" train, the lively days I'd spent with my Zambezi River crew and the mystical visit to Matobo all made that hair-raising night in Doug's car worth it. With over half the country waiting to be explored, I was eager to keep moving.

Nine

EN ROUTE TO MASVINGO, the bus pulled into a large dirt lot next to the highway to drop off and pick up passengers. Outside, a variety of vendors – some seated on chairs with coolers, some on blankets on the ground – were waiting to sell their goods, snacks and chilled beverages. A boy who looked around 11 years old held bags of nuts and a basket of food I didn't recognize. He looked up toward the open bus windows chanting, "Samosa! Samosa!"

I reached down and handed him a few coins. With a beaming smile he passed two samosas up to me in a thin napkin. I bit into one. The outside layer was mildly soggy and reminded me of *inari* sushi pockets. The rice filling lacked spice, its bland flavour and texture nothing like the tasty Indian potato-filled samosas I had eaten before.

As I took a second bite, I noticed some little dark specks mixed into the rice and assumed it was ground black pepper. When I inspected the samosa more closely, I realized the mysterious specks were the tiniest ants I had ever seen. They must have gorged themselves to death.

The dead ants were so damn cute I just couldn't get upset. I finished off the samosa then ate the other one. Nothing like a few ant samosas to whet the appetite. Still hungry, I scanned the row of vendors and saw a woman carrying bags of white buns. I drooled at the sight of them and waved to get her attention. She approached my window and I bought a bag of six.

I opened the bag and inhaled. The little buns smelled irresistible. I took a bite of one and had to stop myself from stuffing the whole thing into my mouth. The bun was buttery, slightly sweet and, oh, so unbelievably soft.

I had found heaven. On a bus. In the middle of Zimbabwe. For the next month, I made sure I was never without a bag of these delicious sweet buns, a jar of peanut butter, and baby plantains.

I arrived in Masvingo with my bag of sweet buns empty. I checked into the hostel for one night, arranged a ride to the Great Zimbabwe ruins and caught a lift there early the next morning.

Before walking around the expansive site, I studied the pamphlet. Spanning nearly 1,800 acres, the ruins were the remnants of a medieval city. The ancient site dates from the 11th to 15th centuries, long before colonialism, and houses impressive fortress-like structures surrounded by walls made of granite stones. Although the origins of the ruins remain enigmatic, most archaeologists credit the Shona for its construction.

As with my visit to Vic Falls, I strolled around the ruins with only a handful of other visitors. With so few people around, it was hard to envision what this medieval city of stone would have looked like in its heyday, when thousands of people lived there.

I followed a rubbly path to the Great Enclosure, the best-known structure within the site, believed to have functioned as a royal palace. The elliptical enclosure was built around elephant-sized boulders. High above, a triangular rocky formation dwarfed the largest boulders, and its unique appearance reminded me of Le Corbusier's Ronchamp chapel.

Only when I stood in front of the massive fortress did I understand its status as a UNESCO World Heritage Site. Its walls, made from lichen-covered stones and brick-shaped rocks, looked to be a hundred metres across with a circumference of more than 200 metres. Even though there was considerable deterioration, the impenetrable walls still stood ten metres high and five metres thick in some sections. A second set of walls was built within the main enclosure, connecting to a conical tower that had to be as tall as two giraffes.

It was after ten in the morning. The scorching sun made me move at a snail's pace. Sticky sweat coated my body. My shoulders and forearms felt like they were on fire. The ruins were fascinating, but the heat made me miss Vic Falls. I longed to douse my body in its cool mist. My only option was to take refuge in the shade of the fortress wall and drink some water.

After cooling off, I explored another area of the ruins where three artists, seated on the ground, were working on some pottery in front of a round, thatched-roof hut. The women wore cotton head coverings and had their long legs stretched out in front of them with their ankles crossed. Unlike me, they appeared to be unbothered by the heat.

The women were completing the final touches on some dark-silver ceramics. I stopped to admire their work. They smiled politely at me but remained focused. Their technique seemed second nature to them as they chatted away to each other. They were applying a material resembling hematite, which gave each piece a smooth, lustrous sheen. I was drawn to the straightforward pattern of dots and shimmery texture, so I bought a tea set, even though I knew it was purely decorative and not food-safe.

I sat down on the grass in the shade to write a postcard and noted the date: April 9th. Another week would mark the halfway point of my journey. All of a sudden I felt a surge of restlessness and urgency. I had a limited budget and two months of travel remaining. Visiting Malawi, Tanzania, Zanzibar and possibly Kenya meant covering an additional 3000 kilometres before my return to Joburg, from where I would fly home.

I would have loved to spend more time in each area I visited, but my desire to see more of the continent outweighed the need to stay in one place for longer. The ruins were impressive, but there was nothing else keeping me there. I explored for another half-hour and caught a ride back to town.

AFTER THE RUINS, MY PLAN WAS to head east to hike in the Chimanimani mountain range near the Mozambique border. The next morning, while I was packing up my belongings, a German named Gabi invited me to accompany her to Lake Kyle, 30 kilometres away from town.

"Sorry, I won't have time. I'm going to Chimanimani and need to catch the early bus if I want to arrive today," I told her.

Gabi's brown eyes were full of determination. "Oh, it's supposed to be very pretty. Why don't you catch the bus at noon instead? I'll make sure we make it back in time."

I sensed she wasn't going to take no for an answer. I'm not sure why I agreed to go, but I did. Reluctantly.

By the time I learned that Gabi's gift of the gab would annoy even the most chatty traveller, it was too late to turn around. Cars whizzed by as we walked along the main road away from Masvingo with our hitchhiker thumbs raised high. Fifteen minutes in, light rain began to fall. Instead of feeling excited about visiting Lake Kyle, I was regretting my decision to go. Not only would it be a rushed visit but I also didn't care for Gabi's company.

A man picked us up and drove us the first 20 kilometres, then dropped us off with several kilometres to go. Gabi and I headed along a desolate road toward the lake in hopes of catching another lift. After we'd walked more than a kilometre, the wind picked up and unleashed its fury. The light drizzle turned into a pelting downpour. Within minutes, my shorts and T-shirt were completely soaked, suctioned to my skin like a blanket of leeches. My regret turned into a boiling pot of frustration. I didn't need any more adverse weather to convince me to keep going.

"This is ridiculous. It's got to be at least another five more kilometres to the lake. I'm heading back to town to catch my bus," I said without hiding my annoyance.

It was rare for me to get mad, but I was fuming: I was furious at myself for agreeing to go with Gabi instead of catching the early bus. Regardless of how she felt, I was turning back.

"Yeah, okay. I'll go with you, then. You're right. This weather is terrible."

We slogged it back to the main road and waited an hour before someone picked us up. Sitting in the pickup truck's cargo bed, all I could think was, *I'd better not miss that goddamn bus.*

Back at the hostel, I towelled off and changed in record time. I rushed to the station and made it onto the bus only minutes before it was scheduled to leave. I was determined to arrive in Chimanimani village by dinner. The ticket clerk instructed me to disembark the bus at a junction before it continued north to Mutare. She assured me a Chimanimani-bound bus would arrive at the junction "sometime in the early afternoon."

It was warm and sunny when I stepped off the Mutare-bound bus. The junction had no notable landmarks save for a small corner store next to a cluster of large shady trees.

Minutes after my arrival, a group of barefoot children appeared and gathered around me and my backpack. There were ten of them in total, ranging from ages 2 to 12.

The first to greet me was a young, smiling girl in a pink-and-grey striped dress, and a boy clad in a pink golf shirt and holding a two-metre-long bamboo pole. The older girl with them wore a faded Mickey Mouse T-shirt and a blue skirt and clutched an orange bowl full of what looked like peanuts.

Two older boys balancing watermelon-shaped gourds on their shoulders offered me huge smiles. There was a young child with an unusually large forehead perched on one of the boy's shoulders. She stared at me with serious, attentive eyes. Her toddler face was dirty, and her stubby legs revealed dry, cracked skin and fresh scars from insect bites. Her large protruding navel poked out the unbuttoned, stained, cotton outfit she was wearing.

The children's animated reactions and smiling faces left me with the impression that few foreigners spent time in their village. They seemed intrigued by my presence. In turn, I was thrilled to make a connection with them.

Two of the younger kids took turns clasping my hand while another linked her arm through mine. Their palms were dry and rough but radiated warmth and affection. The oldest boys could string together some simple sentences in English, but because of the language barrier it was difficult to communicate. Instead, our shared language was laughter while we attempted to talk to each other. This was the first place I'd visited in Zimbabwe where English wasn't widely spoken. It made me wish I had learned a bit of the local language.

To help pass the time, I sang, "You Are My Sunshine," and "My Bonnie," a Scottish folk song my dad sang to me as a child. The children listened intently to my musical interludes. My heart smiled when they clapped along to their own songs. Their angelic voices filled the air as they tapped the long poles against the ground to keep the rhythmic beat.

When I gestured to take their photos, the children squealed with excitement. It was a joy to be around them while I waited for the bus to arrive. They reminded me of the endearing children I'd met in South Africa and Namibia. By Western standards, they had little but they seemed happy. Spending time with them made me think how wonderful it would be to stay in Africa and teach.

Three hours passed. I had serious doubts about the elusive bus to Chimanimani. I looked past the clusters of scrubby trees and the sea of tall, yellow grasses and watched the sun sink below the horizon. It was almost six o'clock. Like clockwork, the children left in twos and threes, returning to homes not visible from the road. When the final pair left my side and waved goodbye, I felt a wave of unease. *Please don't leave me here on my own.*

After I lost sight of them, I was all alone. The remaining light of the sunset faded behind low-lying, wispy clouds. I knew the bus wasn't coming. If by fluke it did show up, it would mean a very late passage in the dark.

Three men joined me at the junction corner. They kept their distance and eyed me with suspicion. I must have looked like a naive woman with poor judgment, waiting on my own in the dark. I didn't feel threatened by their presence, but I did feel vulnerable standing there with no plan to act upon. Nobody knew I was there. I had no idea what to do next. Naturally, thoughts of my parents crept into my conscience.

It was summertime. I was 13, riding my bike along the dyke well after sunset. With the exception of some distant airplanes, the moon and stars were the only lights in the navy sky. A kilometre into my ride, I happened to pass Mom and Dad, who were out for an evening stroll. After Mom realized it was me on the bike, she shouted, "Lisa, what do you think you're doing out here in the dark? Do you want to get attacked? You're *asking* for trouble, girl."

I pedalled furiously away from them and yelled, "Who would ask for something like that?" I was so angry. She'd ruined the night for me. No longer could I enjoy the warm evening breeze against my face and the openness of the clear, starry sky. All I could think about was if someone was lurking in the shadows waiting to pounce on me. *Thanks, Mom.*

I pushed Mom's voice out of my head. Just then, a lorry pulled up and picked up one of the men at the junction. I wasn't about to hitchhike: I needed a plan.

I studied the uninhabited surroundings. There was no flashing neon sign advertising a vacancy at a local motel. Aside from a little corner store, nothing resembling a hostel or lodge existed. I contemplated sleeping outside, away from the road near the store. Fortunately, my common sense kicked in. *That would be very unwise, Lisa.* I wouldn't be able to fall asleep, not to mention I had no idea what wild animals roamed around there at night.

I crept up the stairs of the storefront and peered inside the main window. The absence of lights made it evident the owners had closed up the shop. Filled with reticence and desperation, I walked around to the side of the building and found a small structure with dimly lit windows. I tiptoed toward it, lured by a pleasing aroma of food being cooked over coals in a small hut next to someone's humble home.

Like a prowler, I snuck around to the back of the tiny dwelling. I hesitated before knocking gently three times. The door opened slowly. A woman in her late 20s appeared, looking as if she were expecting me. I wondered what she thought when she saw a lone white woman holding a large backpack standing at her door. Perhaps news of the silly foreigner waiting at the junction had already made its way through the small village.

"Hello. I was waiting for the bus to Chimanimani, but it never arrived. Is there a guest house or somewhere I can spend the night?"

She shook her head and replied in English, "No. No guest house here." Then she invited me in, no questions asked. "You can stay here tonight," she said softly.

This lovely woman introduced herself as Simba. But I'll always remember her as my guardian angel.

Simba had been preparing a meal in the compact cooking hut next to the corner store owned by her cousin. She boarded in a room roughly 50 metres from the store where she worked. Simba brought me to her living quarters then left me on my own.

The room was simply furnished but had everything a person would require: two twin beds pushed together enclosed by a large mosquito net, a four-drawer dresser, a small round table, two chairs, a small lamp.

Twenty minutes later, Simba returned with a steaming bowl of food. She put the meal in front of me. I inhaled the wonderful aromas. The dinner included *sadza*, a cornmeal-based starch that is a common Zimbabwean staple. Its rubbery texture reminded me of Cream of Wheat prepared with not enough liquid. I loved *sadza*'s subtle flavour. It was a perfect accompaniment to the grilled vegetables and tender stewed beef Simba had cooked to perfection. The *sadza* soaked up the savoury sauce like a sponge, ensuring each bite was flavourful.

Perched on the wooden chair in the faintly lit room, I relished each mouthful of the beef stew, feeling safe and grateful for Simba's generosity. This table for one remains the most unexpected dining scenario I have ever experienced, and it became one of my most memorable evenings in Africa.

After dinner, there was nothing else for me to do but get ready for bed. That's when the night took a strange but amusing turn.

Simba said I could sleep in her room in one of the twin beds. A few minutes before I snuggled into bed, an older woman in her 60s or 70s – perhaps an aunt or grandmother – entered the room. She let out some violent coughs to clear her throat before getting into the bed next to me. The woman acknowledged my presence with a wry smile. She muttered a few words in what I assumed was Shona before chuckling to herself. I guess neither of us was expecting the other as a sleeping companion.

Within minutes of her head hitting the pillow, she fell fast asleep. I smiled to myself, thankful I had a full belly and was secure and warm. Despite my being a light sleeper, the sounds of her heavy breathing and snoring didn't keep me awake.

SQUAWKING CHICKENS woke me up at 5:30 the next morning. I got dressed in a hurry: there was *no way* I was going to miss the 7:00 a.m. ride to Chimanimani. I thanked Simba for her hospitality. I thought about leaving money behind for the lodging and meal, but Simba seemed like the kind of person who would have refused the offer. I walked over to the junction. After boarding the bus, I regretted my decision not to leave a few Zim dollars to show my gratitude.

Though it started out as a stressful mishap, the failure to catch the afternoon bus from the junction turned out to be serendipitous. My rash decision to go to Lake Kyle with Gabi had been a hidden blessing. Instead of disaster, I was granted gifts. The precious moments with the wonderful children and Simba's kindness and generosity resulted in a detour I will *never* forget.

Catching the two-and-a-half-hour bus ride to Chimanimani a day late was worth the unpredictable night. The tranquil scenery in the light of dawn was lovely. I focused on the views from the bus window. The green rolling hills reminded me of Matobo. The little huts dotting the landscape fit perfectly into the natural surroundings, looking as though someone had painted them.

The sun broke through the clouds, revealing hundreds of pine trees at the base of the mountains as we neared Chimanimani. The bus pulled up to a row of shops. The undeveloped village boasted a few conveniences: a gas station and two grocery stores selling the exact same toiletries and food products, including expired bread.

After I walked away from the village centre, I was greeted by friendly locals who stopped to say hello. Their warmth made me feel welcome as I walked one kilometre to the hostel.

Despite the friendly reception I received throughout the village, my positive attitude was short-lived. For reasons I couldn't understand, the moment I stepped foot into Heaven Lodge, I felt out of place, as if I didn't belong. The feeling was familiar, like that dreaded day I had arrived at school in Grade 7 to find I had no friends.

The spacious dining room had around 20 backpackers seated at a long table in groups of three and four. They were busy chatting away to one another, sipping mugs of tea and coffee. Maps were spread out in front of them as they discussed viable hiking routes. Many of them seemed to have established friendships already. It felt as though I had arrived at the exact moment when everyone at the lodge was content with their current company. *Thanks, but we met our quota this week. We don't need another backpacker to make small talk with today. Move along.*

Up until that day, I had pushed myself to connect with others. For the most part it happened naturally, without much effort. Now I felt like an outsider. People arrived and departed from hostels all the time. *Am I really interesting enough that they'll want to spend time getting to know another backpacker?*

Before I decided to travel to Africa on my own, two of my closest friends invited me to go to Central America. It would have been easy to travel with them. But I didn't want easy. I craved new experiences without familiar faces reminding me of home. I wasn't willing to compromise my itinerary in order to accommodate others, especially friends. I knew travelling on my own would be a brave undertaking, but I've always enjoyed solitary pursuits. Even when I am alone, it is rare that I feel lonely.

In Chimanimani, however, I felt lonely and insecure. Without the distraction of good company, my mind wandered to how things were unfolding back home. I had sent a few postcards, but I hadn't spoken with my family for a month.

Even though I had been fortunate to form quick bonds with strangers, I never discussed my family worries. These friendships didn't last long enough to move beyond the phase of having fun and revealing the best of oneself. Surely, no one wanted to hear about my depressing family situation back home, and I avoided dwelling on this aspect of my life in the midst of fulfilling my African journey.

I looked around Heaven Lodge. I wasn't in the mood for initiating small talk. I walked upstairs to my room to be alone in my thoughts: I had to ride this one out.

After unpacking my belongings, some much-needed self-talk snapped me out of my negative state of mind. *Stop feeling sorry for yourself, Lisa. You've been really lucky so far.*

I climbed an open staircase that led to a little balcony with peekaboo views of the nearby hills. There, I was greeted by Naomi, a young music teacher from Tokyo who was volunteering in Mutare. I followed her outside after she asked me to join her at the front of the lodge. We sat down on the spacious, sunny patio next to a stocky woman wearing a colourful crocheted brimmed beanie. She was sitting cross-legged with her shoulders slouched forward. Her long, golden pigtails shimmered in the sun. The woman took a drag of her cigarette and gave me an encouraging, "Hey, how's it going?"

I no longer felt like an outsider. I convinced myself, *Okay, you can do this.*

Keelie was from Toronto, in the midst of a cultural studies project funded by an NGO. After chatting, I learned she and Naomi had already visited the Chimanimani Mountains. Keelie was telling me about some of the hiking routes when an Australian woman joined us. Brook was a law student and fellow climber. We hit it off right away. When she invited me to walk to Bridal Veil Falls with her that afternoon, I happily accepted.

By the time Brook and I began the five-kilometre walk toward the falls, my negative frame of mind had improved. I felt more cheerful as we talked about our shared love of rock climbing. My passion for adventure was rekindled after I told Brook about my plans to camp and hike in Chimanimani.

After visiting the largest falls in the world, I didn't expect to be amazed by the sight of another water feature. I was mistaken.

When we arrived at Bridal Veil, I was struck by the sheer natural beauty that surrounded us. Roughly 50 metres high and measuring one elephant wide at the top and five elephants wide at the base, the waterfall was a bucket compared to Victoria Falls, but it was still stunning. The dark, rocky, tiered backdrop gave the illusion that the steady flow of cascading water was travelling down a giant widening staircase. Lush green shrubs and tropical trees encircled a tranquil lagoon. Brook and I ran straight for the pristine pool and waded up to our thighs. At that moment, any lingering insecurities and thoughts of home were washed away by the refreshing water.

THE NEXT MORNING I left Heaven Lodge on my own to explore the nearby hills and get some much-needed exercise. After a casual climb up a wide dirt road, I began ascending Pork Pie Hill through the Chimanimani Eland Sanctuary, a ten-kilometre return hike from the hostel.

I was desperate to get my heart rate up, to push my quads and calves beyond a six-stair ascent onto a bus. Sitting around on my butt was doing little for my atrophying rock-climber physique. Two months into my journey, I felt like quite the pork pie myself. I was looking for any excuse to burn off the sweet buns that already seemed to have lodged themselves in my waist, hips and buttocks.

When I reached the top of the little mountain, I didn't care that stubborn clouds obscured the views of the sanctuary. Beads of sweat dripped down my back, chest and forehead. I felt invigorated. This was the hardest my heart and lungs had worked in weeks.

I must have just burned off two sweet buns. Maybe even three.

I turned around and began the five-kilometre descent down the trail, relishing my small but satisfying feat. I was taken aback when two baboons popped out of the bushes. At first I was curious about their unexpected presence. That initial intrigue vanished the moment their numbers doubled. And then doubled again.

In a matter of seconds, a troop of ten blocked off the trail. Beady eyes peered out from dark furrowed brows. I felt the weight of their cold, untrusting stares: these baboons didn't look like the docile pair I saw in the Drakensberg with Simon and Rowen. A surge of panic ripped through my chest. Back home, I sort of knew what to do if I encountered a bear. But a *baboon*? I was well aware of the crocodile and hippo risks when I paddled the Zambezi. How was it that I didn't read any warnings about baboons in my trusted guidebook?

I looked around. There were no other hikers in sight. My pulse quickened as I contemplated an exit plan. Maybe showing dominance was my key to escape. I kept a close eye on the troop and grabbed a large branch to make myself look larger. In this moment of fear and uncertainty, I had a vague recollection about how baboons can turn vicious when threatened. Running away wasn't an option, but staying calm was easier said than done. One wrong move, and I feared one of them would rip my arm out of its socket and start a game of catch.

I brandished the branch high above my head, lowered my eyes and backed away slowly. The best defence I could muster was a lame, "Get out of here!" I hit the branch on the ground to compensate for the quiver in my voice, but the baboons seemed unaffected by my pathetic intimidation tactics.

Then I remembered: I was in *their* territory.

The baboons became still and quiet. The one closest to me paced back and forth. Its hairless, angry-looking, bulbous butt looked like it could do more damage than its long, canine teeth. The baboon stopped to pick at its matted rump. Then it emitted a few deep grunts followed by a blend of barking and high-pitched squawking before it moved away from me. The peculiar sounds made my heart jump. I hoped it was simply telling the others, *Check out the linebacker shoulders on that one. She's not gonna back down. And she doesn't even have any food!*

After a minute the troop lost interest in me. A train of pink asses followed the leader into the bushes. Perhaps they understood I had nothing they desired, but I wasn't about to stick around to test that theory. I jogged down the hill with my heart still pounding, looking over my shoulder, warning a few hikers along the way.

MY ENCOUNTER WITH THE BABOONS didn't deter me from going to Chimanimani National Park two days later. I was disappointed when I had no luck renting any camping gear. I had to settle for a day trip.

I was fully aware that trekking solo in an unfamiliar mountain range when no one back home knew my whereabouts might have seemed foolish. But, even after my run-in with the baboons, I didn't feel unsafe or ill-prepared. Nor did I have an alternative, except *not* to go.

A couple from the hostel offered me a lift to the park entrance. After a stalled engine delayed us by two hours, I didn't leave Mutekeswane base camp until almost 11:00. It was reassuring knowing there were fellow hikers in the park, but it didn't take long before I was completely alone.

Following the advice of fellow backpackers, I chose Bailey's Foley for my first hike. The first two kilometres of the arduous ascent took me through a mist-filled, rocky landscape. I trudged up the steep route, scrambling ungracefully over piles of scree, jagged rocks and serrated boulders along a poorly marked trail. The occasional cairn kept me on the route. Only once did I have to retrace my steps when the trail seemed to disappear on me. An hour in, the vertical grade relented for the last few kilometres.

After reaching a small hut, I was rewarded with a dramatic viewpoint. The panorama of peaks seemed to extend indefinitely. An ocean of quartzite glistened against a smattering of lime- and forest-green palettes. I was dwarfed by the vastness of the mountains. I was in complete solitude, but I didn't feel lonely. Instead, I was overwhelmed with gratitude by the beauty that surrounded me.

Despite the cloud cover, it was warm and muggy. I wiped the sweat from my flushed face, took off my daypack and pulled out a snack of sweet buns, peanut butter and plantains. I scanned my surroundings – the mountains were all mine.

I was basking in the view and enjoying a brief visit from the sun when some movement in my peripheral vision caught my attention. I looked over. A figure about 50 metres away was heading in my direction. *Thank god*, it wasn't a baboon. This one was human. The man stopped to take in the scenery but kept his distance.

A couple of minutes passed. I assumed he was about to leave. Then, looking a little sheepish, he walked over to me and said, "Thanks for sharing the view."

Like me, this Aussie hadn't seen a single hiker since leaving base camp. We chatted for a while, sharing our abbreviated versions of how we ended up in Zimbabwe. I felt like an inferior adventurer when Paul told me he'd been travelling around Southern Africa by bicycle. Until his arrival, I was content hiking on my own, but I welcomed his company. In Africa, I was learning that beautiful moments were more memorable when shared with another person, even if it was just a fleeting moment with a stranger.

Paul was also hiking for the day and on a mission to cover more terrain. Like a gazelle, he was gone within seconds. I remained a few minutes longer. I took a swig of water and threw on my pack, its dampness cool against my spine.

I was leaving for Skeleton's Pass when two red-faced hikers appeared, out of breath, drenched in sweat. "Oh, are we ever glad to see you," one of them laughed nervously. "We got ourselves a bit lost earlier…weren't sure if we were going the right way."

"Do you want to have a look at my map?" I asked, smiling.

Relief replaced the strain on their faces. The guys walked over, and our getting-to-know-you ritual began. They were around my age, early 20s. Medical students from the UK. Their exhausted condition made me think they spent more time reading human anatomy textbooks and dissecting cadavers than testing the limits of their own bodies.

The Brits invited themselves to hike with me for the rest of the day. I was glad to have them along. My Blundstones were comfortable for walking but lacked sufficient ankle support for hiking. Alone in my thoughts, I could have lost my footing in these isolated mountains. It would have been easy to become distracted by the scenery and roll my ankle – or, worse, trip and bash my head and end up unconscious, with vultures pecking away at my bloody skull.

The thought of being stuck on the trail with an injury made me appreciate the Brits' background in medicine. The guys were pleased to have me as their navigator, though I wasn't quite sure why they thought I was qualified to take on this role.

Darkening clouds threatened rain as we trekked through the rocky, lichen-covered escarpment toward Mozambique. The international border posting was nothing but a faded, rusty sign held up by a pair of sun-bleached timbers nearly three times my height. Aside from the lemon-coloured lettering prohibiting anyone from crossing into Mozambique, there was nothing – and no one – stopping us from illegally entering the country.

We hovered at the invisible border, intent on locating Monte Binga, Mozambique's highest mountain. Like the dunes of the Namib Desert, the Chimanimani Mountains seemed to go on forever, even though the Indian Ocean was just a few hundred kilometres to the east.

Moss-green-covered fold mountains rose up to meet steep sandstone cliffs resembling a sleeping lioness. The landscape sprouted jagged, silvery, quartzite boulders that looked like they had been dusted with icing sugar. No one else was in sight, but life was abundant. Red-orange pincushion plants and blooming proteas were woven into a blanket of maroon grasses. Orange ground thrushes and yellow-throated warblers flitted between the branches of olive shrubs.

While admiring the views, I found it hard to believe the Chimanimani mountain range served as a well-known guerrilla route during the Zimbabwe War of Independence in the 1960s and '70s. The mountain passes were used by guerilla fighters, and mere kilometres from where we stood, land mines still littered the uninhabited landscape. Despite its turbulent history, I found the area peaceful.

This was the remotest place on which I had ever stepped foot. Standing there made me feel alive, proud and brave. Yet all I could think about was the nagging pressure in my damn bladder. I instructed the guys to stay put while I searched for a suitable bush to crouch behind.

I felt rebellious crossing the unmarked border into Mozambique. I lowered my shorts to my ankles and perfected the ultimate squat position. First, a hesitant trickle. Then the contents of my bladder unleashed like the Zambezi. The parched soil drank up my urine like the first rains of the season. Mid-pee, I scanned the ground. Staying squatted, I stretched my arm out and retrieved a soap-sized polished stone. In lieu of toilet paper, I used the rock's smooth texture to dab myself, a trick I'd adopted during one of my climbing trips that proved more effective than using dead leaves or drip drying.

While hiking up my shorts, I became self-conscious, like a performer on stage blinded by a spotlight, unable to see my audience. I couldn't help but wonder if there was a border official observing my bare bum from a hidden post off in the distance, holding binoculars in one hand and a rifle in the other.

After leaving my undetectable mark in Mozambique, we left Skeleton Pass to begin the descent back to base camp. The flat walk through a marshy field of tall, yellow, flowering grasses coated my calves in condensation. Water droplets trickled down my ankles and seeped into my boots. My socks became soggy and cool. By the time we reached the parking lot, my toes were prunes.

I was changing into my sandals when a guy walked up to me to introduce himself. "Hey there. I'm Chris. Let me guess. You're Canadian?"

"How'd you know?" I replied with a smile.

Chris gestured toward my green Mountain Equipment Co-op daypack. His confident grin ballooned into astonishment when he found out I was also from Vancouver. After chatting, I learned Chris had been teaching in Zimbabwe for a year. Then we discovered another crazy coincidence: both of us had graduated from UBC in '94. For four years we'd shared the same campus, yet our paths had never crossed. *Of all the places to meet on the planet, how did we end up here at Chimanimani together?*

Chris's tall, broad-shouldered build made him look like he could hug a small village. His darker, smooth skin and high cheekbones made me curious about his ancestry. *Indonesia? Nepal?* I wondered. Flattering, thin-wired eyeglasses framed his big, dark, accepting eyes.

A petite, fair-haired woman walked over and introduced herself to me. She sounded British. Chris's expression softened when his gaze met Hannah's angelic face. He stroked her wavy locks. She gave him a shy smile. Right away I understood: they were in love.

Despite their blossoming romance, they embraced my companionship and invited the Brits and me to get a lift with them from Mr. Lovemore, a local driver who shuttled backpackers to and from the park. Right away I felt at ease in Chris and Hannah's company. A quick friendship formed during the shared car ride when they learned I was making my way to Malawi.

Back in the village, the three of us shovelled down a vegetarian curry like ravenous hyenas. We devoured a huge bowl of mysterious-flavoured ice cream and talked like we had known each other for years instead of hours. It was reassuring to know we shared the same travel plans for the next few weeks.

If it weren't for my friendship with Chris and Hannah, I doubt I would ever have found romance waiting for me in Harare.

Ten

ON APRIL 15, I left for Harare with Chris, Hannah, Keelie and two of her friends from Heaven Lodge. En route to the town of Mutare, an unsettling vibration radiated throughout the bus before a deafening crash made us jump up in our seats. The explosive backfire forced dust and debris from the floor of the bus while frantic passengers yelled at the driver to stop.

Outside the window, I saw the back of the bus engulfed in hazy blue smoke. The foul smell of burning oil made me certain the bus was on the verge of a complete breakdown and we'd find ourselves stranded on the side of the road.

I couldn't believe the driver ignored the passengers' urgent pleas to pull over. He carried on as if nothing out of the ordinary had occurred. After a few kilometres, and one final resounding backfire, the dust settled and everyone calmed down. I was particularly impressed by a woman sitting a few seats over from me who appeared unaffected by the chaotic scene. She kept her cool while breastfeeding her young baby as if nothing unusual had occurred.

Luck was on our side, though I suspected it was only a matter of time until I ended up on a bus with a mechanical failure. To my surprise, the bus made it to Mutare without any more delays. With an anticipated eight-hour train ride to Harare, we hurried to a restaurant to feed our grumbling bellies. The *sadza* tasted tough and chewy. The chicken resembled elephant skin. Disappointing meal aside, the six of us had fun exchanging some of our travel highlights and challenges. Sharing my stories about the rotting seal corpses in Namibia, my Zambezi River escapades and the memorable ostrich ride with Anna allowed me to reflect on how fortuitous my travels had been so far. The obstacles and unintended detours were all important in shaping my journey.

My downer mood had greatly improved since leaving Chimanimani. This change had a lot to do with the wonderful company I surrounded myself with. When I'd originally set out to see Africa alone, I had been naive. Back home, I often enjoyed bouts of solitude. It was a surprise to discover I wasn't the solo traveller I had imagined myself to be. So far, most of the beautiful moments of my trip had occurred in the presence of the travellers and locals I befriended. *Of course*, the geography was remarkable. But once the landscapes became more familiar and less exotic, it was the moments I shared with people that made my time there so special.

Walking to the train station, Chris asked, "So what are your plans when you get back to Vancouver?"

His question was a natural inquiry into my life. But with my journey almost halfway over, I didn't want to think about life *after* Africa. I had no exciting job or solid school plans to look forward to. Dad's and Russ's physical states would only worsen. Having an uncertain future made me feel stuck. I wanted to be free, to stop making compromises. Not just in Africa, but for good.

Backpacking let me live in the moment. I dreaded the unpredictable circumstances back home. But in Africa I embraced the unknowns. I loved not knowing how things would turn out, or who I would meet next. Even though I always had a rough plan in place, so much was left to chance and circumstance. I controlled how I reacted to each new opportunity.

"I'm not entirely sure yet. I'm going to apply to the education program. I'm thinking about becoming a Japanese teacher and I also want to teach art," I replied.

"Oh, I think you'd make a great teacher, Lisa. You'll have no problem getting into the program." Chris sounded pleased with my plan. But he wasn't the one who needed convincing.

Once we arrived at Harare station, I made the mistake of tagging along to Backpacker's Connection with Keelie and her friends. Keelie and I got along well, but the three of them had already formed a close bond before my arrival in Chimanimani. I quickly felt like the odd woman out. The hostel was far from downtown, so I hopped on the free shuttle back to the city centre and walked over to Sable Lodge. Chris and Hannah were delighted when I showed up.

"Lisa! Good to see you already. Everything okay?" Chris asked.

"Yeah, I didn't realize that hostel was too far from everything. Running errands and getting to the embassy will be a real hassle from there. And, of course, I missed your good company."

"Well, we're glad to have you here," Hannah said.

Right away I was comfortable in their company. It was a bonus that the lodge was nestled in a lovely, quiet property buffered by shady trees, giant aloe plants and flowering shrubs. Despite its popularity, I lucked out finding accommodations. After spending two nights in one of the expensive private dorms, I landed a spot on the communal floor with half a dozen friendly backpackers.

THE SECOND DAY AT SABLE LODGE, I was outside, lying on my stomach, legs stretched out on a lounge chair. The early afternoon sun blanketed my bare arms and legs while I wrote in my journal. Mid-sentence, I noticed an attractive, dark-haired man leave the lodge. Peering over my sunglasses, I spied tan, muscular calves walking away from the hostel entrance. My eyes lingered above the cuffs of his torn jean shorts before moving up to his back and broad shoulders. A vision of me hiking his charcoal T-shirt over my head flashed across my eyes. A hot flush radiated from my cheeks.

Within the hour, he returned, ambling along the front path of the lodge. My heart skipped a beat when he offered a polite smile. His arresting gaze swallowed me up. There was a depth to his dark-lashed, dreamy eyes, as though he could burrow into my head and read my thoughts. His were the eyes of an attentive lover.

Don't be an idiot. Just say hi. One glance at his chiselled features and I became flustered. I looked away, my eyes safely returning to the pages of my journal.

I was completely taken off guard. Instead of 24, I became the reserved 14-year-old version of myself who lacked the guts, experience and maturity to act on my crushes. I wasn't looking for a fling to complement—or *complicate*—my travels. But I knew well that romance sneaks up when it's least expected.

With some help from Al, a fellow floormate from Montreal, I was able to put a name to this beautiful man: Matthias. From Switzerland.

Matthias was travelling with his friend Daniel, a stocky, stern-looking Swiss with short, blond, ringleted hair. Although Matthias was taller than me and had a muscular build, he appeared small compared to Daniel, who resembled a Viking. Matthias had a flattering, trimmed goatee. Daniel donned a full beard. Something about their contrasting appearances made me picture them dressed in medieval attire. Of course, in this fantasy scene, Daniel remained fully clothed at the end of the day.

My attraction to Matthias was intense and immediate. I couldn't think of a clever way to approach him. Naturally, I assumed he would remain a fixture of my imagination and that nothing would transpire beyond me discreetly admiring him from behind the security of my sunglasses.

THE NEXT EVENING, Chris, Hannah and I walked over to the neighbouring diner for a late supper. My pulse quickened the second we entered the small, near-empty restaurant – Matthias and Daniel were already seated at a table, looking at menus. They both turned to look at Chris, Hannah and me. I felt Matthias's sultry eyes on mine. This time I didn't look away.

We took our seats at the table next to them. I was excited to be in the same space but felt nervous at the prospect of speaking to him and making a first impression. It had been a long time since I'd had such a strong attraction to a complete stranger. My sweet-bun weight gain and diminishing climber muscles made me feel doughy and insecure instead of sexy and self-assured.

We were the only customers at the diner – not chatting with Matthias and Daniel would have been odd. It was a relief to have Chris and Hannah at my side to initiate some small talk. Without realizing it, Chris acted as my unofficial wingman while he asked the guys about their travels.

It turned out that Matthias and Daniel were also heading north to Malawi. Getting to this tiny country meant travelling more than 200 kilometres through a narrow strip of Mozambique. We were all waiting for our transit visas to be processed before leaving Harare. A flurry of elation rushed through my body: Matthias would be around for at least a few more days.

Seated just an arm's length away, I felt my heart pound out of control. I was only half listening to the conversation. My eyes were transfixed on Matthias's lips as I imagined them on mine. Somehow I summoned the courage to speak to him directly. Unsure what to say, I kept the conversation safe and pragmatic instead of blunt and honest. *Just thought you should know I haven't been able to stop thinking about you since I saw your beautiful face yesterday.*

After taking a breath, I announced, "I'm also waiting for my visa for Tanzania. I want to visit the Serengeti before I go to Zanzibar."

I hoped he didn't sense how nervous I felt. Or how much I had been lusting after him for the last 24 hours.

To my delight, Matthias replied in perfect English, "Cool…After Malawi, I'm planning to head north. I want to go to Zanzibar too and do some diving there."

My mind raced as I imagined the two of us there together. Zanzibar – the exotic spice island in the turquoise waters off the Tanzanian coast – was at the top of my list of places to see before returning to Canada. I told Matthias about my plan to leave Saturday on the 6:30 a.m. bus to Malawi with Chris, hoping he might join us. My eyes pleaded, *Please be on that bus.*

THE NEXT DAY CHRIS, HANNAH AND I perused the popular Mbare Musika market next to the bustling bus terminal. We had been warned to stay away from the station, a notorious location for sneaky pickpockets and violent muggings. Even though I never worried for my safety while walking around Harare, it was a good reminder not to let my guard down.

In addition to a variety of fruits and vegetables, I was pleased to find several curio stalls at the market. Perhaps if I had slowed my pace, I would have discovered some worthy keepsakes. But I was on a mission to find a *mbira* – a metal-tined musical instrument played by the Shona people. To me, the *mbira* encapsulates the quintessential sound of Zimbabwean music: I didn't want to leave Africa without one. I scanned row after row in hopes of finding one to call my own, but to no avail.

After the market, Chris treated Hannah and me to lunch at an outdoor patio. It was sweet to see the two of them in love, during the early stages of a relationship when neither of them could do wrong. I envied how comfortable they were together. They made it look so easy.

I left them to have some time together, which allowed me to explore Harare solo for the rest of the afternoon. The National Gallery's art exhibit on women in the arts, politics and culture was my first stop.

The spacious, naturally lit gallery revealed crisp, white walls and wide-open spaces to freely roam. Up until this point, I had mostly seen the traditional arts and crafts of Zimbabwe. The exhibit's collection of expressive and contemporary art widened my perspective on modern Zimbabwe beyond the women and men who make woven baskets, handmade pottery and animal carvings.

Before heading back to the hostel, I walked over to the post office to call home. I had sent a few postcard updates to my parents, but over a month had passed since I'd last spoken to my mom. Using a calling card proved difficult in many towns and villages. Harare was my last chance to phone home before leaving for Malawi. I couldn't relax and enjoy myself in a new country until I found out how everyone was doing.

I felt anxious as I dialled their number. Mom usually sounded cheerful whenever she answered the phone. If something was wrong, I could detect her mood by the tone of her voice. I had no idea what her reaction would be on the other end of the line. Relief? Resentment?

The knot in my stomach tightened. It was early in the morning back home. It took several rings before Mom picked it up. When she first heard my voice, she sounded concerned. As soon as she realized nothing was wrong on my end, she reverted to her usual happy self, and the tension in my body unravelled.

"Sue and Dave were over last night for dinner." It was a comfort that my sister and her husband were close enough to visit. "What else is new...Um, Dad's been busy working in the garden. He planted his dahlia bulbs last week. It wasn't that easy for him, but he managed."

Dad's dahlias were a summertime spectacle. By the time I returned home, they would be starting to bloom.

"How's Russ doing?" I asked.

"Well, his balance has gotten a bit worse, and his legs are getting stiffer. It's harder for him to get upstairs now." This wasn't the update I wanted to hear, but it wasn't surprising. A month before my departure he'd had a few falls. One afternoon when I was visiting, Mom and I heard him yelling. We ran downstairs and found him lying on the bathroom floor, unable to get up on his own.

"So where are you now? Hold on a second...What? What are you saying? Oh, geez. Your dad's trying to ask me something." Dad's muffled voice kept interrupting Mom until she finally passed him the phone.

"I *said*, have you ridden any more steam trains?" His question made me smile. As suspected, he didn't ask about my canoeing in hippo habitat, or if I had seen any elephants.

"No, Dad. Just the one steam train. I've ridden a few regular passenger trains, though, including an overnight one with sleeping quarters."

I indulged Dad and answered his train questions before Mom came back on the phone.

"Okay, love, have fun. And please be careful, okay?"

My guilty conscience had been appeased. At least for the time being.

DESPITE PLANS TO WAKE UP EARLY to prepare for Malawi, a group of us went dancing that night. Matthias, a Brit named Bea, Al from Montreal and I joined the locals at the Archipelago Nightclub and lit up the dance floor. This was the first time I would be around Matthias without Sir Daniel the knight keeping watch.

Matthias and I had chatted a few times at the hostel amid the security of others, mostly talking about our travels. He struck me as a bit serious, but I found him to be intelligent and sexy. Whenever our eyes met, I sensed an unspoken attraction. But I was too hesitant to act on my impulses, fearful my hunches were wrong. I felt excited knowing that at the very least we would be on the dance floor together.

We entered the Archipelago Nightclub in Harare and I felt nothing but bliss. The dance floor was packed with sweaty bodies swaying and gyrating to the beat of the deep-tempo music.

I was completely in my element.

When I had turned 19, I wasn't fussed that I could legally consume alcohol – underage drinking in my early teens had relieved me of that curiosity. I anticipated this milestone because I was finally old enough to hit the Vancouver nightclubs. I *loved* to dance. Without the aid of liquid courage, I felt uninhibited and euphoric when I danced. Like a whirling dervish or Masai entranced in a traditional jumping dance, something took hold of me when the music came on. I was spellbound for hours until the lights came on to signal closing time.

In the midst of dancing, Matthias and I gravitated toward each other until there was little space left between us. I savoured the raw pleasure of being so close to him without worrying about what to say. Before I had time to think, he moved in closer and leaned into my ear to say something. The loud music drowned out his voice. "I can't hear you!" I yelled back with a smile.

His cheek grazed mine. I felt drunk from the heat of his breath. When his lips brushed up against my hair, I felt a ripple of pleasure at the centre of my body. I rested my hands on his waist and inhaled the sweet scent of his shirt while we moved to music together.

Matthias's eyes drilled into mine. With one hand on the small of my back, he pulled me close and pushed a lock of hair behind my ear. He stroked my cheek. When our lips met, tufts of soft whiskers tickled my lip, making me laugh. The kiss was tender at first. Then urgent and eager.

Now that we were surrounded by a dozen dancing sweaty strangers, our bold actions confirmed my hopes. I was elated by our connection on the dance floor. It was a huge relief to know our attraction was mutual. We kissed and danced the rest of the night. I couldn't stop beaming when Al, who knew about my crush on Matthias, waved across the dance floor to give me his thumbs-up seal of approval, as though I had fulfilled a long-awaited conquest.

With Matthias as my drug, this state of euphoria lasted all night. We stayed out dancing until 3:00 a.m. With no privacy at Sable Lodge, I kept my expectations realistic. We kissed good night and headed to bed in separate rooms. His musky scent lingered on my skin, keeping me in a trance until sleep took over.

I WAS EXHAUSTED when I woke up late the next day, yet my elation lingered. I stood up and stretched. The tightness in my calves and glutes reminded me that the night on the dance floor hadn't been a dream.

While Matthias had gone early into the city on his own, I spent the morning at the hostel, relishing the intimate moments we'd shared on the dance floor. Every time I closed my eyes, I felt his mouth on mine and imagined the two of us undressing one another, our hands, arms and legs intertwined, navigating through unknown territory.

By dinnertime, I was ready for another night out. The same group of us had plans to catch a live show at Harare's local Carleton Club. This time Daniel decided to come along. Right away his presence stifled the bond between Matthias and me. We walked hand in hand but didn't show our affection as openly as we had the previous evening, even though my attraction for him was unchanged.

Matthias and I sat next to each other during a supper of *peri peri* chicken at a Mozambican restaurant. I delighted in our knowing glances and felt the warmth of his calf rub against mine. When his hand grazed my forearm, carnal urges raced through my body. I longed to be alone with him, but with Daniel close by, things felt guarded. It seemed strange how intimacy complicated things so quickly.

At the Carleton Club, a group of us began playing a round of pool. I took pleasure in studying Matthias's movements, admiring the focused expression on his face before he set up each shot. In between turns, I let my eyes linger on his.

I walked over to him. Images of us on the dance floor kept replaying in my head. Having grown up feeling reserved in matters of love and sex, I hated the invisible boundaries I sometimes still put up: I didn't want to hold anything back.

"Last night was a lot of fun," I said with a look of longing.

Matthias grinned back. "Yeah, it was," He chalked up his pool cue.

I took a deep breath. "In case it wasn't obvious, I couldn't stop thinking about how if we had a private room, I wouldn't have hesitated to sleep with you." As soon as the words left my mouth I realized how vulnerable I had made myself. *What did you just do, Lisa?*

Matthias's eyes widened. The club was dimly lit, but I'm sure his cheeks turned red. Though it was hard to read his expression, I could tell he was caught off guard. He paused for what seemed like five excruciatingly long seconds. I'm not sure how I would have reacted if I had been in his position. Not to mention that English was his second or third language.

"Oh, okay. Wow," he said, nodding, his lips turning upward into a smile. "I thought about that too. But, yeah, it's hard to find privacy at the lodge." He pulled me in for a quick kiss before I took my next shot.

After a few rounds of pool, a group of men challenged Bea and me to a match. Their arrogance and sexist remarks about women pool players annoyed us, but we gladly accepted and gave them a run for their money. It wasn't until an hour later, when the music began, that we realized two of the patronizing pool players were members of the band.

I was happy to be on the dance floor again, but the reggae-inspired beats soon turned monotonous. We danced until our boredom could no longer be feigned.

My blunt words had little effect on Matthias. After we left the club, nothing transpired between us beyond walking arm in arm. On the way back to the lodge, however, my mood perked up.

"Daniel and I are thinking of leaving for Malawi on the same bus as you and Chris," Matthias announced. "Hopefully, we will have everything we need by tomorrow."

"Really? Oh, that would be great," I said, hoping this meant he wanted to spend time with me. Maybe my bold confession wouldn't send him running for the hills after all.

AFTER AN EARLY BREAKFAST I picked up my visas and did some last-minute errands downtown. Chris and I were catching the 6:30 a.m. bus the following day, but Hannah was staying in Harare to meet up with a friend.

I recharged at the hostel before heading out for the third night in a row. A popular Zimbabwean musician named Andy Brown was playing at one of the hotel clubs in Harare: I couldn't wait for an excuse to go dancing again, but Matthias remained at the lodge, saying he was tired.

I was stoked to see an African musician perform live in an intimate venue. When Bea, Al and I entered the club, I was happy to see that the majority of the people were locals. I was unfamiliar with Andy Brown's music but knew that his most recent album, *Gondwanaland*, had been a huge success in Zimbabwe.

The crowd let out a big cheer when Andy appeared on stage. His long, black dreadlocks were pulled away from his forehead to reveal a slender, handsome face: dark almond skin, high cheekbones, a faint moustache and a heartfelt smile.

As soon as the band started playing, I was drawn to Andy's resonant voice, his gifted guitar playing and the varied traditional instruments and background Shona singers that accompanied him. Immediately, the dance floor filled up with local fans moving to the band's captivating beats.

During the third song, a stoic-looking man stared in my direction. I glanced over my shoulder to see if there was someone else he was looking at. The man had to be at least twice my age, but had some of the best soul dance moves I'd ever seen. His whole body moved like a sea creature, his hips, shoulders and hands behaving as separate entities.

His bloodshot, light-hazel eyes seemed to challenge me to a showdown on the dance floor. I took him up on his unspoken offer. Without us touching, an electric current passed through our bodies as we moved seamlessly to the music. My impromptu dance partner was a complete stranger. I had no physical attraction to him and let my guard down. No judgment. No expectations. Not worrying about making an impression.

We danced in sync the rest of the evening. Our bodies never touched, but we shared a rare, platonic connection. I'll never forget the intensity of my older dance partner's mesmerizing eyes and masterful maneuvers. My last night in Zimbabwe turned out to be one of the most memorable evenings of my trip. And, to my surprise, it had nothing to do with my lustful feelings for Matthias.

I've never been a night owl, but somehow I stayed up until 3:00 a.m. again, knowing full well I had to wake up a few hours later to catch the bus. I tiptoed into the communal room at Sable Lodge, careful not to trip over the sleeping lumps all over the floor. It looked like an adult slumber party as I shimmied into my sleeping bag.

Seven of us were fast asleep on the floor when the door creaked open. A ribbon of light from the hallway stung my eyes. I groaned, then felt a gentle tap on my shoulder. Chris, who *hadn't* been out late dancing, was kneeling next to me.

"Lisa…It's time to wake up," he whispered. "Our taxi will be here at five." It was 4:30 a.m., and I had barely slept an hour. My stomach felt acidic and my brain was fuzzy. I rubbed my groggy eyes and mumbled, "Sorry, Chris…I need more sleep. Just go without me."

"Are you sure?" he asked. I mumbled yes. Then Chris walked out of the room and closed the door behind him.

Ninety minutes later, I arrived by taxi at the bus station with Matthias and Daniel. *Yes*, my wish to ride the bus with Matthias came true, even if it meant Daniel was along for the ride.

The bus terminal was a chaotic scene. Blaring horns made my head throb. Workers shouted from the rooftops of buses. Noxious fumes spewed out of idling taxis. Women balanced large bags upon their heads as if they carried nothing but air. A group of men glared at us like jackals. Right away, I understood the station's reputation as a haven for criminals preying on trusting travellers and distracted passengers.

We boarded the bus at precisely 6:30, but I was puzzled by Chris's absence.

"That's strange," I said to Matthias. "I thought Chris would've been the first one on the bus."

"Yeah, that is weird. Maybe there was another bus that left already?" Matthias suggested.

Our driver didn't pull out of the dusty dirt lot until 7:45 a.m. He made five unexplained stops before fully committing to the road. But I was too exhausted to care – I just wanted to close my eyes and wake up in Malawi.

I was happy to be travelling with Matthias. But once we boarded the bus and sat next to each other, I felt a bit of tension. Showing affection in Daniel's presence was uncomfortable, at least for me. It felt as if we had a big, disapproving brother watching over us.

Across the aisle, Daniel exchanged a few words with Matthias in Swiss-German. I interpreted their tone as serious, but Matthias gave me a reassuring smile once the conversation ended. I had no idea what they were discussing. I suspected Daniel was unhappy I had joined them. I couldn't help feeling as if my presence disrupted their dynamic-duo travel routine. But then it was hard to know exactly what Daniel was thinking – unlike Matthias, he had limited English and he didn't say much around me.

Hours later, the bus slowed to a halt and pulled up to the Mozambique border control. Unhurried border officials clutching rifles inspected our travel permits. After we crossed into Mozambique, views of the Tete Corridor started to unfold, revealing clusters of thatched-roof homes, rocky outcrops and emaciated cattle resting in red-clay landscapes.

Driving through this skinny strip of Mozambique meant we would arrive in Malawi in a few short hours. I felt energized at the prospect of arriving in a new country and spending more time with Matthias. I closed my weary eyes. Instead of worrying or reading into things, I tried to relax.

I didn't know how long I had been dozing when tumultuous sounds from the bus's engine startled me awake. The anticipation of getting some rest and arriving in Malawi with Matthias came to a halt. Before reaching the border, our bus had a complete breakdown. Al from Sable Lodge had joked with Chris and me two days earlier. His premonition haunted me now: "Just you wait and see. You're going to end up on a *chicken bus!*"

Of course, we had scoffed at his prediction. "Chicken buses," unlike luxury coaches, were notorious for their mechanical unreliability and for being overcrowded with passengers transporting large amounts of boxed cargo and giant sacks of dried goods.

And, *yes*, there was usually at least one person on board carrying a live chicken.

Everyone exited the bus and stood around for two hours on the side of the highway until a replacement vehicle arrived. All the luggage was transferred onto the roof of a bus that was already at capacity. Among the passengers, two women were breastfeeding. No one gawked while the babies suckled at their mothers' nipples.

Back home, this would have been a rare sighting. I admired how this simple act of love and nourishment wasn't kept hidden from society.

We shuffled along the bus aisle like penguins. The spaces between the seats were packed with an assortment of goods: bags of dried food, plastic bowls, boxes of ballpoint pens. All the passengers crammed into the second bus's tight quarters. Some were sandwiched three to a seat, while others were left standing for the rest of the journey.

I would have been happy with Matthias at my side, but a man holding two chickens in a small crate became my travel companion for the rest of our unpredictable ride.

Chicken bus, indeed.

An hour later, the driver pulled off the highway into a bustling terminal a quarter of the size of the one in Harare. He parked the chicken bus snug up against another bus. I thought it seemed odd that two men were standing on the roof waiting for something to happen.

Matthias and I peered out the window and watched the scene unfold. One of the men hopped onto the roof of our bus and rifled through the jumbled pile of bags, boxes and backpacks. When Matthias saw the man transfer some of our luggage onto the roof of the other bus, he stuck his head out the window and shouted, "What are you doing? Leave those alone!"

Matthias, Daniel and I ran outside to make sure our packs were still there. After hearing about the thefts and muggings at Harare bus terminal, we weren't taking any chances.

"Hey! That's my bag. Put it back!" I yelled, using my best *don't mess with me* tone.

The men looked at me as though this was routine business. Then one of them threw my pack back onto our bus.

After the tiresome journey, it was a huge relief to cross the border into Malawi. Matthias, Daniel and I arrived at Doogles Lodge in the city of Blantyre in time for an early supper. The hostel was set on an open, grassy property. It had thatch-roof dorms and an inviting swimming pool much cooler than the one at Ai-Ais.

Our host greeted us with freshly barbecued hamburgers and ice-cold drinks. Seated in the dining area, munching on a burger, I felt as if we had just been transported into an episode of *Happy Days*. I looked around but didn't see a jukebox.

It was at Doogles Lodge where my love-hate relationship with Western pop music began to unfold in Africa. Here I was, my first day in Malawi, and Counting Crows's "Mr. Jones" was blasting out of the dining room speakers. The song had been a huge hit back home, but I never expected to hear it in Malawi. Since most hostels were run by foreigners *for* foreigners, it made sense. Familiar tunes comfort travellers when they're far from home. Even I had given into this guilty pleasure back at Shaka's Spear in Bulawayo, when I cranked k.d. lang and Massive Attack on the jukebox.

After the second hour of hearing Counting Crows, though, I wanted to escape this little compound of Western culture. I didn't feel like we had arrived in Malawi yet.

I AWOKE TO SUNNY SKIES, but the brisk morning air made me shiver. I pulled on my sweater and strolled outside. I found Matthias playing a game of *bao* on a shady patch of grass with one of the hostel workers, a native of Malawi. I took a few minutes to admire him from afar. I snapped a photo then walked over to watch them play.

I was familiar with this traditional East African game for two, but I hadn't fully grasped its rules. *Bao* is a rectangular wooden board with 32 hollowed-out pits and 64 small seeds that opponents try to capture from one another. The game appears simple, but its appearance is deceptive.

While observing Matthias play, it occurred to me that *bao* and love share similarities. Both are more complicated than what meets the eye, making it difficult to predict your partner's next move. Ever since making my intentions clear to Matthias, I was waiting for *him* to make the next move. Now I wondered if he had second thoughts about me. Maybe I'd scared him off.

After breakfast, Matthias, Daniel and I went into the centre of Blantyre to get some supplies. While walking down the main street, we were surprised to run into Hannah, who appeared to be alone. Her face lit up the second she saw us. "Hi, you guys! It's so good to see you again."

"Hannah, how are you? Where's Chris?" I inquired naturally.

"Oh, you won't believe what happened." Her smile disappeared. "He's been stuck in Harare. The morning he left to catch the bus, he got mugged."

A terrible sinking feeling filled my stomach as Hannah went on to describe Chris's horrible fate. Since he had pre-booked his taxi the night before, the police suspected the driver had helped orchestrate the mugging. The cabbie stopped the taxi in a deserted part of the bus terminal. No one came to Chris's aid when three thugs circled him before helping themselves to his belongings.

I felt terrible about what had happened to Chris, but it was a relief knowing I had escaped this unfortunate turn of events.

Matthias, Daniel and I left Blantyre to travel southeast to the tiny mountain village of Mulanje. We had read about its rolling hills full of tea plants and couldn't wait to do some hiking and camping near Mount Mulanje. Because our transportation experiences were playing out like a comedy of errors, none of us were fazed when the afternoon bus to Mulanje was delayed and the 90-kilometre journey took over three hours.

It was already getting dark, the night air humid and warm, when we arrived at Mulanje Motel. The lobby smelled of mildew but was immaculate. A man around my age popped out from the office and greeted us with an eager smile of perfect white teeth. He looked very professional in a navy collared shirt and black dress pants.

"Hello, friends. Welcome to Mulanje Motel! My name is Mike. I am very happy to assist you this evening."

Mike looked hungry for business. From what I could see, we were the only guests at the motel. I introduced myself and asked Mike about himself. He was a college student who worked at the motel full-time to pay for his tuition. He seemed to be the only one in charge

TEN

when he asked us, "So I trust you will be needing two rooms this evening?"

I shook my head and smiled. "Actually, we only need one room for the three of us."

Mike's friendly demeanour turned businesslike. "I am very sorry to inform you, miss, but we have strict rules. It is against policy for men and women to share a room. Unless, of course, you are married? Or perhaps related. Is this the case?" he asked with a hopeful smile.

I shook my head again.

Mike let out a disapproving sigh and appeared concerned and hesitant to bend the rules. I thought I could put his mind at ease by offering him a plausible explanation:

So, Mike, you see the dark-haired, sexy one? I've been lusting after him for days. I would love to have my way with him, maybe dirty the sheets in one of your lovely motel rooms. But I'm pretty sure he must be a Swiss prince or something. The tall blond is making damn sure my civilian hips don't get anywhere near his precious royal loins.

Or maybe this explanation would have been more believable:

Oh, you don't need to worry, Mike. They're Mormons, in the middle of their two-year mission. I managed to cast a spell on Sultry Eyes for a few nights. He almost gave in to my sinful ways. But Big Blondie steered him away from the temptations of my flesh and put him back on the righteous path. He won't be making any moves on me tonight. Or ever, for that matter.

Once I convinced Mike nothing indecent was going to happen between Matthias, Daniel and me, we negotiated a preferable rate for a dank-smelling room for two.

Sharing a motel with Matthias seemed as if my fantasy had come to life, but between Daniel's looming presence, my growing insecurity, the unbearable humidity and the pungent smell of mould, *nothing* was going to happen between Matthias and me.

Mike served us a simple meal of chicken stew with vegetables and *nsima*, Malawi's equivalent to *sadza*, in the hotel's quiet, clean dining room. He beamed when I asked him if he would teach me some Chichewa after dinner.

I've always had a knack for learning languages, a trait I likely inherited from my mom. In addition to speaking her native Dutch and hometown dialect *Sneekers* and learning some Frisian, at school Mom studied English, French, German and Latin. My Vancouver-born father, however, lacked such linguistic prowess. In France, I was so embarrassed by Dad's mispronunciation of *bonjour* when he greeted a Parisian couple in the hotel elevator. As an adult, I went on to appreciate Dad's honest effort to speak a bit of French. Since then, I've always prided myself on mimicking accurate pronunciation in whatever language I take on.

I sat down at one of the dining tables. Mike returned with a steaming teapot and a proud grin. "Let us drink Malawi tea," he said, and poured me a cup.

He retrieved a ballpoint pen and a sheet of soft beige paper from the front desk. I blew into my cup and took a sip. The second Mike sat down next to me, he took on a serious teacher role. He sat up straight in his chair and held the pen with purpose and confidence. His lesson began with a list of basic expressions and commonly used words: *Muli bwanji?* (How are you?), *moni* (greetings), *Ndili bwino* (I'm fine) and *zikomo* (thanks).

Mike wrote them down and then said them aloud. Slowly. Clearly. He had me repeat each one four, five times, until he was satisfied. "Yes, that's right. Very good, Lisa," he commented each time I successfully echoed his pronunciation and intonation.

My favourite words were *zikukoma* (this is so fantastic), and *kudya* (eat). I love making up corny mnemonic devices to help me remember foreign words and couldn't resist. "Mike, *kudya* get me something to eat?" I quipped. Initially, my joke was lost on him, but after I explained the pun, he let out a hearty laugh. "Oh, that's a good one, Lisa. I like it. I will have to remember that. *Zikukoma.*"

Mike watched as I wrote some words phonetically in *katakana* to help me with the pronunciation. He became interested and asked me to teach him a few Japanese words. It was fun taking turns, swapping our teacher-pupil roles.

My hope was that these Chichewa greetings would be a simple way for me to connect with the locals, and I couldn't wait to put them to use. After the hour-long lesson, I tucked the paper into my travel journal. Looking at Mike's writing takes me right back to the motel's humble dining room and our shared love of learning.

As suspected, Matthias, Daniel and I were the only guests staying at the hotel that night. With my lesson done and the lethargic bartender closing up early, the three of us retired to our hot, dank room.

I tossed and turned, trying my damnedest to get comfortable in the narrow cot while Matthias lay sleeping an arm's length away. It wasn't long before Daniel was snoring heavily, ensuring another night would pass without me having any physical contact with Matthias.

My frustration grew like mutant mould spores as I stared at the stained ceiling, wide awake.

MATTHIAS, DANIEL AND I were up by seven to go hiking after breakfast. I was heavy-eyed from my sleepless night. But it was April, the tail end of Malawi's rainy season, and the moist morning air invigorated me as soon as we stepped outside.

The sub-rainforest and tea plantations surrounding the village were spectacularly green and lush. Walking away from Mulanje Motel, I felt the misty rain beading onto my smooth, tan skin. Despite the persistent drizzle, we were determined to hike toward Mount Mulanje. Within half a kilometre, we came across a semi truck the length of almost two school buses parked on the dirt road. At least 60 labourers, likely in the tea or timber industry, stood in the open, cobalt-blue cab, waiting to get a lift to work. A few men and women were standing on the ground, chatting among themselves. We looked at each other with mutual curiosity.

A nearby baobab quickly diverted my attention. The enormous tree had delicate white blossoms woven into its elaborate root system.

The scale of the tree and massive truck distorted normal proportions and created an amusing illusion: everyone nearby looked miniature, yet there was nothing small about their presence.

Matthias, Thomas and I meandered up the gradual hill toward the mountain. We passed by tiny homes made of stone and clay. The voices of children spilled out from a small structure constructed of bricks, mortar and wood. I peeked inside and saw stacks of timber. Just then, a boy and a girl around age 6, and a younger girl who was maybe 4, popped out from behind the structure and ran toward us.

"Hullo, hullo!" they chirped.

I sang back, "*Moni! Moni! Muli bwanji?*"

The little boy couldn't contain his infectious grin. "*Ndili bwino,*" he replied to my delight. *It worked! It worked!* If only Mike had been there. He would have been so proud of me.

The boy looked like a little man wearing black shorts and a gold, short-sleeved collared shirt. The older girl was adorable in a floral, oversized pale-green dress. The youngest covered her toothy smile and tugged shyly at her stained, striped polo shirt. The three of them followed us barefoot along the path. After a hundred metres or so, they turned around and waved goodbye until we were out of sight.

Thankfully, our elevation gain got us above the cloud cover and out of the rain. A local guy named George around our age was out walking and joined us for part of the hike. With things between Matthias and me increasingly unclear, I welcomed George's company. He led us to a fenced lookout perched upon a steep cliff that boasted panoramic views of Mount Mulanje. The tranquil scenery of tea plantations and treed landscapes seemed to go on for miles and distracted me from the confusing Matthias situation.

When we came back down the mountain, the three children ran over to greet us like old friends. Aside from these lovely children and George, we only encountered a handful of people during the hike. But the locals we met in the village were very friendly, and I was thrilled to put Mike's Chichewa lesson to use.

Once we descended back into the village, the rains started up again, putting a damper on our plans to explore other areas by foot.

For the rest of the day, stubborn clouds hugged the hills and mountains, the unfavourable weather matching my circumstances with Matthias to a T.

DESPITE WORKING THE EVENING SHIFT, Mike showed up to the motel early the next morning dressed for work. He bid farewell to Thomas and Matthias, then turned to me. "Lisa. I would like to be your pen pal. Can we exchange addresses, please?"

I smiled at his request. "Of course, Mike. I would love that too."

I had him write down his address on the paper he gave me for our lesson. I started to write out my Vancouver address on some scrap paper, then changed it to my parents' permanent address, in case I moved.

From Mulanje, we caught a bus to Zomba village 70 kilometres away. Matthias had a tent, and the three of us would share this tight sleeping arrangement for a couple of nights. Camping with Matthias and Daniel was reminiscent of my cozy camping with the Aussies in the Drakensberg, only this time it wasn't so comfortable. I still had feelings for Matthias, but I felt like the third wheel. I was certain that Daniel would have preferred me to go my separate way.

After we exited the bus, a dirt road took us through Zomba village. A mountain of neatly folded, second-hand clothing was piled high onto a large wooden platform. A man sporting a McGill University sweatshirt managed the distribution of donated pants, shorts, T-shirts and sweaters. There had to be at least a few thousand items.

His face lit up when I told him I was Canadian and that I had been to the McGill campus in Montreal. I wondered if this man ever had a connection to university life beyond wearing someone's gently used varsity apparel.

Matthias, Daniel and I continued along a red dirt road away from the village centre. Aside from the odd thatched-roof home, the area appeared desolate at first. Further down the road, a group of six children were having a blast with a well-worn Frisbee. I was warm in my shorts and a cotton tank top, but these children, despite their bare feet, were wearing red and pink sweaters, pants and long skirts, reminding me of the schoolchildren Anna and I had met near the Cango Caves.

The kids seemed overjoyed to have us join their Frisbee game. It didn't take long for more children to appear. Eight of them gathered around towering Daniel, fascinated by his tight, blond curls and six-foot-two stature. He shed his usual stern countenance and looked like a gentle giant, smiling joyously from ear to ear from all the attention.

One of the girls threw the Frisbee. It flew over my head and landed a few metres behind me. As I ran to retrieve it, I recognized some tall, flowering plants: poinsettias. I looked around. They seemed to be everywhere.

Back home, the sight of poinsettias depressed me – I never understood their appeal at Christmastime. I thought they looked dejected and out of place in their plastic containers and cellophane wrapping. I think it was their inevitable demise that bothered me so much. It was only a matter of time until they were forgotten. The soil would dry up and crack. The red-and-green leaves would shrivel up and fall off. The plant would be discarded, spending its last days clinging to life at the bottom of a garbage bin before being sent off to the landfill.

Dad's and Russ's declines had made the last five Christmases a sorrowful time for me, especially when Dad's melancholy and talk of suicide surfaced. Celebrating meant pretending nothing was wrong. I dreaded the days leading up to Christmas – Christmas trees, poinsettia plants, decorations, songs, lights – and I couldn't wait for Boxing Day to arrive to signify the passing of the holiday.

Here in Zomba, though, I loved seeing the cheerful poinsettias in a natural setting among indigenous perennials. They were free. Bursting with life. Instead of depressing me, they uplifted me.

I retrieved the Frisbee and threw it back to the smiling girl who was waiting with outstretched arms. She caught it with two hands and the younger kids jumped up and cheered.

THE STUBBORN RAINS from Mulanje followed us to Zomba. In the middle of the night, I woke up in the tent with a runny nose. My throat throbbed. I felt miserable. Grumpy. Circumstances were *not* working in my favour regarding Matthias. There was no hand holding, no lingering looks. Things between us had come to a complete standstill. And now I had caught a goddamn cold.

Despite the cloud cover and my sickly state, the scenery in the Zomba Plateau didn't disappoint. Steady rainfall kept the region lush. The area boasted views of rolling hills, cedar groves and a cultivated forest of skinny pine trees planted in perfect rows.

I didn't know what to expect at Chingwe's Hole, a large chasm located on the western side of the Zomba nature reserve. We snaked along a wide dirt path flanked by yellow gladiolus flowers, their bright, joyful blooms obscuring the area's unsettling history. Chingwe's Hole was believed to house spirits known as *mizumu*. Legends of chiefs throwing their enemies into the abyss were widespread. There were rumours that the pit had also been used to discard the remains of lepers, and that the mentally ill were thrown in to meet their death.

I wondered if it had crossed Daniel's mind that Chingwe's Hole would have been a perfect place for me to disappear into.

After the 14-kilometre hike, the three of us relaxed in the comfort of the Ku Chawe Inn lounge. It was tempting to treat ourselves to some sweets, but I passed on the exorbitantly priced crème caramel, one of my all-time favourite desserts. Instead, we limited our luxuries to tea, coffee and soda.

Our final day of exploring the Zomba Plateau came to an end before dusk. We were leaving the next day for Cape Maclear, the popular lakeside resort, and wanted to get an early start. My hope was that, once we had a change in scenery, Matthias and I would resume whatever it was we'd started.

Surely, Lake Malawi's sandy beaches and romantic sunsets would bring us together again.

Eleven

I AWOKE WITH A START when the bus hit a pothole. My makeshift pillow – my forest-green Taiga fleece jacket – had slid down during my snooze, and my cheek and temple bumped up against the window. The bus was half-full. Matthias was sitting alone across the aisle from me, reading a book. Daniel was in the seat behind him, sleeping. I stretched out my legs and rubbed my eyes.

"Matthias, what time is it? How long was I asleep for?"

He looked over and smiled. "You had a good sleep. It's almost 11:30. You probably slept for an hour? The driver said we should be in Cape Maclear in about 30 minutes."

I took a sip of water to moisten my dry mouth and let out a little groan of exhaustion. "I can't wait till we get there. It will be so nice to swim in the lake."

Matthias was quiet for a moment. Then he got up and joined me. His knee rubbed up against mine ever so slightly, and my pulse quickened.

"I've been thinking. Since we're travelling together, I think it's better if we keep things friendly. I don't think it's a good idea for us to sleep together." Despite English being his second language, he was a far better communicator than I could have ever hoped to be when dealing with such matters.

His words were crushing, but I wasn't clueless. I had sensed something was off.

"Yeah, you're probably right. I understand," I replied, masking my disappointment.

"Daniel only has a week left before going back to Switzerland. Our plan in Cape Maclear is to go diving almost every day. And we'll be staying at the campsite in the tent."

"Yeah, I get it. I don't want to interfere with your plans," I said coolly.

"Okay. But I still want us all to hang out."

"Sure, of course."

After processing this change in dynamic, I felt some relief. It had been exhausting, sleeping in a cramped tent in the rain with a nagging cold and awkward tension for two nights. The cosmos had been working against us, or at least me. My insecurity was mounting: I needed some time on my own.

I was thankful Matthias had told me on the bus instead of delaying the inevitable or ignoring the awkward scenario – my usual tactic. Maybe his feelings had changed, and this was his way of letting me down easy. Or maybe he really felt it was better to just be friends. After all, he and Daniel had been travelling together for six months. I was never part of their plan.

We arrived at noon and went our separate ways.

It didn't take long for me to figure out why Cape Maclear remains Malawi's most visited lakefront destination. As soon as I got off the bus, I was captivated by Thumbi Island off in the distance. Cape Maclear's warm breezes and inviting beaches made it the kind of place where I could relax and not worry about making too many plans. I sensed I wouldn't be in a hurry to leave.

I checked into my humble accommodation for one at the Gap Beach Resort. In spite of its alluring name, this was by no means a luxury resort. For the next week, I slept in a tiny clay room merely big enough to house a narrow single bed and a wooden chair. It was basic and cheap. Since I planned on being outside every day and didn't anticipate any overnight guests – Swiss or otherwise – it fit my needs perfectly.

I spent my first day in Cape Maclear exploring on my own. The shoreline was a hub of fishing activity. Hand-carved wooden canoes and small fishing vessels were plentiful. I couldn't walk more than 20 metres without passing by clusters of fish drying racks of tiny *usipa* (sardines). No space was wasted – women and children used the spaces between the fish racks to hang dry their hand-washed clothes in the sun. In time I would learn the humidity made this chore challenging.

I chatted with some local fishermen eager to hook me up with a freshly cooked dinner. In the late afternoon, their assistants walked up and down the shore, promoting the daily catches and taking customer orders. A few hours later they would return with hot, savoury fish and side dishes. My mouth watered just thinking about it.

I became intrigued when I learned over a thousand species of multicoloured cichlids lived in Lake Malawi, making it a popular destination for scuba divers. A few signs advertising diving piqued my interest. I popped into Cape Maclear Sports to ask about courses and studied the brochure: a five-day course cost USD130 – economical compared to Canadian prices but still spendy for my budget. I decided to hold off until I had a chance to talk to other divers.

The sun dropped behind Thumbi Island as I walked toward the beach that evening. The sky had turned a brilliant lavender. Vibrant streaks of orange and yellow clouds glowed above the horizon. Everything I saw made me think I had arrived in paradise.

I headed to the outdoor bar, assuming it was a logical gathering spot for locals and travellers alike. I walked in and looked around: a lone bartender wiping down the counter was the only person there. I took a seat at the bar.

"Good evening, miss. What can I get you? And will anyone be joining you?"

"No, I'm on my own tonight. I'll have a Carlsberg, please."

He placed the chilled bottle in front of me. When the music started playing, I couldn't wipe the stupid grin off my face. I'm sure the bartender thought I was unusually happy. Here I was, in the middle of Malawi, with Billy Ocean taunting me with his "Loverboy" song. By the time I finished my beer, Billy's best-known songs, including "Get Outta My Dreams, Get Into My Car" and "Caribbean Queen," had echoed across the lake from the bar's speaker.

Thanks to Billy, I wasn't really alone after all.

By the second day, it seemed Billy Ocean's *Greatest Hits* was the only cassette tape at the bar. Though I was a fan of alternative music and indie bands, I secretly appreciated a good pop love song. Billy Ocean put a spell on me: I couldn't stop myself from singing along to his corny lyrics for days on end. I didn't cringe at the bar's repetitive playlist. Instead, I basked in Billy's soft-rock hits. I never pictured myself belting out Billy Ocean pop songs at any point in my life. But his smooth, bellowing voice remains one of my first and fondest memories of Cape Maclear.

ON MY THIRD DAY, I was sitting on the sandy beach, chatting with a group of affable teens, when a petite, bubbly Brit strolled up. Emma looked to be about 20, but exuded the self-assurance of an old soul. Her wispy ash-blonde bob was damp with perspiration. The Malawi sun had turned her pale complexion into a painful flamingo hue reminding me of Sion after our river safari. She rubbed her fingers over the top of her shoulders and neck and removed a few layers of peeling skin that resembled paper-thin, curling bark on arbutus trees back home.

Emma threw us a smile that radiated unbridled enthusiasm. She won me over the instant she placed her hands on her curvy hips and asked, "Do you fancy a swim over to Thumbi Island with me later today?"

I squinted against the bright sun and glanced across Lake Malawi toward the uninhabited island. At one and a half kilometres from the shores of Cape Maclear, Thumbi looked far but not impossible. *Sure, why not?* I thought to myself.

I agreed like a devout follower. I had no idea what I was getting myself into.

"Brilliant. Let's meet back here in a few hours. Say one o'clock?"

"Sure, see you at one," I replied as Emma sauntered off.

The boys looked at me. "You are swimming to Thumbi?" one of them asked.

"Yeah, it looks that way."

I stared at the close-to-perfect mound in the distance and my confidence wavered. The island seemed to be mocking me, questioning my ability to swim that far: *What makes you think you can make it all the way there?*

As a child, I spent countless hours in my family's above-ground pool, which was heated by my do-it-yourself dad's collection of solar panels. Sue and I enjoyed judging each other's Olympic dive techniques despite the pool's five-foot depth. We earned ourselves the flawless reputation of saving dozens of children from drowning while role-playing our "Millie the Dolphin" routine.

I could comfortably tread water for long periods of time and swim shorter distances in lakes and the ocean, but I'd never considered myself a proficient swimmer. I never even mastered the front crawl. The breaststroke, with my head *above* water like my mom, had always been my go-to swimming style. I was counting on my basic skills and sheer will to get me all the way to Thumbi.

I met Emma on the beach, determined to complete the swim. We didn't waste any time with small talk. She plunged into the lake. I followed in after, leaving my doubts behind on the shore.

The water was calm and warm. With Emma swimming just a few arm lengths away, my confidence returned. During the first hundred metres, my triceps were tight and achy. It didn't take long for me to find a consistent rhythm, and soon my strokes and breathing became fluid. I steadily glided through the water with my head *underwater* to keep up with Emma's swift pace.

I kept my eyes closed tightly to avoid messing up my contact lenses. Each time I came up for air, a blurred image of Thumbi Island bobbed up and down in my line of vision. Around 20 minutes in, Emma stopped to tread water. She looked over her shoulder in my direction.

"I think we must be halfway!" she trumpeted.

I looked back at Cape Maclear, then toward Thumbi. We had definitely reached the point of no return.

I took Emma's exuberant announcement as an invitation to rest. I turned onto my back and floated, catching my breath, gazing at the infinite sheet of azure above me. The absence of clouds, birds or planes made it impossible to gauge the depth of the sky, as if we'd entered an alternate dimension. With my face hovering above the surface, the delineation between my skin and the lake water disappeared. A feeling of calm overtook me. I closed my eyes, relishing the sun's warmth on my cheeks and forehead. From space, my body registered as nothing more than a minuscule speck floating in one of Africa's largest lakes. But I didn't feel insignificant.

"Lisa, ready? Let's keep going!"

Even with my ears submerged underwater, Emma's muffled voice was a drill sergeant, snapping me out of my meditative state. We were off again.

My pace quickened as I tried to stay in sync with Emma. Never before had I been so far from land with the strength of my body keeping me afloat. This wasn't the time to falter.

Emma and I swam in silence until the island was within reach. We pushed up onto our forearms and dragged our bellies and thighs onto the large, smooth, beige rocks like inelegant seals. After scrambling onto the island, I cried out an exultant "We did it!" Emma double high-fived me and I beamed with pride. This was no English Channel by any stretch of the imagination, but it was the longest swim I had ever done.

Emma and I celebrated our feat by relaxing on the rocks, warming our damp skin in the afternoon sun and admiring the view back toward Cape Maclear. A few minutes passed before a French woman showed up and sat down on a nearby rock. She and a friend had come over to the island by boat for the day. They were about to head back to the mainland.

As she was packing up, the woman turned to Emma and me and half-jokingly remarked, "You know that crocodiles live in Lake Malawi, don't you?"

Oh, right. Now that you mention it...Fuck. Nooooo.

The possibility of encountering crocs had *never* crossed my mind when we began our swim. Emma and I exchanged nervous laughter and looks of disbelief as we contemplated our swim back to Cape Maclear. Trepidation drowned my previous state of calm. The wind picked up, creating ripples across the lake. I shivered. Goosebumps covered my skin, making my fine arm hair stick straight up.

I knew the risk of a crocodile attack on the beaches of Cape Maclear was low, but I had no idea about their populations on Thumbi Island. The woman must have read our minds: she offered us a ride back to the mainland in her friend's boat. Emma and I accepted without hesitation. Under the circumstances, there was no room for pride.

As it turned out, the lake breezes on the return trip were not to our advantage. Crocodile risk aside, it would have been a strenuous, nerve-wracking undertaking had we been forced to swim back. The small boat battled the wind and fought choppy waves all the way back to shore.

Back at Cape Maclear, some local fishermen confirmed that crocodile encounters on Thumbi were rare but not unheard of. They told us croc sightings were more common in the shallow parts of the lake on the beaches up north.

Had I known about any potential risk, I wouldn't have agreed to swim all the way to Thumbi with Emma. But I had no regrets. Our swimming escapade was definitely a case where ignorance was bliss.

Emma and I gathered at the beach for dinner with Matthias, Daniel and Emma's brother, Mark. Now that my status with Matthias had been downgraded, I could relax instead of trying to figure out what he was thinking. It didn't change the fact I still liked him, but it was a relief that I didn't have to resort to any awkward avoidance tactics.

We watched the sun sink below the horizon while waiting for the fisherman's assistant to show up with dinner. I dug my heels into the soft sand to enjoy its last traces of warmth. Thumbi Island was now a silhouette surrounded by streaks of lilac and tangerine shimmering across the rippled lake water. I couldn't believe I had swum all the way there.

Moments later, a light breeze delivered scents of grilled *chambo*, coconut-infused rice, and steamed veggies. Feasting on this locally prepared meal among friends against a dramatic backdrop was the perfect way to commemorate my lake adventure with Emma.

By 10:00 p.m., I was tired from the sun and swim. After returning to my tiny hut for one, I crawled into my sleeping bag and fell asleep to the sounds of the water gently lapping against the lakeshore.

Sometime around midnight, I was woken up by a horrible pinching sensation all over my body. I jumped up in bed like I'd been electrocuted. I assumed it was just another Lariam nightmare, but I was too groggy and disoriented to comprehend dream versus reality.

The second wave of painful pinches felt like my leg hairs were being plucked out. I reached for my headlamp and shone it into my sleeping bag. It only took a second for my eyes to adjust to the bright light. I was horrified: a hundred ants were crawling over my ankles, legs and torso, biting me in their tracks. I screamed in disgust, bolted out of bed and ran outside, dragging the ant-infested sleeping bag with me. I stood outside the hut, shaking it out like a madwoman. A handful of backpackers were up late chatting. They shot me looks of concern and disapproval.

"Don't worry...I'm okay," I explained with a nervous laugh, vigorously brushing off every inch of my body.

After returning to my room, I located a horde of ants storming through a small hole in the base of the wall next to the bed. In addition to my pepper spray, my small arsenal included an oversized bottle of insect repellant. I sprayed in and around the hole with such fervour I thought I might pass out from the toxic smell. I shone my headlamp toward the floor. The swarm of ants had been stopped dead in the midst of their militant march and were floating in a shallow puddle.

After my revulsion subsided, I headed back to bed, but the foul odor prevented me from falling back to sleep. Wide awake, my mind began to wander. *You know that crocodiles live in Lake Malawi, don't you?*

Panic torpedoed through my stomach and landed in my chest. Shutting off my brain at night was like trying to master the front crawl in the Namib Desert. I shuddered to think what would have happened if Emma and I had actually encountered a crocodile while swimming.

With my thoughts racing out of control, I dwelled on my failed romance. *Does Matthias even think about our night in Harare?* Trying to forget about him was proving more difficult than expected.

After settling back into my sleeping bag, I rested my head on my pillow and attempted to talk myself into a calmer state. *Stop being ridiculous. Nothing bad happened today.* I took a deep breath and imagined myself floating on the lake again beneath the clear blue sky.

This late-night disturbance wasn't how I had envisioned the end of my triumphant day with Emma. I suppose a mid-slumber attack by an army of ants was definitely better than getting shredded by the jaws of an irate crocodile. But I would have welcomed a late-night wake-up attack from Matthias instead.

THE NEXT NIGHT, a group of us went out to dine and dance at the popular Ba' Blu outdoor club. Aside from the female tourists, I noticed few if any local women dancing there. It was fun dancing with the local men and tourists, but I wished I could have befriended more Malawian women. It occurred to me that perhaps it wasn't culturally acceptable for them to go out late at night. Or maybe they were at home, tending to domestic duties.

After the club closed up for the night, we gathered at the beach. Backlit by the moon, Thumbi Island was barely visible. Some teenage boys draped in oversized T-shirts and baggy jeans joined us. They seemed free to roam around late at night without consequence, and we enjoyed their good-natured company. After two of them began giving free shoulder massages, I might have inadvertently started a beach business on their behalf when I suggested they charge for their services.

The boys reminded me of my rebellious teenage years. With my best friend Cathy, I sometimes went out at night without my parents' knowledge under the guise of hanging out at her house. Mom and Dad were much stricter than any of my friends' parents. They *always* seemed to know when I wasn't where I was supposed to be. I suppose dealing with my older brothers and sister made them wearier and wiser by the time I began testing the waters. But I resented how they applied a different set of rules to me because I was a girl.

One night Dad found a group of us hanging out in the parking lot of a shopping plaza. My best friend Cathy was tipsy and couldn't stop blabbing to Dad. "Ohhh, Mr. Duncan. You have a wonderful daughter. Lisa is such a good friend. She keeps me out of trouble. You don't need to worry about her...sheee's great." Dad politely nodded and didn't comment on her slurred speech.

A different night, after dropping me and two friends off at a community dance, Mom drove by while we were crossing a major street, heading in the opposite direction from the rec centre.

"Lisa! *Vhere* do you think you girls are going?" she yelled from the open window, her thick Dutch accent commanding us back into the red Chuck E. Wagon. "Get in the car *now*!"

I wonder what my parents would have thought about me sitting there on the beach in Cape Maclear, hanging out late at night. When I was a teen, their strictness had irked me. But as an adult I grew to appreciate their efforts to keep me safe and instill a sense of responsibility in myself and others.

THE NEXT MORNING I had to decide if I wanted to enroll in the diving course. Scuba diving had never been something I felt I had to try, but now that I was there, I wanted to do something out of my comfort zone while exploring the depths of Lake Malawi.

Matthias and Daniel were pleased with the dives they had done so far and weren't concerned about crocodiles. After speaking with a few travellers who were happy with the course, I began the class immediately. During the theory class, the South African instructor Nigel looked in my direction when he saw me blowing my nose.

"You can't dive with that cold," he said. "Sorry, but you're going to have to wait until your sinuses clear up."

His words were discouraging. I debated quitting while I could still get some money back. But on the second day my thoughts turned to my brother, and I decided to stick with it.

Four years earlier, Russ had travelled to Maui to visit his best friend. Despite his failing health, he was determined to dive in the tropical waters of Hawaii. Spending time on the island was a temporary escape from his dire prognosis. Diving let him hang onto his diminishing mobility just a little bit longer.

Two years later, our family travelled to Maui for my sister's wedding. A winding path from the hotel led us to the sandy beach for the intimate ceremony. I watched with a heavy heart as Russ struggled to descend the downward path using his cane. He looked like a toddler who hadn't mastered how to walk yet. At any moment I expected him to fall.

Russ's disease hid, lurking in murky waters, waiting to strike. After that trip, his balance worsened. His fine motor skills diminished and his limbs succumbed to spasticity, forcing him to use a walker. Russ never went diving again.

By the third day, my cold was gone, and Nigel gave me the green light to dive. After suiting up, he instructed me to sit on the edge of the boat, explaining it was easier and safer to fall backwards into the water. As awkward as it felt, he was right. My body entered the water with one swift roll and I popped upright.

We swam away from the boat, staying a few metres below the surface, but I was disappointed. The water was cloudy, and we didn't see any cichlids. After practising our buddy signals, we resurfaced and Nigel laid out our plan: we would all be going down to four metres for 15 minutes.

When we descended back down, I felt comfortable in the water. My buddy Michael was never far from my side, reassuring me with a thumbs-up. Once we reached a depth of four metres, though, water seeped into my mask. It felt like someone had jabbed cotton swabs deep into my nostrils. My breath quickened. I felt flustered and out of control. *Get a grip, Lisa.*

I tried to relax but no longer trusted the scuba apparatus. The pressure in my nose intensified. The pain made me panic and I bolted to the surface like a torpedo.

Nigel swam over and gave me a stern lecture: "Don't ever do that again. That's an absolute no-no. It can be very dangerous, especially when diving at greater depths."

"I know. I'm sorry. My nose really hurt, and then I panicked."

Of course, I knew the risks of surfacing too quickly. But at that moment staying calm and rational had proved impossible.

The next day the lake water was a pleasant 24 degrees but still murky with only ten metres of visibility. Nigel led us underwater for 45 minutes at a depth of three metres below the surface. After an hour break, we went back for a second dive and swam down to six metres. This time, we were rewarded with schools of vibrant yellow-and-purple-striped cichlids swimming all around.

Despite my initial reluctance to sign up for the course and my brief panic episode, I was glad I never gave up. Nigel made me feel competent. After my initial shaky start, I never panicked again. I completed five dives, staying at a depth of 13 metres for half an hour.

I assumed this favourable trajectory would continue. On the second-to-last day of the course, we were puzzled when Nigel failed to show up. We heard rumours that were quickly confirmed: Nigel had been taken into police custody after an officer noticed damage to his car while completing a routine firearm inspection. The police suspected Nigel of hitting a motorcyclist and then fleeing the scene.

With Nigel gone, we missed a session of diving. His partner took over the course, but this meant we had to complete four dives in one day to meet the minimum required hours for certification. The woman didn't bother with logbook entries and skipped our debriefing session.

Luckily, a second replacement instructor, a lovely man from France, led our last day diving. Since only three of us showed up that morning, we received more one-on-one instruction. This small stroke of fortune was the silver lining to an otherwise disappointing finale.

For our final exam, we gathered at the local clubhouse. Without any supervision, students talked among themselves and openly shared answers. Backpackers not enrolled in the course sauntered in and ordered beers at the bar.

In the end, I never received my diving certification. Cape Maclear was the last time I ever went diving.

AFTER A FULFILLING WEEK, I was ready to leave the comforts of Cape Maclear. With my backpack in tow, I strolled past the pub and waved goodbye to the bartender. "Loverboy" Billy serenaded me one last time, demanding I get into his car. This song made me chuckle, just as it had when I first arrived. I contemplated the absurdity of the lyrics given my location – not only was car ownership in Malawi extremely rare, but, out of context, the chorus sounded like the threats of a predator. Hardly the makings of a romantic proposition.

Emma, her brother Mark, Daniel and I waited for the bus to the Monkey Bay ferry terminal. We were travelling 300 kilometres north across Lake Malawi to Likoma Island. Matthias was staying behind in Cape Maclear a bit longer.

"I'm going to spend a few more days here before heading up to Senga Bay. I'll see you in Nkhata Bay in a week or so, okay?" Matthias sounded certain we'd meet up after my island exploration. I wasn't counting on it, though.

"Sure. Have fun. See you in a week."

I considered the possibility that he had met a new love interest. Or maybe he just wanted the freedom to travel on his own now that Daniel was returning home. Either way, I hoped that with some distance between us and a change of scenery I would stop thinking about what might have been.

Twelve

WHEN TRAVELLERS CLAIM, "I survived the *Ilala*," it is no small exaggeration. The moment I boarded the overnight ferry to Likoma Island, I was under no illusion it was a luxury boat. The MV *Ilala* had been completing weekly trips across Lake Malawi for 45 years before I came along and added my name to its roster of unlucky passengers.

Emma, Daniel, Mark and I bought our third-class tickets, naively thinking economy class would be perfectly adequate for our simple backpacker standards. *Of course*, we wanted to travel as the locals did. The ferry service had eliminated all second-class tickets and increased the economy fare price by 300 per cent. We'd heard rumours about massive overcrowding on the lower third-class floor but had no idea what was in store for our long journey across Lake Malawi.

We schlepped our backpacks to the only vacant corner of the partially covered cargo area. Large wooden crates and stuffed burlap sacks covered most of the deck floor, but we had clear views of the lake, which seemed like a vast ocean.

"I'll be right back…I'm just gonna have a look up top," I told Emma.

I crept halfway up the stairs leading to the first-class deck, straining my neck like a pesky rodent sniffing the air. A dozen well-dressed passengers sipped ice-cold drinks through straws under cloudless blues skies from the comfort of their reclining deck chairs. The fresh-smelling lakeside breeze carried their carefree laughter across the gleaming hardwood deck. A pair of glaring eyes met my look of longing. I scampered back down to the cargo deck.

As soon as the ferry set sail, I had one mission only: to scour the crowded boat and find a spot, no matter how small, to call my own for the 36-hour voyage. The door leading into the enclosed passenger area was as heavy as lead. I used the weight of my body to push it open. The inside air was sticky and suffocating. I was assaulted by the smell of sweaty, sour-smelling bodies. The stench of stale urine and feces leached out from the toilets.

I held my breath and did a quick scan. No one else on board appeared repulsed by the putrid odors. Families sat huddled together, taking bites of home-cooked meals, their palates seemingly unaffected. Children were sleeping on the floor next to unwashed feet. Flies buzzed all around, landing on one face before travelling to the next.

The toilet smell was too much for me. Vomit trickled up my throat. I covered my mouth and nose and rushed outside. It seemed the only place I would find reprieve was the cargo deck.

After a few hours adapting to our new environment, Emma shrieked, "Oh, fuckin' hell. I just saw a bloody rat run across that railing!"

I rushed inside one more time to search for an open spot, trying not to breathe through my nose. I walked past a small industrial kitchen. The scent of rancid cooking oil wafted out, clinging to my hair and skin. Two cockroaches scuttled across the unwashed, rust-stained floor. What I was most perturbed by, though, was the sight of a kitchen worker struggling with an animal carcass.

The man's sweat-filled, furrowed brow was fraught with desperation. His gaze turned toward me, his eyes locking with mine for a few seconds, looking as though I'd just caught him in the midst of an unspeakable crime. The bloodied meat was pressed heavily against the unsanitary floor by the weight of his left arm to prevent it from slipping. The veins of his sinewy biceps popped like pythons as he hacked the large mass into smaller pieces with a butcher knife.

This was the exact moment I decided to stop eating meat for the rest of my trip.

By the afternoon, Emma, Daniel, Mark and I had accepted our ferry fate. We made our tiny corner on the cargo deck as cozy as possible. It was a relief that the air was fresh-smelling compared to the ferry's foul interior and that it was sunny and dry.

My oversized backpack doubled as a mini sofa. I spread my legs onto a pocket of warm sun. I looked down at my calves and cringed. They were toned and tan, but I hadn't shaved them since arriving in Cape Maclear. This practical decision was no longer sitting well with me. The hair on my legs wasn't thick or dark, but as far as I was concerned, it wasn't helping matters in the sexiness department.

Even though it was convenient for travelling, my decision to cut my hair shorter than its usual shoulder length made me feel less feminine. My backpacker wardrobe consisted of a limited selection of loose-fitting cotton clothing that had acquired a subtle funky smell from hand washing using lake water. I didn't bother with makeup except for a bit of mascara on the odd evening out. Even with Matthias out of the picture, having smooth legs again would allow me to cling onto one last thread of desirability.

The leg hair would have to go.

Nobody seemed to care when the four of us laid our sleeping bags across the heap of stuffed burlap sacks at bedtime. I nestled into my makeshift bed and marvelled at the full moon shimmering above. The stars flickered alive against a sea of black velvet, making the ferry ride tolerable.

WE WOKE TO A SECOND DAY of clear blue skies. It would take another six hours until Likoma Island appeared on the horizon, but as we counted down the last few hours, our negative experience faded, morphing into an anthill on the scale of things to whine about. One thing Africa had taught me was that it is better to embrace life's small wins instead of dwelling on short-term grief and inconvenience.

The MV *Ilala* chugged up to the water's edge. We bid farewell to Thomas, who was continuing on the ferry to Nkhata Bay before heading home to Switzerland. Emma, Mark and I stepped off the boat and waded to shore. A stream of islanders carrying bags over their heads climbed aboard to replace us.

The clean island air and calm waters made me believe the filthy ferry ride wasn't for nothing. Emma, Mark and I walked over to our quaint, one-level bungalow. As far as I could see, it was the only lodge in Likoma village. The little house boasted pastel-coloured tiles and polished floors. Red cast-iron window frames revealed a small court-yard surrounded by cacti. Brilliantly coloured roosters with crazy crests of feathers roamed freely. It was perfect.

After being confined to the boat for so long, I left Emma and Mark at the lodge and jogged over to the closest beach to do some writing. I plopped my body on the edge of the shoreline: feeling the warm, smooth sand against the backs of my legs and the soft waves against my feet was exactly what I needed. Once again, the lake disguised itself as an ocean, but without the salty residue.

I watched a handful of charming pied crows wearing their Sunday best peck away at a fish carcass. Residents were filling up large jugs with lake water. A few women went about their routine washing. They appeared unworried, knowing full well that crocodiles lurked in the deceptively tranquil waters.

An hour later, I walked back toward the lodge to explore the village. In the centre stood a sprawling baobab. I had seen plenty of baobabs while riding in buses, but none this magnificent. A permanent bench encircled the massive tree, with seating for more than 20, making it a popular gathering spot for locals.

The village had a few conveniences, including a grocery store, a post office and a tailor shop. I grew up believing sewing was women's work. I was delighted to see a middle-aged man working outside on the verandah, his feet pumping methodically as he guided brightly patterned fabric through the antique Singer.

With few tourists around, it was refreshing to have a break from the backpacker scene. Interacting with the islanders required nothing beyond stepping outside. A pint-sized beer shack sold chilled beverages when the island's fickle electricity supply was up and running. It didn't take long before a group of older men sipping lukewarm beers invited me to join them outside the shack at sunset. They had a good laugh when I tried speaking Chichewa to them – though a few of them understood me, most Likoma residents spoke the Nkamanga dialect.

Despite my elation at escaping the ferry, it only took 24 hours for me to discover there was little to do on the island aside from socializing at the baobab tree and walking along the shoreline. As much as I wanted to swim in the lake, locals advised against it because of the crocodile risk.

I was glad to have the company of Emma and her brother. Beyond their fine, chin-length hair, fair skin and button noses, the siblings shared few similarities. Emma was petite, curvaceous and lively. Mark was as lanky as a beanstalk and spoke at a minimum.

Despite his introverted nature, I didn't mind hanging with Mark in small doses. He was low-maintenance and kept things tidy. We both enjoyed listening to Billy Bragg's music. I didn't feel obliged to make conversation or invite Mark along when I wanted to explore on my own.

I did feel disappointed, however, when two days in, Emma shamelessly announced, "So I'm heading over to Mozambique to see my lover. I'll be back in a day or two."

"Lover? When did that happen?" I asked.

Mark rolled his eyes and lit a cigarette. Emma read the puzzled look on my face. "Oh, you don't remember? It was the guy I met while we were all dancing at the Ba' Blu last week. God, he's gorgeous. Malawi men are such gentlemen," she said, looking enamoured, her eyes brimming with lust. "He's working in Mozambique, 30 minutes away."

Two hours later, Emma hopped onto a boat and travelled to the mainland, leaving me with her brother. As soon as she left, I felt a void. Emma had been a sweet, sugary can of soda, but Mark was tonic water that had lost its effervescence. Without Emma's boisterous personality to balance out his quiet demeanour, some of Mark's quirks began to annoy me.

By the next day I realized he was perfectly content hanging out at the lodge, smoking cigarettes and playing his coveted Oasis CD at high volume from his little portable stereo. To me it was another case of a foreigner overplaying Western music in an obscure East African town. Even though I had been guilty of the same thing a few times, it reminded me of how the British had imposed their religious and cultural beliefs on Africans for so many decades. This time Mark was to blame.

After Emma's abrupt departure, I wanted to see more of the island beyond its sandy shores, meet some locals and seek out some adventures on my own. Likoma is less than eight kilometres long and is only three kilometres at its widest point. With no cars or buses, the only way for me to get around was by foot.

I walked out of the lodge in a hurry, leaving Mark alone with the Gallagher brothers' "Wonderwall" bouncing off the patio wall. As I passed the post office, a man came out carrying a small box wrapped in brown paper. This was the first foreigner I had seen in the village.

The man greeted me, curious about my presence in Likoma. After chatting, I learned John was a dietitian and Peace Corps volunteer who had been working on the island for eight months.

In Malawi and on Likoma Island, it was impossible to ignore the AIDS/HIV epidemic spreading throughout the country. It was shocking that some Malawians believed God had created AIDS as a form of punishment, and that Joshua Nkomo – the vice-president of Zimbabwe at the time – claimed whites had planted AIDS in Africa.

Posters featuring sex education campaigns and free condom distribution were widespread in Malawi. The rate of HIV infection among men was on the rise, and many carriers didn't know they had been infected. AIDS aside, the residents of Likoma had to contend with their own set of health concerns. John told me illnesses among children caused by poor water quality were a grave concern. He had been trying to set up a proper water system but was frustrated by the slow progress.

The islanders had long been accustomed to receiving handouts and subsidies from the mainland. According to John, there wasn't a lot of motivation for them to improve their standard of living and become self-sufficient. Many believed they would be cursed if they became more successful than their relatives on the mainland, who often helped support them. I saw evidence of this dependence in the crowds of people who gathered on the shores of the beach, waiting for the boat carrying supplies and packages to the island.

John wished me well and I wandered inland. Without a map, my instincts guided me as I walked up a gentle slope. Roughly half a kilometre later, a large church came into view. I hovered outside the entrance, pausing a few minutes to take in this unexpected sight.

This was St. Peter's Cathedral, one of Africa's largest churches, built by Scottish missionaries between 1899 and 1903. Even though I had read about it in my guidebook, it was strange to be confronted by such an enormous religious structure dominating the natural landscape in what seemed like the middle of nowhere.

My feet gravitated toward the faint, harmonious notes of a soulful choir spilling out of the church. I stepped inside and stood in the nave of the cathedral, looking up in awe toward the naturally lit ceilings. The interior was spacious and pristinely maintained. The cathedral boasted intricate, patterned wooden flooring, colourful stained-glass windows and a long row of pointed arches typical of Gothic architecture. One look at the ochre-coloured stone walls and my mind travelled back to the Namibian dunes and my Rabbit crew.

I sat in one of the long wooden pews and looked around. There was seating for 200, but there were at most 20 of us there. I listened to the talented choir for several minutes before realizing I was the only woman sitting among the men. This made me wonder if segregation between the sexes was an expected practice, or if it just happened by chance. I never found out.

It was strange to sit in a church and not want to leave. For as long I could remember, Mom had ensured I attended the United Church

near our home every week. I willingly went to Sunday school when
I was little, but by age 11 I attended the church's youth group with
growing skepticism. The New Wave music the older kids played at
church dances was my only saving grace. That year I wised up when I
discovered helping out in the church daycare got me out of attending
sermons.

As a teenager, I loathed the arrival of Sunday morning, and this
feeling lasted a decade after I stopped going to church. My family's
double standard always bothered me. *Hockey Night in Canada* was
Dad and the boys' religion of choice. I couldn't understand why I had
to attend church with Mom and Sue every Sunday.

When Dad and the boys did make a rare church appearance at
Easter or Christmas, we watched closely until Dad nodded off minutes into the sermon. Each time he exhaled, a ridiculous puffing
sound escaped from the corner of his mouth, like an air compressor
releasing its final breath. As soon as the snoring became obvious, one
of us gave him a nudge in the arm to bring him back to consciousness.

All those years, and I never made a connection to the Christian
faith, Jesus's teachings or the concept of a heavenly father. Nothing
resonated with me: I never understood why a person needed to attend church or study the Bible to be a caring, decent human being.
As a stubborn teen, I was dead set against church. Mom struggled to
keep me going until I refused outright around age 14.

So it came as a surprise when, years later, world religions became
one of my favourite university courses. I grew to appreciate my religious upbringing. I had a frame of reference to compare faiths, and
my knowledge of Christianity proved useful when I majored in art
history and travelled to Europe. I had rejected my own religious upbringing but was fascinated by other world views and loved learning
different interpretations of life's mysteries.

When Russ and Dad first got sick, I prayed for them. But deep
down I knew praying was nothing more than a temporary effort
to cope with grief and despair, a desperate attempt to fix things I
couldn't control or make sense of. Praying, or believing in "God's
plan," wasn't going to make them better.

I've never really believed in God, at least not in the Christian sense. But I do believe in gifts: the gift of health and an unfailing body, the gift of adventure and friendship. These gifts I could never take for granted. These gifts I could hold on to.

I was in no hurry to leave St. Peter's. If only Mom could have seen me contently seated there in the pew. Of course, I wasn't seeking her approval. I was there on my own terms, enjoying the lovely music and marvelling at the impressive architecture.

This was my kind of sermon: one without words.

I left the church and roamed inland toward the other side of the island. I was delighted when two teens befriended me en route. Gift and Advice lived in the smaller neighbouring village a few kilometres away. Gift was the taller of the two and spoke English like an articulate adult.

"What did you think of the church?" he asked.

"Oh, it's very beautiful. I've seen some wonderful cathedrals before, but St. Peter's is just as impressive."

"Did you know the cathedral's crucifix was made from a branch of the tree where David Livingstone's heart was buried?"

"Really? No, I didn't know that. Fascinating."

Gift continued. "Yes. *And* the founders of the church brought dirt all the way from Jerusalem and placed it under the high altar."

"All the way from Jerusalem?" I asked. "Wow, that's a huge effort." Unlike me at 15, Gift didn't seem to reject the influence Christianity had on the island.

"I'm trying to get to the other side of the island. Am I going the right way?"

"Yes, that is the way. Why don't you follow us, Lisa?" Gift suggested. "We are very happy to show you the way."

Gift's afro was thick on top and trim on the sides. His chipmunk cheeks contrasted with his lanky stature. He wore bright orange, knee-length shorts and a flowy, blue-and-orange checked shirt. Advice was half a foot shorter and timid compared to Gift. He hid his eyes behind reflective aviator sunglasses, and he hardly made a peep.

A few minutes into our walk, Gift turned to me and announced, "I think Malawi people are bad. They think all white people have money."

I laughed out loud. Gift sounded wise beyond his 15 years, but I thought he needed some perspective. "Well, we do have poverty and homelessness in Canada too. But compared to people in Malawi, most Canadians are quite wealthy."

Gift nodded as if he agreed, but it was a hard comparison for me to make. I tried to imagine someone from Malawi having the financial means to travel to Canada just to go backpacking. It seemed like an impossible, frivolous dream.

The boys led me along a rock-strewn trail that snaked up to a viewpoint looking west toward Chizumulu Island. While climbing up the hill, I noticed Gift's legs. His calves and ankles had gaping tropical ulcers oozing with pus. The wounds looked raw and painful.

"Gift, your legs. Aren't the sores painful?" I asked.

"Oh, I don't notice them anymore. They don't really bother me." He brushed off my concern like it was nothing. I wasn't convinced.

"If you come back to the village with me, I can use some antibiotic cream and bandages from my first aid kit. Maybe it will help heal the sores," I said, hoping he'd accept my offer.

An hour later, we sat down outside the lodge on the verandah. I introduced the boys to Mark, who was slouched onto a chair with his legs crossed, reading a book. Billy Bragg's *Don't Try This at Home* album was playing on the stereo. Gift and Advice bobbed their heads to the beat of the song and moved their hands up in the air joyously.

"This music is great!" Gift exclaimed with a broad smile.

"You like it? Brilliant. You have good taste, kid." Mark grinned with a nod of approval.

I retrieved my first aid kit from inside. After I dressed Gift's wounds, his initial lack of concern turned to gratitude.

Before dinner, Gift, Advice and I were near the lakeshore when a loud commotion 20 metres away took us by surprise. We ran toward the yelling and saw a man lying helplessly on his back, writhing in pain. I looked down in shock: a deep laceration on his knee was bleeding profusely. The man had been cooling off in the lake when a crocodile's tail struck his leg like a whip.

Two locals ran for help, while Gift, Advice and I stayed behind with him. Together we put my first aid kit to use a second time, bandaging up the injured man's leg until he could receive proper medical care. The violent tendency of this elusive species had finally revealed itself, reminding me to be extra vigilant while spending time close to the lake.

THE NEXT MORNING I went to the post office to mail a few letters. When I asked the operator to use the private phone to call home using my calling card, I wasn't prepared for her curt response.

"That won't be possible," she replied, sounding annoyed.

I pleaded a second time, but she wouldn't budge. I felt my chest tighten. Mother's Day and Russ's birthday were around the corner. Phoning home made me worry less. Now that I was faced with being unable to contact them, my guilty conscience resurfaced.

I returned to the lodge feeling frustrated and, surprisingly, homesick. With little to do on the island, I was restless. I dwelled on the fact that I only had five weeks left. Instead of getting excited about Tanzania, Zanzibar and Kenya, I thought about all the things I wanted to do when I returned to Vancouver.

Cycle along Spanish Banks to UBC. Have a coffee and biscotti at Ecco Il Pane. Go climbing in Squamish. Crank my Prince and George Michael albums. Go out dancing. Cook pasta with garlic and prawns.

As if this passing nostalgia weren't enough, I started thinking about Matthias *again*. I assumed once I set sail, I'd forget about him. But there were few distractions on Likoma to take my mind off our time together. Even though I had believed nothing further would happen between us, I hoped to see him again in Nkhata Bay.

After lunch, a wave of nausea hit me hard. I ran to the bathroom and vomited. I lay holed up in bed for the rest of the day and night, convinced I had contracted bilharzia or, worse, malaria. My patience was waning. I was consumed by the sudden urge to call it quits and get off the island as soon as I was well enough to leave.

With infrequent ferry sailings, I decided to catch the *Ilala* back to the mainland the next evening if I felt better. I had really hoped that Emma, who had returned to Likoma the night before, would join me. Instead, she announced she was heading back to Mozambique the next morning to see her new boyfriend for a few more days.

When I told Mark my plan, he replied, "I think I've had my Likoma fix too. If you don't mind, I'll catch the ferry with you."

"Sure," I said, even though I wanted to leave on my own.

I WOKE UP THE NEXT MORNING with no signs of nausea. Whatever had wreaked havoc on my stomach had exited my system. Aside from feeling lethargic, my body was more or less back to normal, and I regained an appetite.

I was eating a bowl of rice porridge, halfway through Alice Walker's *Possessing the Secret of Joy*, when Gift and Advice popped by the lodge to see how I was doing. I snuck a peek at Gift's legs. Two of the bandages were hanging off like lifeless leaves. Despite our efforts, his sores were still raw and bright pink: clearly, the humidity and unfavourable water conditions wouldn't allow his ulcers to heal.

Gift told me about the local healer William, whom he simply referred to as the witch doctor. Gift piqued my interest when he suggested we attend one of the services together.

"Doctor" William was seated in the bar looking like a regular fixture when we found him just before noon. He appeared to be in his mid-50s and was very distinctive with his long, matted dreadlocks and wide, bulbous nose.

Gift took a seat next to him and introduced me as "Lisa, the Canadian." William brought his bottle to his lips and sipped vigorously. Beer dribbled down his chin and onto his lap. He nonchalantly wiped his mouth on his sleeve, then mumbled something to Gift, who translated for me.

"The doctor invited us to come by this afternoon. Would you like to attend a healing ceremony?"

I was desperate for something – *anything* – to bring an end to the tedium. I didn't need any convincing. "Oh, yes, I would love that, Gift." It was exciting to have something to look forward to again.

Gift and Advice picked up Mark and me from the lodge. I shook my head and chuckled. The boys were singing my favourite Billy Bragg song, "Sexuality." Clearly, Mark's tunes had made an impression on them.

We walked along a dirt path flanked by a smattering of mango and baobab trees. Before arriving at the witch doctor's quarters, Gift stopped and instructed us to fetch some cassava branches.

"We will present these branches to the doctor as an offering." Gift explained that William once had a vision of his deceased mother in spirit form. She was holding a cassava branch in her left hand, and from there this tradition was born.

Like most Westerners, I had zero experience in the realm of witchcraft. I had no idea what to expect but arrived with an open mind. A thatched building the size of a small classroom housed the ceremony. There were around 40 adults and children already snugly seated together on the clay floor when we entered. At the front of the room there was a small stage with a white altar covered with red-painted hospital symbols. The area above and behind the stage had an assortment of wall coverings: white flags with red crosses, GOD is LOVE and GOD is GREAT slogans, a calendar, an iconic image of a white Jesus with lambs, an election campaign poster and a Misozi Hospital sign.

A small choir in faultless harmony began the procession with five back-to-back hymns. Their beautiful singing was followed by a dramatic entrance: Doctor William dashed in with his head held high, moving about with an air of authority. Then he stood still as a statue for a few seconds so everyone could give him their undivided attention.

I studied William from head to toe. His unruly dreadlocks were tied up securely with a bold fuchsia bandana. He wore a crisp, white, short-sleeved jacket resembling a clinical gown that draped down past his hips. A blue-and-tan shell-patterned sarong covered his short legs down to his ankles. William held a short staff in one hand. In the other he clutched a stick with what looked like a full head of black straight hair attached. He spent a few moments preaching before proceeding with his first patient.

John, the headmaster from Gift's school, was also present. He sat next to me and quietly translated some details for my benefit. The ceremony began with a 39-year-old woman who had been a talented and renowned dancer in the community. John explained she had become paralyzed the previous month while walking in the village. She appeared to have lost muscle control but still had feeling in her legs. I was struck by her appearance. Her atrophied muscles and unexplained symptoms reminded me of multiple sclerosis, though I knew the disease was rare in Africa.

William concluded her condition was linked to a curse that an evil person had placed upon her. Accompanied by a skilled drummer, Doctor broke into song. The woman remained seated but moved her shoulders and arms joyously to the frenetic drumbeat until she slumped forward, apparently fatigued. William lifted her chin and held a frothy remedy to her mouth. After drinking some of the liquid, she regained some energy and danced until her exhausted body became limp and lifeless again.

Her family sat by her side. They presented William with payment in the form of a covered bowl full of maize flour. He proceeded to cover his face with the flour, although I never learned the significance of this action. During this part of the ceremony, I had to contain my laughter: William incorporated bouts of wide-mouthed yawning in the midst of chanting his mantras. I looked around the room at all the stoic faces. Apparently, I was the only one amused by this unintended comic relief.

The next patient was a young, thin woman who had to be around three to six months pregnant. John told me she had been possessed by two spirits, one male and one female. At first, she resisted coming up to the front altar. Her distraught state made me suspect she was there against her will.

The woman's high-pitched voice wailed uncontrollably. She had already spent three weeks in a state-run hospital, but no one discussed her medical condition. I assumed her hysteria and madness were symptoms of an untreated illness like malaria.

Doctor William called out to ask the spirits what remedies they wanted. He stopped to listen. The spirits responded by requesting the blood of two doves and a chicken. William gave the woman a herbal concoction. A minute after taking a few sips, the foamy liquid erupted from her closed lips before one big gush poured onto her sagging breasts and frail body. When the vomiting ceased, a family member wiped the drool from her mouth, chin and chest with a cloth.

William delivered his final oration and then ended the service in prayer. Immediately after, he orchestrated a spectacle by encouraging a photo-taking session featuring none other than himself. He left the room for a few minutes and reappeared donning a bright-red gown that looked like an outfit taken from a theatrical props chest. William posed for us in a variety of positions, looking poised and contemplative, relishing his celebrity status.

Up until the ceremony, my scope and understanding of medical treatments was limited to mainstream Western medicine, a bit of naturopathy and Chinese herbal medicine. I was familiar with some alternative treatments for MS – primrose oil, emu oil and bee venom therapy – that Russ had tried without success. African witchcraft was not something that made sense to me. But it wasn't for me to decide if it was an effective or legitimate practice. From what I witnessed, William's rituals seemed harmless, save for the birds involved. I wasn't there long enough to see the effects on those he attempted to heal. But I *could* relate to what the families were going through as they sought any means possible to help their loved ones get better.

Since witchcraft was such an important aspect of island life and for most Malawians, I was grateful to be able to attend the healing ceremony. It changed my impression of Likoma: instead of being mild and mundane, the island could be an unpredictable and evocative place.

I snapped some photos and thanked William before leaving. Mark and I followed Gift to Chinyanya village to meet his family. The late afternoon sun warmed my shoulders as Gift led us along a narrow path through a spectacular vista of thick-trunked baobabs. Peekaboo views revealed the shimmering lake and the magnificent mountains of Mozambique.

After a two-kilometre walk, we arrived at Gift's one-level clay home. The small structure was topped with a large, umbrella-shaped, thatched roof. Rows of washed clothes were strung between two mango trees to dry despite the island's moist air. A large, crude firepit made of stone sat in the middle of the grey dirt yard.

Gift's mother was the first to greet us out front, followed by his four younger brothers. His older sister was lying in bed, recovering from malaria. Her listless demeanour perked up a little when I popped in to say hello.

We gathered outside on the sunny patio. Gift and his mother served us tea and cassava treats. It was wonderful to be in the presence of his family – they made Mark and me feel like relatives the moment we arrived at their doorstep. Gift beamed with pride as he translated for his mother as we made small talk.

As dinnertime neared, Gift reminded us, "You have to leave soon before it gets dark. I will walk you back to the start of the trail."

Gift's mom clutched my hands tightly in hers when I thanked her and said goodbye to her sons and daughter. Just as we were leaving, a man rushed over to their house. He was out of breath and clearly in distress. His shaky words were fraught with sadness and shock. After he ran off, Gift translated the man's dire message.

"A woman was attacked by a crocodile…at the lakeside. They don't know how bad, but he thinks it is serious."

Gift raced over to his neighbour to find out more details. He returned and delivered the news with a look of shock across his face. A 30-year-old mother had been fetching water in a nearby marshy cove with her baby strapped to her back: the crocodile attack killed them both.

A few sombre minutes of silence passed. Then the sounds of wailing echoed all around us, filling the air with sadness and grief. Villagers sang sorrowfully as they gathered to begin the difficult task of preparing for an unplanned funeral for the mother and child.

A feeling of unease settled into me. I looked at Mark but had no words. As an outsider, I felt out of place in this tight-knit community that was now ensconced in tragedy. I told Gift it was best for us to leave: I didn't know what else to say.

Gift led Mark and me to the trail, then left with a rushed and frantic farewell. The fading light between the tree branches quickly disappeared. Darkness nipped at our heels all the way back to the village. I stopped at the big baobab tree and broke the tragic news to the locals, who shook their heads in disbelief.

Mark and I packed up in anticipation of boarding the evening ferry as planned. Eating supper as though nothing had happened seemed callous while villagers were mourning the loss of the woman and her baby. Yet there was nothing we could have done. These tragic deaths were completely out of my Western realm of experiences. Aside from the guilt of not feeling more affected, little emotion came over me. The tragedy seemed like a horrible dream divorced from reality.

An hour later, we waded through the shallow lake water, holding our backpacks high above our heads, *praying* that no crocodiles were skulking nearby. Mark and I boarded the *Ilala* with only seconds to spare.

The overnight journey to the mainland removed me physically from Likoma, but emotionally part of me was still there. This wasn't what I had expected for my last memory of the island. Sadly, it still stands out for all the wrong reasons.

Thirteen

IF SOMEONE HAD BEEN SELLING "Give the *Ilala* Ferry a Second Chance!" T-shirts, I would have gladly stood in line to buy one. My expectations were low given our disappointing voyage from Cape Maclear, but our second trip aboard the infamous ferry was a vast improvement. I didn't spy any rats or cockroaches this time around, which seemed like a big win. With the town of Nkhotakota only 110 kilometres from Likoma, the overnight trip was tolerable, with the ferry pulling into the mainland shore early the next morning.

The deaths on Likoma were still heavy on my mind as I walked up and down the main street of Nkhotakota. One glance and I knew a day and night would suffice in this tiny town. Aside from some banking and getting some rest after the late ferry ride, there was little to do there. I did, however, find a place to use my calling card and got hold of my mom. Dad sounded stable. Russ's symptoms hadn't worsened. After the disturbing end to my time on Likoma, I exhaled a big sigh of relief, knowing I didn't have to worry about family.

With only one day in Nkhotakota, I made it my mission to rent a bicycle. My desire to go cycling in Africa had been growing. With the exception of biking in Oudtshoorn with Anna and my short ride with Sion over the Zambian border, I hadn't ridden a bike since leaving Canada. I missed the freedom of self-propelled transportation. Travelling in buses and cars all the time made me feel lazy, and I didn't like always being on someone else's schedule.

After making a few inquiries around town, I almost gave up. For most Malawians, owning a bike was a luxury, almost as rare as owning a car. I was overjoyed when I found a man willing to rent me a bicycle for 20 kwacha.

It was a rare sight to see a woman riding a bike in Malawi, or in any other African nation I had visited. Factor in my fairer complexion and light-brown hair, and I made a lot of heads turn when I left town on two wheels.

This reaction from the locals felt familiar. After a month of my Japanese host mom chauffeuring me to and from school, I opted to ride a bicycle instead. I loved pedalling along the rural roads, snaking through the tranquil landscape of rice paddy fields and bamboo groves. My wavy, dark-blonde hair set against my grey-and-white sailor uniform made the rural folk gawk as if they had just seen Gojira stomping through the countryside.

I pedalled away from Nkhotakota, grinning from ear to ear, exhilarated by the warm breeze against my face. My enthusiasm, however, was short-lived. Roughly half a kilometre from the town, I discovered the bicycle was in dire need of some maintenance. After five or six pedal rotations, the saddle would slope downward. Only minutes into the bike ride, I had to stop repeatedly to adjust the angle of the seat. I knew I looked about as graceful as I did riding that ostrich in Oudtshoorn.

Given my transportation track record in Africa, the bike's condition shouldn't have surprised me. Without repair shops, the only viable alternative was for me to ride out of the saddle. Despite the bicycle's poor form, I came close to mastering the art of sitting on the bike without putting all of my weight on the seat.

While cycling along a compact dirt road away from Nkhotakota toward the lakeside, I discovered it wasn't sandy like Cape Maclear. The grassy, marshy surroundings reminded me of the dyke near my family home. The setting and funny scenario made me think of my mom.

My parents moved our family from hilly Vancouver Island to pancake-flat Richmond when I was a baby. Mom had always loved to bike, since it had been a common transport mode for her growing up in the Netherlands. One day she told me a story I've never forgotten.

"For my birthday, I think you might have been around 1 or 2, Dad bought me a second-hand bicycle. I rode that bike every week." Mom's eyes were bright and vibrant as she reminisced. "Back then in the '70s, you just didn't see people riding a bike for fun. Or for exercise. Everyone drove or walked. Whenever I rode through our neighbourhood or on the dyke, people turned their heads like they couldn't believe their eyes. As if I were riding a spaceship or something!" She laughed, revealing her beautiful smile.

By age 3, I joined Mom as her co-pilot in the seat at the back of her bike. I looked forward to our weekly bike trips along the dyke and through farmland to buy fresh produce at the farmers' market. Sitting behind her with the summer wind blowing through my hair remains one of my fondest childhood memories. By the time I was old enough to bike on my own, I was hooked.

After a few more kilometres, the road ended close to the shoreline. The wheels of the derelict bicycle spun in the sandy dirt until they stopped completely, forcing me to push it toward the water. A guy about my age was sitting cross-legged on a log, reading a book. His messianic presence almost made me believe I was seeing an apparition. There wasn't another soul in sight: the mid-morning sun seemed to be shining just for the two of us.

Sensing he was friendly, I walked over. When he saw me approach, he closed up his book and gave me his full attention when I said hello.

"Nice to meet you. My name's Christmas," he said with a genuine smile.

Of course it is, I thought to myself.

Christmas was a year younger than me. His stylish hair was thicker and unkempt compared to most Malawian men. His borderline skinny, muscular physique was clad in a Rastafari-inspired T-shirt and knee-length shorts. In perfect English, Christmas told me he was a college student in Lilongwe, 200 kilometres away. His family lived nearby.

We made a quick connection when I told him about my little bike adventure and how the area reminded me a bit of home. Christmas was keen on asking me about life in Canada. For nearly an hour, we sat chatting about our studies and travel.

"Do a lot of Canadians smoke ganja?" he asked out of the blue.

I was taken off guard and let out a nervous laugh. "Ah, I wouldn't say a lot. I've never been much of a pot smoker myself," I admitted.

He laughed out an incredulous, "Really? Why not?"

Between my last year of high school and university, I had tried marijuana enough times to know it wasn't for me. "It always makes me paranoid," I explained. "I hate feeling out of control...so I just avoid it altogether."

"Well, too bad that happens. I don't smoke it a lot. Just sometimes, when I want to relax."

My parents rarely drank and never did drugs. They once had an open bottle of wine on top of their fridge that stayed there for nearly six months. I suppose my attitude toward mind-altering substances was conservative despite my teenage experimentation with drinking. But when Dad and Russ fell ill, I wasn't about to risk doing any damage to my healthy body, nor did I have a desire to do drugs.

Christmas talked about world events and global problems. His open-mindedness and wide range of knowledge – including Canadian geography and American politics – surprised me. Aside from Mike in Mulanje, my limited interactions with local men, mostly fishermen and shop owners, made me think that most Malawians weren't exposed to outside influences and world views. Meeting Christmas revealed my ignorance and made me realize I still had lots to learn.

"Have you been to the Livingstone Tree already?" he asked.

"No, not yet."

"C'mon. Follow me then," he said with an easygoing smile.

Three young children recognized Christmas and ran toward us. Together we walked a few hundred metres over to the famous tree. I couldn't resist climbing onto the lower branches of the sprawling baobab. A small crowd of children observed my every move as they climbed up the tree to show off their agility. They stood up on the higher branches and grinned down at me.

Weeks earlier I had read a blurb about the Livingstone Tree in my *Lonely Planet*, but it never occurred to me that it was located right here. Christmas was happy to explain its significance:

"They say David Livingstone camped under this tree, and this is where he met Chief Jumbe, a Swahili-Arab slave trader. Livingstone was trying to get him to stop the slave trade back in 1863…He convinced Jumbe to sign a treaty, but the slave trade continued. It took another 30 years before Nyasaland saw the end of slavery."

I beamed at Christmas. This history lesson from a local was much better than reading anything from my guidebook. Spending time with him was an unexpected gift. Unlike Christmas the holiday, I didn't want my time with Christmas the person to end so soon.

"I wish I could hang out longer," I told him, "but I promised the guy who rented me the bike I'd only be gone a few hours. I gotta get going. Thank you for everything, Christmas."

"It was my pleasure. Enjoy the rest of your stay in Malawi."

I got on the bike and waved goodbye. I pedalled back to town, my clenched buttocks hovering over the saddle for most of the ride back.

For our one night in Nkhotakota, Mark and I stayed at a small lodge with spotless rooms, save for the peeling paint. The next morning we were packing up to leave when two young boys walked past our room. They looked to be around 8 or 9 and wore shiny, oversized watches that hung like bracelets. Their shimmery, pristine soccer jerseys and matching shorts were two sizes too big. Compared to the faded second-hand clothing worn by most Malawi children, these boys stood out like Liberace.

They kept going in and out of a room where an older German man was staying, two doors over from us. Mark asked them if they were also staying at the motel.

"We're visiting our uncle," one of them replied proudly as he played with the silver watch dangling from his small wrist. As far as I could tell, there was no European blood running through their veins. "Our mother knows we're here."

The brothers seemed happy to have this wealthy Westerner spoil them. Aside from their flashy outfits, I didn't think much of the scenario.

A few minutes later, a door slammed shut and some unintelligible sounds and laughter spilled out of their open window. Mark shook his head in disgust. "What kind of perv hangs out with two young boys? Sick bastard."

My chest tightened. I had no idea if Mark's hunches were right and shuddered to think about the man's questionable interactions with the boys behind closed doors.

"You think something weird is going on?" I asked Mark.

"It sure looks that way to me." More laughter escaped out of their room, and a sick feeling filled my stomach. "C'mon, we gotta go or we're gonna miss the bus," Mark said.

I left Nkhotakota feeling perturbed, wishing I had never witnessed Mark's reaction, praying he was wrong.

THE THREE-HOUR bus ride to Nkhata Bay was a backpacker's dream: the coach featured clean cushioned seats, minimal stops and *no* breakdowns. Not long after driving through tropical, lush scenery and an enormous sugar cane plantation, we arrived in the bustling town.

Rows of food shacks, a large outdoor market and artisan craft stands lined the main street of Nkhata Bay. Looking out the bus window, my salivary glands went into overdrive as we passed all the food signs. Pizza. Pasta. Curry. Banana Pancakes. I had arrived in culinary heaven. Having so many food options in one place was overwhelming but divine.

As soon as we exited the bus, a huge downpour chased Mark and I into a small pizza joint. We were getting acquainted with a British couple and comparing our MV *Ilala* horror stories when a rain-soaked guy ducked into the restaurant. He sat down at our crowded table without waiting for an invitation.

"How'd ya do? Hope you don't mind me joining you. It's raining buckets out there. My name's Duncan."

Water dripped from his frizzy rat-tail dreadlocks and beaded onto the arms of his plastic raincoat before pooling onto the table. It was hard to take this Brit seriously with his unflattering mop head, but his affectionate smile reeled me in. After I told him my last name was Duncan, he got excited and said something like, "Fantastic. That means we're *almost* like kin."

I pictured the Duncan clan tartan and wooden plaque that hung on display in my parents' living room. My aunt had bought it for Dad during her trip to Scotland. "What does '*Disce pati*' mean?" I had asked Dad, curious to know more about our shared heritage. "Learn to suffer," he replied matter-of-factly. These words seemed like a cruel joke, not words to put on a plaque and certainly not words to live by. Hadn't Dad and Russ suffered enough?

I couldn't help myself when I asked Duncan if he was aware of my family's clan motto. "It's kind of hard to get excited about a name that means 'learn to suffer,'" I said with a dry smile. Just as the words left my mouth, I regretted them. I didn't want to come off as a killjoy with someone I'd just met.

Duncan's reply was quick. "Well, from what I recall, the more ac- curate meaning is learn to *endure*, not suffer."

That one word made all the difference. Maybe hundreds of years ago something got lost in translation from the original Latin into Old English.

"Huh, I never thought about it that way. I much prefer that inter- pretation. I'll have to tell my dad that one."

THE RAINS DRIED UP BY THE MORNING. I spent most of the day on my own strolling the local beaches and exploring the town centre. In addition to all the food signs, there were many more billboards and posters promoting safe sex compared to Cape Maclear. I learned it was common practice for health clinics to give out free condoms since AIDS was still on the rise in the country.

Duncan joined Mark and me for curry and a Carlsberg at dinner. I was happy to have him along as he balanced out Mark's wallflower persona. After our meal, we ambled along Chikale Beach and then plunked ourselves on the sand to watch the sunset. Without a word, Duncan lit up a joint. Mark took a few tokes and offered it to me.

I shook my head. "I think I'll pass. Pot and I don't mix well together. Paranoia isn't my idea of fun," I explained, feeling like little Miss Goody Two-Shoes.

"Suit yourself. This stuff is pretty chill, though. You could try a bit and see," Duncan suggested.

I didn't feel any pressure. *What the hell. Why not?* It had been a few years. Maybe this time it would be different. Worst-case scenario, I'd have a bad trip. Then I would avoid it again.

I took the small joint from Duncan and inhaled. The smoke burned my throat, but I was thankful I didn't break into a coughing fit. By the fourth or fifth toke, I felt a warm, tingly sensation. Minutes later my mind started to warp. I couldn't feel my legs: I thought I was floating. I sat quietly for a few minutes, staring at the golden surface of the water. The remaining pale-yellow light of the sunset shimmered across the lake like clusters of dancing moths.

My eyes moved from the lake to the shoreline. I was transfixed by a cluster of egg-sized rocks sticking out of the sand. They turned into a pair of crocodile eyes glaring at me. A minute later, the eyes morphed into a walking cartoon cactus. When a second cactus appeared, I couldn't stop giggling.

"You guys can see that cactus over there, right?"

"Um, no. I can't see it." Duncan chortled, his voice cracking like a pubescent boy's. "But you better not touch it!"

His reply made me laugh even harder. I waited for Mark to respond, but he didn't utter a word. He was staring off into the night sky with a stoner look on his face. Rarely had I seen Mark's expression reveal excitement or joy, but I detected a little smile cross his thin lips.

By bedtime, my normal state of mind returned, and I didn't see anything beyond the harmless crocs and cacti. I'm not sure why I decided to smoke up with Duncan and Mark that evening – maybe because I was removed from my family responsibilities – but I'm glad I did.

BY MY THIRD DAY AT NKHATA BAY, I had established an enjoyable albeit predictable routine. In the morning I walked into town for mouth-watering banana pancakes before strolling over to Chikale Beach, where I found a secluded spot to sunbathe topless. Later in the morning, I gathered with the local families for a swim. Ever since the croc attacks on Likoma, I stayed close to shore where the lake floor was visible.

After a shallow dip, I read, wrote in my journal and perused the local markets before heading over to watch the charismatic craftsmen work on their wooden sculptures. In the evening I drank a beer and smoked a bit of pot with Mark and Duncan.

Two days in, I became enthralled by a handful of Malawi chief chairs. This style of chair consists of two pieces of carved wood that, when fitted together, resemble an asymmetrical X from the side. They only stand a few feet off the ground but can be taken apart and stored flat in one swift move.

One craftsman's chief chair stood out from the rest. It featured a detailed scene of daily village life. On my second visit, I stayed an hour and watched the woodcarver work his magic and transform the chair into an exquisite work of art. The intricate composition had two small houses, trees, a riverbed and three people washing their clothes. By my third visit, it was complete: I knew it was *the one*.

I purchased the Malawi chair, a *bao* game and some smaller wooden curios, and headed straight to the post office to ship them home. When I went to pay, I couldn't believe it: the postal rates had doubled in less than a month. This increase, along with residents complaining about inflation and the troubled economy, indicated all was not well in the country.

FOUR DAYS INTO MY STAY at Nkhata Bay, Matthias strolled into town looking as dreamy as ever. Over a week had passed since we'd last seen each other at Cape Maclear, and I had begun to wonder if our paths would ever cross again.

He had travelled up from Senga Bay with a German woman. From what I could surmise, their relationship was platonic – he was tenting it alone at the campground. When I ran into him at Chikale Beach that afternoon, I couldn't deny the strong attraction I still felt. I invited him to join a group of us for dinner. Though we had left things friendly, now that Daniel was out of the picture, I thought this might be my last chance to see if things could be different.

After dinner our group left Moses restaurant and settled into an outdoor cafe for dessert. I was disappointed that Matthias never showed up. Instead, a freshly baked chocolate cake the colour of his eyes sat on display behind glass, a beacon of desire tempting us with its decadent sweetness. Someone in the group suggested we order the whole cake. Everyone chimed in with an enthusiastic "Yes! Yes!" as though we'd been denied carnal pleasures our whole lives.

We eyed the server like panting dogs. He cut the cake into eight equal pieces with the precision of a surgeon. Before plating each slice, he turned his attention to a large French press and poured steaming hot water onto *real* ground coffee, not the instant, why-bother chicory concoction I'd been drinking since my arrival in Africa. The grounds swirled and floated then settled at the bottom. We waited. Scents of caramel, vanilla and bitter roasted beans permeated the air around us. The server brought over the cake and cups of coffee. Someone pretended to moan. We all laughed.

My mouth watered. I took the first bite of the divine, dark cake, letting the smooth frosting coat my tongue. I savoured its moist, creamy texture before taking a second bite. Everyone at the table was in various stages of ecstasy – the cake was *so damn good.*

I devoured my last few mouthfuls, sipped the heavenly coffee and scraped up every last speck of icing with my fork. I looked up and saw Matthias walking toward us. My body tingled, then I tensed up.

"Hey, glad you finally showed up," I smirked coolly, trying to contain my excitement. I felt like I had Sophie B. Hawkins's "Damn I Wish I Was Your Lover" playing at full volume in my head. But I wasn't about to tell him that.

Matthias sat down at the table with us and initiated a round of *bao.* My pulse quickened. I studied his face, admiring his fine features, waiting for him to make a move. He was so close, but there was an unspoken barrier between us. *Remember, Lisa...you can look, but don't touch.*

I was dying to know what was on his mind, but I remained tight-lipped instead of making myself vulnerable again. After all, he was the one who had suggested we keep things friendly. For all I knew, he had met someone else. I was annoyed with myself for not being able to shake this lack of confidence. Almost a month had passed since we'd first met in Harare. I knew if nothing transpired between us that night, it would be time to move on.

After our game, we changed venues a few more times. One by one, I watched nervously as everyone went their separate ways. By the end of the night, Matthias and I were the only two remaining.

An elixir of caffeine, sugar and adrenaline pumped through my veins. I felt alert and jittery. My heart was an out-of-control metronome about to explode into a hundred pieces. One second I broke into a sweat. Then in the next I grew excited thinking about what might happen between us.

We headed to Safari's for a drink and closed the small bar down. By then, my sixth sense was kicking in – Matthias was definitely *not* looking for someone to join him in an all-night *bao* marathon.

After leaving the bar together, he placed his arm around my waist and pulled me in tight. We walked down the dark, empty road. The heat from his body penetrated my skin. It felt like Harare all over again. Hip to hip, we wandered aimlessly. The faint yellow light of a street lamp lit up his beautiful face, casting gold flecks onto his dark locks. Then he stopped and faced me, and our lips locked.

In the midst of our kissing, three giggling boys snuck up behind us. They came in close to gawk while making suggestive whistling sounds. Matthias took my hand and led us away from the boys. They followed us like mosquitos, hoping to see more of a show. I found their presence amusing. Matthias became irritated.

"Get out of here!" he snapped.

The boys just laughed. We walked in the opposite direction until they finally gave up and left us alone.

"Where should we go now?" I asked, with a nervous yearning bouncing off every syllable.

"We can't go to the campground," Matthias explained. "There are too many tents and campers. What about Africa Bay?"

I weighed this option for a split second. "Mark and I are sharing a hut...Maybe we can find an empty one?" I proposed, feeling hopeful.

We hurried over to Africa Bay in search of a vacant hut. These ultra-basic beachfront accoms were small rectangular rooms made out of cheap plywood, raised off the ground with stilts. We found two that were empty, but neither of them had a mattress, or any other sort of furnishing suitable for intimate acts.

My heart sank. *Why do things have to be so goddamn complicated?*

Matthias and I ended up at the only open bar in town, playing a second round of *bao*, wallowing in the sting of defeat. After our bedless search, I gave up on the idea of sleeping together. We had nowhere else to go.

This wasn't how I'd envisioned our night together. Something – perhaps karma, the cosmos – was making sure *it* didn't happen. Maybe I was being punished for not ending things properly with my boyfriend. I wondered if Doctor William had put a curse on me during his witchcraft ceremony.

After this failure, I didn't think the night could turn more disastrous. In the midst of our *bao* match, I felt a sharp pain in my stomach. "I'll be right back," I muttered. I rushed off to seek refuge in the bar's squalid outhouse, ten metres away, fearing I might not make it in time.

I sat on the toilet. It felt like a dozen doll-size daggers were stabbing away at my intestines. I broke into a sweat. My skin turned clammy and hot. I sat in silent agony, willing the pain to *please please PLEASE just get the hell out of my body.*

My stomach percolated like a pot of boiling witch's brew before erupting into wicked cramps. Then came the diarrhea. Just for good measure.

As I sat hunched over in the outhouse, it never occurred to me to check the toilet paper supply. There was barely enough to wipe a rat's ass.

The hurricane in my stomach subsided, but I didn't know how long the calm would last. I completed the walk of shame back to Matthias and casually mentioned, "Oh man, my stomach is really upset." Even if a miracle presented itself in the form of a private room for two, there was *no way* I would be getting close to Matthias that night.

We resumed some awkward game playing, the silence between us deafening. Matthias looked around in disgust. Then he said something like, "What's that smell? It smells like shit. It must be coming from the toilet."

I just about died. Where was Chingwe's Hole when I needed it? I would have gladly jumped into the deep, dark abyss to escape this misery.

At midnight we called it quits. Matthias walked back to the campground.

Alone.

It was never my mission to have a sexual conquest in Africa. But I was crushed. Humiliated. I had to wrap up my time in Malawi. I would spend one more week here, tops, before heading north to Tanzania. Even though Matthias and I had talked about visiting some of the same places, I couldn't stay in Nkhata Bay longer in order for us to travel together.

I was feeling depleted in both the love and self-esteem departments. I was in no frame of mind for romance. I was convinced that

Matthias was done with me. It had been fun to imagine us having a few days together in Zanzibar. But I accepted my fate: *nothing is going to happen between us.*

THIRTY-TWO HOURS LATER, with the embarrassing events still heavy on my mind, I walked to the bus loop. I wanted to leave on my own and have a fresh start, but Mark followed me like a faithful basset hound. After having him around for almost two weeks, I didn't have the heart to tell him the rest of my journey didn't include him.

The bus pulled up. Its arresting facade was hard to miss: the entire bus was painted bold indigo with orange trim, advertising Chishango condoms. I stared at the large silhouette of a couple linked arm in arm and contemplated the campaign's motto, *Kuphelera basi*: just wear a condom. It was one last jab reminding me of my failed night with Matthias.

I was sitting next to an open window, *begging* the bus to pull away, when I heard a bubbly voice call up to me: Emma had come to say goodbye.

She yelled up to me for all to hear, "Lisa! Did you and Matthias *snog*?"

I grinned down at her, my voice full of hesitation. "Ah, yes?"

My comprehension of the British colloquialisms *snog* and *shag* was fuzzy. I wasn't sure if I'd admitted to kissing Matthias or having sex with him. Either way, Emma was thrilled by my response.

"Woo-hoo! Good girl!" she cheered back.

Her unstoppable optimism lightened my sullen mood. Even though the night had been a disaster in my mind, I didn't have the heart to tell Emma all the details. She seemed so proud of me. I didn't want to let her down.

As the condom bus pulled away, I left Nkhata Bay feeling sick to my stomach. But the emotional weight I'd been carrying began to lift. I was glad to be leaving it all behind.

FIFTY KILOMETRES AWAY, Mark and I settled into a dormitory in the little town of Mzuzu for the night. The next morning I was woken up by excruciating abdominal pain, ten times worse than my night with Matthias. I felt wobbly. Drugged. I hobbled to the women's dorm bathroom like an injured bird before painful diarrhea glued me to the toilet seat.

I sat there in a foggy haze with the bathroom stall door ajar. I was lightheaded and dizzy. Lodgers walked by. I could feel their eyes on me, but I didn't care.

It seemed like I hadn't moved in hours. A woman found me hunched over with my head and hands resting on my knees. "Do you need some help?" she asked, sounding concerned.

I nodded a feeble *yes*.

She helped me off the toilet and called a cab. Mark escorted me to the hospital. Even in my weakened state, I felt apprehensive about spending time in any sort of medical setting considering the high rate of HIV/AIDS. Given my precarious situation, though, I couldn't be choosy.

After a no-nonsense admission into the hospital, I was brought to an immaculate, spacious room for one. It felt like Shangri-La compared to the humble accommodations I'd grown accustomed to. Even in my woozy state, I was impressed by the hospital's cleanliness and professional nurses and doctors. My fears of unsanitary equipment and contagion vanished. The diarrhea, however, was flowing like Victoria Falls. My fever spiked. I couldn't walk more than a few steps without feeling like I would pass out. Or shit my pants. Or do both at the same time.

While I was lying in bed, the third or fourth wave of bloody diarrhea hit me – not British *bloody*, but actual blood. It felt as if someone had pummelled my rectum then set it aflame. Walking the 20 metres to the toilet down the hallway wasn't an option. In my semi-lucid state, the only logical solution I could think of was to hang my ass over the oversized sink in my room.

And I was worried about *other* people spreading disease.

I had barely eaten anything since leaving Nkhata Bay. I couldn't understand how it was humanly possible to have anything remaining – solid or liquid – in my body. I was confident every last morsel of those irresistible sweet buns had been extracted out of me for good. I couldn't retain any liquid and became severely dehydrated. I sipped small cups of water only to have it come out the other end minutes later. The nurse hooked me up to an IV hydration drip. Over the next 24 hours, I fell in and out of a sleep-rest cycle.

The next day I got my test results. The good news: not malaria. Instead, I'd contracted something much sexier: dysentery. "You have an infection that causes inflammation of the intestinal tract and colon," according to the young doctor. Medical jargon aside, it was the absolute worst pain of my life.

Even though I had stopped eating meat after witnessing the carcass butchering on the *Ilala*, the doctor said it didn't matter what I had eaten, since dysentery can be caused by parasitic worms, bacteria or even a virus. It was just my luck that the early symptoms revealed themselves during the last few moments I spent with Matthias. Our failure to find a private room that night had actually been a blessing.

After the pain subsided and the diarrhea lessened, my spirits lifted. Lying in bed hooked up to the IV, my thoughts turned to Dad and Russ. Compared to their incurable diseases, dysentery was nothing more than a tiny blip in my medical history. A good story to tell my friends when I got home: *Yeah, and then, you wouldn't believe what happened. I started peeing through my bum! Ha ha ha!* In a day or two, I would walk out of the hospital, my health returning to normal.

By the third day, the repugnant flow of liquid and mucous had ceased. My body was weak, but I was given the all clear to leave the hospital.

Mark arrived to pick me up. He had waited for me instead of continuing north as planned. At the risk of sounding ungrateful, I had hoped he would leave during my convalescence. I couldn't very well ditch him now.

I left the hospital with Mark and headed to the bus station. We were only there for a short time when Matthias showed up unexpectedly on his own. To my surprise, I was no longer lusting after him. It was as though my body had expunged both dysentery *and* any remaining lovesickness.

It would take a while before I found the humour in how things ended with Matthias, but I didn't regret what happened between us. Or more specifically what *didn't* happen. Of course, I had wanted things to work out differently. But there was only so much humiliation and self-doubt I was willing to put myself through.

It's hard to pinpoint what exactly went wrong. I could have blamed it on my vacillating confidence. Or bad timing. Or, like the cheesy Milli Vanilli song, I could have just as easily "blamed it on the rain" after all our drizzly hikes. And, of course, there was Daniel.

In the end, I think it didn't work out simply because it wasn't supposed to. Having a fling or romance likely would have invited disappointment, heartache or compromise.

Despite our crappy ending, I will never be able to remember Malawi and my last days in Zimbabwe without thinking about Matthias with fondness. Few women can claim they had the pleasure of "snogging" a smart, sexy Swiss man in the middle of a steamy, packed nightclub in Harare.

But I can.

The northbound bus arrived. Matthias told me he was heading back to Nkhata Bay. I figured he must have met a woman who could keep her shit together.

I boarded the bus. Mark followed.

I never saw Matthias again.

Fourteen

A BUMPY, 200-KILOMETRE BUS RIDE brought us to the sparsely populated village of Chitimba. Mark and I had planned to hitchhike the 16 kilometres to the hilltop village of Livingstonia the next morning once we found someone to drive us.

A handsome Dane joined us for this leg of the trip. Morten's upbeat company was exactly what I needed. Aboard the bus, we chatted with ease. Mark, on the other hand, hardly said a word. His antisocial behaviour made me wonder why he'd bothered to wait around for me in the first place.

It was dark when the bus driver dropped the three of us off at the turnoff for Chitimba Beach. He pointed down the road, claiming we'd find a rest house close by. We headed along the obvious road leading to the lakeshore. There weren't any houses or street lights to guide us along the one-kilometre walk. Halfway there, three young locals popped up out of the darkness, offering to escort us to the beach. This scenario had the perfect makings for a mugging, but the teens only wanted to help us find our way.

I had barely moved since leaving the hospital. The short, flat walk exhausted me. We arrived at the beach to find there was no motel or lodging of any sort. Our only option: an empty campsite. And none of us had a tent.

When the rain began, my frustration grew into an angry abscess. It was late, and I was too tired to walk back to the main road to search for the elusive rest house. Mark, Morten and I set up our sleeping bags inside an abandoned thatched-roofed open-air bar located on the beach.

Gale-force winds made setting up our mosquito nets futile: we gave up after the second attempt. For most of the night, heavy rain invaded our makeshift sleeping quarters, ensuring we stayed wet, cold and miserable all night long. To make matters worse, the grating sounds of vicious dogs barking kept me on edge for hours. Sometime after midnight, a security guard showed up and blinded us with his bright flashlight. The possibility of getting any rest disappeared with each passing hour.

I can't say I "got up" the next morning because I was awake most of the night. By sunrise, the wind and rain had subsided. Misty views of Lake Malawi appeared as if to say, *Oh, so sorry about the rough night!* I left the bar and walked to the shore. The sun's first rays had broken through the clouds, creating playful streaks of steam across the rain-soaked sand. A group of men gathered around wooden, hand-carved canoes resembling brown bananas. A few metres away, a black lab lay chewing a stick between its large paws. This tranquil scene wasn't worth the sleepless night, but it did make me hopeful that our day would get better.

Small wins.

Mark left to inquire around the tiny village for someone willing to drive us up to Livingstonia. A local man agreed to pick us up from the main road at noon, allowing us a lazy morning to recover from the turbulent night.

It was hammering rain when the driver showed up at 1:30, his truck already full of passengers. It took everything in me not to blow a gasket when he said, "Sorry, but no more room," as though it were of no consequence.

Three hikers walked past us eagerly, their boots and calves splattered in mud before their long trudge had even begun. For a fleeting moment, I considered joining them. But hiking up 16 kilometres in mucky conditions would have been foolish, especially in my weakened state. There was nothing we could do except wait.

Within an hour the rain let up. We passed the time hanging out with a group of sweet children on the verandah of a nearby brick structure. Their joyful voices and laughter made my heart sing and melted away my frustration. A lovely woman named Mercy shared some of her delicious *nsima* with us. Her patient manner and generosity reminded me to accept the situation instead of giving in to anger.

A few hours later, I spotted a pickup truck barrelling down the hill. I squinted: the driver appeared to be alone. Until then, no vehicles had come down. I had to act fast or risk getting stuck in Chitimba for a second night. I jumped out onto the road and waved my hands at the driver like a madwoman. He slammed on the brakes and the truck skidded in the mud before coming to a full stop. I heaved a sigh of relief when he agreed to give Mark, Morten and me a lift all the way up to Livingstonia.

As the truck clambered up the muddy dirt road, we passed the backpackers who were hiking up. They were five kilometres in. At that pace, they couldn't possibly arrive before ten at night, exhausted and cold in their rain-drenched clothes. In ideal conditions, the slog up was supposed to take three hours. It would take them more than five.

An hour later, the truck pulled up to the Old Stone House. I stepped into the dry, warm lodge, overjoyed to finally arrive at our destination. By the time I settled in, it was after dinner and pitch dark: my walking tour of Livingstonia would have to wait until morning.

Having regained some of my appetite, I prepared a packet of Knorr instant mushroom soup and carried a large bowl into the living room. I was taking comfort in this warm meal, chatting with an Aussie who volunteered in Burundi, when three South Africans entered the room. Their lively banter paired with my love of their homeland was the perfect invitation for me to connect with them. Before I knew it, the guys were seated across from me, asking about my South African adventures.

"What'd you think of Durban? I assume you went to Golden Mile beach?" the dark-haired one asked.

"No, I never made it to Durban. After Joburg and the Drakensberg, I bused it to Port Elizabeth and travelled along the Garden Route."

"You never made it to Durban? Ah, shame. That's our hometown. Don't worry. We won't hold it against you," he teased.

The guys were friendly and down-to-earth, not to mention attractive. It was no surprise that they were all spoken for, with girlfriends waiting back home.

From what I had seen, it wasn't common for South Africans to explore their own continent. Those who had the means to travel, mostly wealthy whites, went abroad to Europe, North America or Australia. Pete, Felix and Sollie's enthusiasm to explore their neighbouring countries was palpable and contagious.

GIVEN ITS REMOTE HILLTOP LOCATION, Livingstonia seemed like an odd place for travellers to visit. Its claim to fame is its humble colonial stone and red brick structures – remnants of a missionary effort removed from the malaria-infested shores of Cape Maclear. My hour-long exploration around Stone House revealed there was little to see and do in Livingstonia beyond a visit to the museum that housed artifacts from the first European missionaries. The mountaintop scenery was lush and pretty, but the thick cloud cover made it impossible to view Lake Malawi. The novelty of the missionary setting was short-lived. The austere architecture reminded me of dreaded Sundays when Mom made me go to church. Livingstonia's cooler, secluded setting made me miss the warmth of the lakeside villages.

Mark, Morten and I ventured over to Manchewe Falls. It was wonderful to be outside and feel my body come back to life. For almost the entire four-kilometre walk, though, Mark stomped ahead of Morten and me, keeping his head down. He puffed on a cigarette like a fuming dragon while his lanky legs took giant strides.

"Is there something wrong with Mark?" Morten asked.

"Honestly, I have no idea. He's not much of a talker, and I can't understand his head space right now." Mark's behaviour was awkward, but I wasn't about to let his foul mood take away the beautiful stroll. The three of us took cover under an expansive overhanging rock that functioned as a roof partway up the falls. White, skinny ribbons of water plunged over a hundred metres into the calm pools below. Beyond its beauty, we were curious about Manchewe's history. Behind the waterfall lies a path leading to a cave. Legend has it that a century earlier, the Phoka tribe hid from Ngoni slave traders in this cave. We never got far enough to locate it, but locals confirmed the story.

After returning from the falls, Morten and Mark went into the rest house. I stayed outside to talk to the South Africans. Sollie, affectionately called Pa by Felix and Pete, was repacking some supplies into the cab of a Toyota 4Runner. He was quiet and shy and easily could have been an Abercrombie and Fitch model but didn't seem the least bit conceited.

Pete and Felix were crouched down, inspecting the wheels of a beige vintage truck with its hood open. The truck's wood-panelled box cover brought a huge grin to my face. The hatch featured a purplish-brown, wide-mouthed hippo and the words "Isuzu Imvubu Africa 96" in bold green and red. The right side of the box had the image of a wildebeest and was lined with a colourful row of iconic hand-painted African animals and symbols. A giant African continent, with each country painted a different colour, covered the left side. A drawing of a snapping green crocodile protected the driver's side door. The love and energy the guys had put into transforming the old truck into a one-of-a-kind caravan warmed my heart.

"Hey, Pete. Hi, Felix. Sollie. Everything okay?" I asked.

The guys looked up. Pete was the most sociable of the trio, ruggedly handsome with dark brown hair, a wide smile and a Roman nose. His brown eyes sparkled when he spoke. "Morning, Lisa. Just doing some maintenance...giving Isuzu Imvubu a little TLC before we hit the road ahead. Her brakes might need some work."

Felix grabbed a rag and checked what I assumed to be the brake fluid. His fox-like eyes were framed in wire-rimmed spectacles that made him look like a young professor. His conservatively cropped light-brown hair was mildly untamed due to time spent on the road.

"I love all the artwork you guys did. It's really impressive," I said.

"Thanks. But don't let her good looks fool ya. We should have named her the 'farting hippo' since she's prone to loud bursts of backfiring...not to mention she's big and brown." Pete chuckled, then explained for my benefit. "*Imvubu* means hippo in Zulu."

I laughed. "When are you guys leaving for Tanzania?"·

"We're trying to get to Dar by the end of the week. You know, we have space for one more if you want to catch a lift with us. We're leaving tomorrow."

Pete's invitation thrilled me. I didn't need any time to consider my reply. "Oh, I would love that. Yes, I will definitely get a ride with you guys."

"Great. We have a Kiwi named Vanessa joining us too. It will be awesome to have some company besides these two. Felix can't shut up. Sollie misses his girlfriend. And driving the 4Runner on my own gets lonely."

Felix gave Pete a playful punch in the arm. "Trust me, Lisa. You're doing us a favour. Sollie and I could use a break from Pete. You will, too, after one day in the truck with him. I hope you brought earplugs. I highly recommend nose plugs too!"

That afternoon, Pete introduced me to Vanessa, a short, tan woman with wavy dark hair. The blue tie-dyed T-shirt and black sarong she wore made her look easygoing. She put out her cigarette when I approached.

"The guys have been fantastic. I don't know what I would have done without them." Vanessa sounded calm, and her stoic expression hardly changed as she described her experience two days before. During her long trek up to Livingstonia, she had been robbed at knifepoint. Minutes after the mugging, Pete, Felix and Sollie happened to drive by and picked her up. Despite her misfortune, Vanessa was lucky the guys appeared when they did.

Pete, Felix and Sollie had been exploring Southern and East Africa in their four-wheel-drive trucks for over a month. Isuzu Imvubu had taken on a personality of her own. Beyond the quirky exterior, the guys converted her cargo area into a functional kitchen and pantry. No space was wasted. They kept her well stocked with delicacies: salami, wine, chocolate and cheeses were in ample supply. The South Africans definitely knew how to travel in style.

Their second vehicle, a dependable 4Runner four-by-four, was equipped with a rooftop tent, allowing the guys the freedom to camp pretty much wherever they wanted. The idea of travelling by truck to Tanzania seemed extravagant compared to the slower, less reliable buses I was accustomed to. All Vanessa and I had to do was pitch in some money for petrol and food.

It took the South Africans' vibrant company to make me realize how much Mark had been bringing me down. My connection with the guys was natural and effortless, reminiscent of the bond I'd shared with my Zambezi safari companions. Being around Pete, Felix and Sollie ignited my excitement to visit Tanzania and experience the final leg of my trip.

Travelling with the guys meant I had a legitimate excuse to sever ties with Mark. Since he had waited around for me in Mzuzu, I felt bad telling him my new plans over dinner.

"So, Mark, the South Africans offered me a ride to Dar es Salaam. I'll be leaving with them tomorrow morning."

Mark swallowed a bite of pasta. He didn't say anything for a few seconds. His wispy bangs shielded his eyes. He kept his gaze down and muttered, "Good for you. I'm sure you'll have fun with them. I might stick around for a few more days before I bus it to Tanzania." He finished his plate of food then went to the communal kitchen.

Mark hardly talked to me the rest of the night. I couldn't really blame him. First his sister ditched him, and now me. Despite his loner facade, I think Mark needed someone to latch onto, someone to follow. I just couldn't be that person anymore. With three weeks remaining, I wasn't about to pass up on a once-in-a-lifetime opportunity because of added guilt.

This ride was the exit plan I needed.

Fifteen

DRIVING AWAY FROM LIVINGSTONIA brought me a sense of completion and satisfaction. Riding with Pete and Vanessa, I felt alive and excited about our arrival in Tanzania. I was ready to leave Malawi before my positive impressions soured any further. I had moved past my failed romance with Matthias, regained my strength since my bout of dysentery and no longer had to deal with Mark's melancholy. The unpredictable albeit adventurous bus rides would be put on hold while I travelled in style and comfort with the South Africans.

After a brief stop to sort out Vanessa's police report, our small convoy drove north 100 kilometres. My last night in Malawi, in the township of Karonga, was bittersweet. My connections to the people, both locals and foreigners, and to the landscape were profound. Yet, as we neared the Tanzanian border, it felt liberating and reassuring to know that, no matter where we stopped, we would have food, shelter and fulfilling companionship.

Vanessa and I fell asleep like lionesses in the cozy sleeping tent quarters above the 4Runner, while the guys slept on the ground in a tent. The next morning, before crossing into Tanzania, I took in the vanishing views of Lake Malawi. Considering how tiny Malawi is compared to the other countries I visited, I never expected to spend a full five weeks there. As I gazed out the passenger window, I said one final *zikomo* to the little country that took me by surprise and gave me so many rich gifts, despite the obstacles thrown my way.

Isuzu Imvubu had a brake fluid leak in need of repair. Our first stop in Tanzania was a mechanic shop in the city of Mbeya. The surrounding area was flush with banana, coffee and cocoa plantations, but urban Mbeya had little appeal. The truck repair would take a few hours, so the guys dropped Vanessa and me off at the popular outdoor market. We went our separate ways and agreed to meet up an hour later.

While I was dawdling at the market, three Masai tribesmen caught my eye. The Masai, along with the Samburu tribe, are semi-nomadic people who still live in Tanzania and Kenya today. Their lean frames and short-cropped hair or shaved heads make them highly recognizable.

Long, bright-beaded earrings dangled from the men's stretched-out earlobes onto their bare, bony shoulders like Christmas ornaments. Their giraffe-like anatomy and bold red clothing were striking and made the plainclothes Tanzanians and foreigners like myself appear as dull as pigeons. I tried not to gawk, but they were too beautiful to look away.

I was buying a wooden fertility doll when I heard Vanessa's voice behind me. "You'll never guess who I ran into. Mark. He was by himself, a few stalls over. He was quite rude to me. When I said hi, he ignored me and walked away. I *know* he saw me."

"Really? That's weird," I said, puzzled by her account. "He must have been really pissed at me for abandoning him and took it out on you. Guilty by association, I suppose."

I finished my purchase and we started walking together, stopping at the odd stall. "Did you ever think maybe he liked you? You know, romantically?" Vanessa asked.

"What? No, definitely not." The thought had *never* crossed my mind. If Mark had an unrequited attachment for me, he certainly kept it to himself. I would have never travelled with him had he liked me in that way. It would have been too awkward.

After hearing how Mark gave Vanessa the cold shoulder, my guilty conscience vanished. I couldn't be responsible for Mark's journey any longer.

With Isuzu Imvubu's repairs complete, we travelled northeast 340 kilometres to the Iringa region. The landscape opened up into spacious plains and grassy savannah punctuated by shrubs and standalone acacia trees. With the topography transforming before my eyes, it became evident we were in a new country. The change in scenery brought new emotions. Knowing my days in Africa were numbered, I felt a greater need to savour my time there. In a matter of weeks, I would be back in Vancouver: I wasn't ready to go home yet.

THE NEXT DAY WE ENTERED Mikumi National Park. Measuring over 3200 square kilometres, Mikumi is the fourth-largest game park in Tanzania. The park wasn't as well known as the Serengeti, but there was an abundance of wildlife there, including the "big five" – lion, leopard, elephant, rhino and buffalo – along with zebras and hippos. My eyes scanned the landscape from the comfort of the Toyota. Now that we were in Tanzania, I couldn't wait to see the likes of elephants and giraffes up close.

The guys kept slowing the convoy down in search of a suitable spot for off-grid camping. Pete pulled onto the side of the highway, his voice bursting with glee.

"Lisa, get over here. Quick! You gotta see this."

Pete jumped out of the truck and jogged down a little hill. He stopped and stood up tall like a meerkat. I bolted after him like a cheetah, my heart pounding with excitement. He was pointing between some tall grasses and a large cluster of trees.

"Look…There's a small herd of elephants right over there!"

When I reached Pete's side, I squinted and scoured the area in front of us. My anticipation was replaced by confusion. I couldn't see any elephants. I looked over at him. No longer was he masking the smirk on his face or the mischief in his twinkling eyes.

"Oh, god. The look on your face, Lisa! That was priceless." Pete was laughing. I glanced over at Felix and Sollie. They were behind us, keeled over, chucking hysterically.

My eyes scolded the three of them sternly. "Not funny. Damn you, Pete! You know how much I want to see an elephant." But even I couldn't contain my laughter.

We got back into the trucks and kept driving. Vanessa, who was seated next to Pete in the front, asked, "What's that in the middle of the road?" Pete screeched the truck to a stop. Pete and I jumped out and walked over to a flattened, motionless mass plastered across the yellow median line.

"Whoa, look at the size of that bloody python!" Pete called out excitedly.

The snake's beautiful cocoa-brown, beige and gold scales were still intact. But half of its tubular guts had spilled out from its split belly, drying up in the hot sun like roasting link sausages. Despite its advanced state of decay, the python was still intimidating at three metres in length.

Pete kneeled down to the ground. He looked playful in a brightly coloured, geometric T-shirt and striped *kikoi* sarong wrapped around his waist. I crouched down next to him and inspected the snake's shrunken head using a small stick. Its skinny, shrivelled tongue was sticking out of its mouth like a dried worm. A warm breeze picked up, filling our sinuses with the stench of the rotting snake corpse. In unison, Pete and I let out groans of disgust mixed with laughter and we covered our noses.

"Oh, jeez that's foul," Pete said, shaking his head in repulsion. "Let's get out of here."

We had been back on the road less than an hour when the guys pulled the trucks over again, claiming to see an elephant. I ardently climbed the small ladder leading to the top of the Toyota to get a long-awaited glimpse, only to find a landscape devoid of wildlife. I looked down to see the guys laughing below, amused by my gullibility.

I only allowed their cry-elephant ploy to fool me twice. As determined as I was to see an elephant or giraffe, I wasn't about to fall victim to their convincing claims and teasing taunts a third time.

Mikumi's flood plain provides the perfect habitat for the eland, the world's largest antelope. In addition to the abundant variety of wildlife, the park is home to over 400 species of birds. The terrain was decorated with a variety of flora, including baobab, acacia and tamarind trees. Small, scrubby plants provide shade to the otherwise barren but breathtaking landscape.

In spite of what Mikumi had to offer, affordable accommodations were sparse, and we encountered few travellers. Since both the Toyota and the Isuzu had off-road capabilities, we located the perfect rogue campsite 20 kilometres outside of the park, tucked away and undetectable from the main highway. Having this piece of paradise all to ourselves was an incredible gift.

The guys prepared a delectable curried rice dish for dinner. We sipped red wine and stuffed our bellies with Pete's special *bungie* banana cake laced with pot that he lovingly cooked over coals. Silhouettes of birds darted between the acacia trees while we ate, laughed and watched the orange sunset unfold.

The five of us sitting around the campfire in the middle of the Tanzanian savannah remains one of the most magical moments of my entire trip. It had all the ingredients of a flawless evening: superb company, sumptuous food and a setting one can only dream about. Now that I was there, living and breathing the experience, I no longer had to imagine someone else's reality on the big screen. This was *my* reality, a film nobody else could have created.

I loved every minute of it.

THE NEXT MORNING, while driving on the highway toward Dar es Salaam, the guys pulled the trucks onto the shoulder for a little break. Lean, tan and shirtless, Felix and Sollie were clad in nothing but black running shorts and leather sandals. They looked like 1930s Olympic track stars as they trotted toward a small thicket of tamarind trees and thigh-high grasses.

They were grinning widely and waved me over to see something grazing in the distance. This time the guys *weren't* pulling my leg: less than 30 metres from the road, a lone giraffe was munching on a breakfast of buds and leaves.

I rushed over to join them. My heart skipped a beat. Even though I'd had a few fleeting glimpses of giraffes near the Zambezi River, this was my first time seeing the majestic animal up close and not from a fast-moving vehicle. I felt like a little kid again. This gentle giant seemed unaffected by our silent admiration. Just in case, I made myself as quiet as possible, fearing any disruption might cause it to bolt into the trees. For all I knew, this was my last chance to see one.

In elementary school I loved drawing and writing. In Grade 4, I was so proud of the giraffe book report I wrote. Sadly, I included hand-drawn, colour illustrations depicting giraffes being chased down and captured by fervent, khaki-clad men riding in a safari Jeep. No doubt my detailed drawings were inspired by the grainy photographs from one of the *National Geographic* magazines my family kept in the train room next to our Encyclopedia Britannicas.

I later grew up believing wild animals should be free and protected. The troubling photos of ensnared giraffes must have fed my curiosity about Africa and the increasingly vulnerable animals that call it home. As a child, I had always hoped to see giraffes in their natural habitat. Now I was here, my dream fulfilled. This rare chance to admire one up close made the guys' teasing worth it.

That's why I couldn't believe my eyes when, a few moments later, a mama elephant emerged from the thick grassy plain with two waddling calves at her side. After three months in Africa, it was the culmination I had been waiting for. My heart soared. This was my own special edition of *National Geographic*: "Lisa Arrives in Animal Heaven."

I looked over at Vanessa and the guys: they looked as beguiled as I felt. We basked in the elephants' presence, none of us wanting the moment to end. After the elephant viewing, the floodgate opened up. Herds of buffalo and impala appeared, the latter consisting of one ram among a flock of 20 ewes. A second small herd of elephants showed up right before two more giraffes sauntered over, only metres from the road.

I was so grateful to see all these animals, but equally grateful to have wonderful humans with which to share the experience.

WE LEFT THE PEACE AND TRANQUILITY of the savannah to be confronted, three hours later, by Tanzania's most populated city. By the time the five of us arrived in Dar es Salaam, we had formed a natural bond. Pete, Felix, Sollie and Vanessa were like family to me.

In addition to our growing friendships, Pete and I shared a few flirtatious exchanges. Aside from a bit of innocent teasing over a bottle of wine, neither of us dared to act on our unspoken attraction for each other. I respected the fact that he was in a committed relationship, and after Matthias, I wasn't looking for romance. There was no need to disturb the order of things and spoil the memory of our time together.

Compared to the subdued pace of Malawi and relaxing days camping off-grid, Dar overwhelmed our senses with its high-rise buildings, traffic and the smell of burning garbage. It was a relief to pull into the laid-back Salvation Army campground, ten kilometres away from the busy urban centre. Staying there suited our modest tastes and allowed us to moderate how much time we spent in the large metropolis. Our bodies were fatigued from being on the road. Lounging around at the campground, amusing ourselves with food and drink, and playing Trivial Pursuit, was our preferred pace.

The next morning Pete, Felix, Vanessa and I hopped onto the hot, stuffy bus to the city centre, while Sollie stayed behind at the campground. Upon our arrival, we separated and agreed to meet back at the popular Sno-Cream ice cream parlour a few hours later.

Once a thriving fishing town, urbanized Dar es Salaam was often mistaken for the capital, with a population of more than two million. After walking around for 20 minutes, my initial impression of the city was that it was sprawling and unsightly. The streets were layered in dirt and dust. The rotting bags of garbage were nauseating on some of the streets, causing me to hurry along instead of trying to appreciate my new surroundings.

Malodor aside, the city had several conveniences in the form of international restaurants, upscale hotels and inviting gift shops. But for me, Dar was nothing but a stopover on the way to Zanzibar, a two-hour ferry ride away. After a week-long visit to the tropical island, I planned to join a safari in Serengeti National Park.

There was no shortage of travel agencies in the big city. In no time, I was seated in one of them, exploring the endless safari possibilities. It was reassuring to learn there were plenty of tour companies based out of the western city of Arusha. I felt no pressure to book anything right away.

I still had to figure out the best way to get back to South Africa for my flight home to Vancouver. The travel agent suggested a flight to Harare to help cut down on my travel time, but the USD330 ticket price wasn't remotely within my budget. I left the agency without any travel bookings, feeling unsettled that I still hadn't planned out my final days.

An hour later, I met up with Vanessa and accompanied her to the New Zealand embassy to sort out some post-mugging documentation before heading to the train station to book her ticket to Nairobi. While walking along a car-free street, I noticed my money belt bulging at my waistline under my tank top. Vanessa and I ducked into a small shop where I discreetly removed it and placed it into the zipped pocket of my daypack for safekeeping.

A few minutes later, we were meandering in and out of the storefronts when the humid, ominous, grey skies opened up. The rain pelted down like rubber bullets, forcing everyone on the street to flock to the sidewalk and take cover under the store awnings.

In a matter of seconds, Vanessa and I were sardined among dozens of pedestrians, hovering to avoid the showers. A man several inches taller than me was standing uncomfortably close and looked deep into my eyes. He smiled apologetically then said, "Sorry, so sorry, miss," over and over, as if he had no control of his movements.

He kept pushing himself against me, his raised forearms against my shoulders, which forced me to take three short steps backward. As I moved away from him, my back inadvertently pushed up against the guy behind me and I couldn't escape until the brief downpour came to an abrupt stop. It was as if a raindrop control switch had been shut off to let the sun back in.

Vanessa and I scurried away from the crowds and headed toward the train station. We stopped at a kiosk selling pirated CDs, insipid trinkets and chilled beverages. I reached into my pack to get a few shillings to buy a ginger ale. When I didn't feel my money belt, I frantically searched. A torrent of panic shot through my chest. "Fuck. Fuck. My money belt is gone!"

Vanessa looked at me in disbelief. "Oh, shit. Are you sure? What was in it?"

My fingers pressed against my eyebrows, then along my temples, as I thought about everything I'd lost. "Pretty much everything…my passport, a hundred US dollars. I had 45,000 shillings. And my credit card and bank card. Oh, shit, and my yellow fever vaccination card was in there too, which I need to get into Zanzibar."

Anger swelled up in me like a swarm of wasps. But I felt more foolish than angry. Those smooth operators, disguised as innocent bystanders escaping the rain like everyone else, had tricked me. Someone must have tipped them off after seeing me remove my money belt. They seemed to know exactly where to find it.

Vanessa suggested we go to the police station, but without ID, reporting the theft and going to the Canadian embassy would have to wait. The thin silver lining was that I'd had the good sense to lock up a colour photocopy of my passport in Isuzu Imvubu's safe, along with a bit of cash and some traveller's cheques.

We continued to the station, where Vanessa purchased her train ticket, before returning to Sno-Cream to meet Pete and Felix.

After my sobering incident, Vanessa treated me to a caramel ice cream sundae.

I had ravaged over half of the tasty mound when Pete stormed into the ice cream parlour. His usual happy, upbeat personality was nowhere to be found. I was about to recap my unfortunate turn of events, but Pete beat me to it and he didn't hold back his foul mood.

"*Ag*! Bloody hell, man. You won't *believe* what just happened to me."

It turns out I wasn't the only one who had been outwitted by smooth criminals, and no amount of ice cream was going to make him feel better. Pete's first task in Dar had been to exchange some money. Instead of paying an inflated transaction fee at a foreign exchange bureau, he took his chances on the street. Some local money exchangers took him aside in a nearby alley. As he described this dubious scenario to me, I couldn't help thinking, *No! Don't do it! What are you thinking? Don't go with them, Pete!*

The slick city-street banker counted out a thick wad of Tanzanian shillings right in front of him. "He counted them not once *but twice* to prove I wasn't being swindled. I swear...all the notes were right there in front of me."

Moments after the money exchangers split, Pete checked the money again only to find he was holding a small fraction of what he thought they had given him. He had no idea how they'd pulled it off. I'm sure these thieves had gained plenty of practice prior to Pete. I suggested that perhaps they were business associates of the same guys who stole my money belt, but Pete wasn't amused by our shared affliction.

Unlike me, Pete was only out 50 American dollars. Felix found some humour in the fact that Pete, *an African*, had fallen victim to their tried-and-tested trickery. My situation, however, was no laughing matter and would prove a major setback. Even though I had locked up my last 80 American dollars and Canadian traveller's cheques in the truck's safety deposit box, I realized my cheques were useless without proper documentation. To top it off, I couldn't leave the country without my passport.

The four of us bused it back to the campground. Pete and I felt the sting of our misfortune, wallowing in our contempt for the city while trying to laugh at our fate. In Arabic, Dar es Salaam translates as "the house of peace," but there was nothing peaceful about our experiences in the city that day.

I RETURNED TO DREADFUL DAR early the next morning, feeling vulnerable and less secure. I filed a report at the police station. As suspected, my efforts to retrieve any of my stolen items were in vain. From the police officer's perspective, the theft was nothing more than a daily nuisance, a minor crime that would not be investigated.

All things considered, I had been quite lucky. I'd never experienced the kind of violence Vanessa had during her mugging in Malawi. Up until then, I'd had nothing but positive interactions with strangers. Even when things could have easily gone wrong, I ended up walking away with at least a memorable story to tell.

I began the tedious process of replacing my passport at the Canadian consulate. It was a Friday: little could be done. I was relieved when the agent told me I was smart to have a photocopy of my passport. Even though it would speed up the replacement process, I still had to wait seven days for a new one.

With less than a hundred dollars in my possession and no passport, my travel options were slim. Zanzibar wasn't even a possibility for me – the island was independent of Tanzania and required visitors to carry a passport. It was so frustrating to be in downtown Dar, just steps away from the ferry terminal, and not be able to leave my troubles behind.

I walked over to the posh Kilimanjaro Hotel. Its clean, bright, wide-open spaces and eye-catching artwork and jewellery shops were a welcome distraction. But I wasn't there to shop. I used the hotel phone to call home. After explaining what happened, I asked Mom if she could call my bank, order me a new credit card and arrange a bank transfer. With the time change, this seemed like the best solution.

"How could you be so careless?" she replied. I wasn't expecting her curt reaction. She sounded annoyed and unsympathetic to my situation. I sensed Dad's and Russ's illnesses were wearing her down, but we didn't have time to get into any details.

"Don't worry about it, Mom. I'll try calling my bank directly." I hung up with Mom's disapproving voice repeating in my head. *How could you be so careless?*

After I got hold of my bank, my mood improved: a new credit card would be couriered to the hotel in a few days. The bank transfer would arrive shortly after.

In less than 48 hours, Dar had exhausted our collective patience. Vanessa's backpacking adventure was coming to an end. Pete, Felix and Sollie were getting ready to travel south to enjoy the unpopulated coast for a few days.

"C'mon, why don't you join us? You have to wait around anyway. A desolate beach with three handsome lads is definitely in order," Pete insisted.

I was torn. A visit to Tanzania's white-sand beaches with the guys was beyond tempting. But without adequate documentation, money or a credit card, I didn't want to be a burden. Once I had everything in order, I wanted to head straight to Zanzibar. I made the difficult decision to stay behind.

The five of us spent our last night together in the affluent neighbourhood of Oyster Bay, ten kilometres from the campground. These final moments were bittersweet. Over two bottles of red wine, we laughed ourselves to tears and reached a healthy state of giddiness hours after the sun went down. Of all the people I met during my travels, I felt closest to these three men. Now we had to go our separate ways.

WE ALL AWOKE with nasty hangovers. My head throbbed. It felt like a carpet of mossy dirt had taken root in my tongue. Pete's blood-shot eyes peered into the dorm room I was sharing with Vanessa. He looked as rough as I felt and delivered one final jab of affection before I stumbled out of the bottom bunk bed.

"Dear god, Miss Duncan. *Please*, do us all a favour and stand downwind. And wipe the drool from your chin."

"I'm going to miss you too, Pete." I really was.

A pang of loneliness invaded my heart as I watched Pete, Felix, Sollie and Vanessa drive off in the caravan. A plume of dust and dirt filled the air, leaving me with a newfound sense of emptiness. It felt like I had said goodbye to long-lost family members I might never see again. The guys had talked at length about visiting Vancouver. All I could do was take solace in the possibility of meeting them again one day.

Without their presence, the barren campground lost its warmth and appeal. I couldn't bear to stay there any longer. Unable to travel freely, I only had two options: stay in Dar and wait for my new pass-port and Visa, or explore safari packages on a shoestring budget.

The Serengeti, Mount Kilimanjaro and Ngorongoro Crater were all viable places to visit. I stashed some of my belongings at the campground locker. Two hours later, I arrived at the bus station and bought a ticket to Arusha, relieved to leave Dar behind for a few days.

Sixteen

OF ALL THE THINGS TO REMEMBER about my 600-kilometre bus adventure across Tanzania, I assumed the sweeping scenery of Mount Kilimanjaro and the exotic savannah would have stood out the most. However, it was Phil Collins and a fellow passenger who made this leg of my Africa trip so unforgettable.

My protective shield was thicker than usual when I stepped onto the Arusha-bound bus. As soon as the bus left the station, the driver loaded what seemed to be Phil Collins's greatest hits into the cassette tape player: "One More Night," "Separate Lives," "Another Day in Paradise," "I Wish It Would Rain Down." Hearing his familiar soft-rock tunes helped me relax. Little did I know these songs would play on repeat for the entire eight-hour bus ride.

With two older brothers, I grew up listening to Genesis. Phil's voice took me back to the early '80s when I frequented the local Stardust. "Misunderstanding" and "Turn It on Again" would echo across the roller rink as I refined my backward skating technique, just in case the opportunity to slow skate with a boy presented itself. Of course, it never did.

A few years later, I was too cool for rollerskating, and Stardust eventually closed its doors. But when Phil Collins began his solo career, I found myself drawn to some of his catchy pop songs and love ballads, despite being a fervent fan of the Cure and the Smiths.

Lip-syncing to Phil's songs became second nature to me. The first few hours on the bus I softly sang along to his hits, perfecting my lyrical knowledge with each repetition of the cassette tape. I couldn't help but smile and think of Billy Ocean in Cape Maclear. This time I found Phil's serious tone better suited my circumstances. His music made me feel calm as I headed into unfamiliar territory on my own.

By the third loop of the cassette tape, a quiet, attractive male passenger sitting across the aisle initiated some small talk. Samuel was a Tanzanian native travelling to Arusha for work. He seemed genuinely interested in my trip and offered me a sympathetic ear when I told him about my recent mishap in Dar. I enjoyed our casual chit-chat. Along with Phil's hits, this new friendship helped pass the time.

Despite his soft-spoken, polite nature, I sensed things were taking an uncomfortable turn when Samuel's questions turned more personal.

"Tell me. Why are you travelling without your husband?" He gestured toward the silver band on my wedding finger. Wearing my best poker face, I replied, "My husband's back home in Canada, working. He's arriving next week so we can travel together."

Samuel nodded but appeared skeptical. Of course he had no way of knowing fact from fiction. I looked out the window, trying my best to appear aloof. Phil's "One More Night" was playing in the background as Samuel started his well-crafted line of questioning.

"Were you hoping to have a special memory of your time in Tanzania?" Samuel asked with a hesitant grin. I smiled awkwardly, unsure what he was alluding to.

"You know, something *very* special so you can remember your time here?"

A wave of unease filled me. *I really hope this is not going where I think it is.*

"Oh, I've had some pretty special memories so far. Mikumi park was amazing," I said, referring to my time with Pete, Sollie, Felix and Vanessa.

Despite the implications, Samuel's respectful tone made me think maybe I was reading into things. That was, of course, until he delivered his last question.

"Perhaps you might, you know – just for example, I'm saying – have sexual relations with someone here so you can have a very special memory of Tanzania? Would you like that?"

Up until then, I had played the naïveté card, hoping I was wrong about his insinuations. When he proved my suspicions, my jaw clenched. I raised my eyebrows and shook my head.

"No, Samuel. I'm not looking for that kind of memory, thank you." My body language turned cold, and Samuel realized I found his proposition absurd.

He squirmed in his seat and apologized. "I'm so sorry. I was mistaken. I'm sorry if I offended you. I just thought…"

Samuel's suggestive method of interrogation ceased. I opened up my guidebook to buffer myself. Once my frustration subsided, this distraction began to work.

During the last hundred kilometres of the bus ride, I marvelled at Mount Kilimanjaro jutting out from the plains, showing off its unflinching, subtle beauty. It was clear and sunny. I was thrilled to take in the unobstructed views, as the mountain is often shrouded in cloud cover and heavy rain. Kibo summit still had remnants of snow. It was as if the gods had gently sliced off the mountain's peak before rounding off the edges into a convex form. It was impossible to know just by looking that the mountain was home to three separate volcanic cones.

Gazing out the window, it was fun to imagine myself joining a trekking expedition up the majestic mountain. Kilimanjaro, Africa's tallest mountain at 5895 metres above sea level, is an arduous multiday hike best suited for the physically fit. Even with my rock climbing and hiking experience, the ascent would be a huge undertaking, especially with the added complexities of high altitude. I was so close to this once-in-a-lifetime opportunity, yet my body was in no shape to take on such a goal.

I flipped through the pages of my guidebook and read the section on Kilimanjaro anyway. Reality sunk in and squelched my fantasy: typical ascents took five to seven days and it could cost up to 400 dollars to join a guided trek. At least I had a safari to look forward to.

As the bus neared Arusha, Phil Collins's "Do You Remember?" played on the speaker. Across the aisle, I felt Samuel's eyes on me, but I couldn't meet his gaze. I sensed he felt bad about what had transpired. If anything, Samuel should have been pleased. He got his wish of giving me a memory of Tanzania I will *never* forget.

It was dinnertime when we arrived in Arusha. I was famished, but finding lodging was my first priority. As a lone, foreign woman, I was easy prey for hungry travel agents. As soon as we all exited the bus, safari recruiters and hotel workers pounced on me like predators in the Serengeti. One man insisted he had "the perfect place to stay," while another claimed he could arrange "the best safari adventure ever," if only I were kind enough to follow him.

These men were pushy but harmless. They were just trying to make a living. But I was feeling jaded. The only person I could trust was myself. I told the agents I'd already booked a room – my second lie in five hours. With purpose and direction in my step, I walked away from them, having no idea where I was going.

Two minutes from the bus dropoff, by fluke I located an uninspiring motel that was written up in my guidebook. Two young guys insisted on accompanying me to ensure my safe arrival. A few moments after I settled into the small, dismal room for one, the banging on the door began. Ignoring their persistent offers for me to book a safari was the only way to get rid of them.

When the coast was clear, I snuck out to town. After a quick bite, I headed to bed early, desperate for the day to end. I was feeling alone *and* lonely. I missed the reassuring company of the South Africans. I longed for companionship, someone familiar to share my experiences. The good *and* the bad.

I WAS WIDE AWAKE when the sun streamed through the sheer white curtains before seven. Eager to escape the room and explore Arusha by foot, I headed to the main street. After reading a few signs, I realized it would be another hour before any of the shops opened.

Arusha appeared pleasant, quiet and clean. Nestled at the base of Mount Meru among coffee and maize plantations, the surrounding landscape was bursting with vegetation thanks to the spring rains. The town centre had a variety of conveniences within a half-kilometre walking distance: grocery stores, a Chinese restaurant, pizzerias, curio shops and a plethora of travel bureaus. I looked around the green, sun-drenched landscape and felt much better about my decision to leave Dar.

Navigating through the long list of safari companies was overwhelming. I'd been warned that many of the businesses had folded. Some were run by scam artists. They would take a full payment or a deposit then fail to show up, or worse, leave customers stranded in the countryside. Only a two- to three-day safari fell within my budget. There was no way I was going to risk signing up with a company that might leave me shillingless.

I popped into the hostel to seek the advice of fellow backpackers and met a Scottish woman named Claire. She was frustrated and angry. Two days earlier she'd put down a 300-dollar deposit for a safari in the Serengeti and Ngorongoro Crater. The driver never showed up. The company returned 200 dollars, but she had no luck retrieving the rest.

Claire and I discussed going to Moshi together for a one-day hike from the base of Kilimanjaro, but I wasn't optimistic: the forecast called for rain, and it was getting too late to make arrangements. With no concrete plan, I felt stuck.

That evening Claire and I dined with an American woman. I listened intently as she talked about her safari experience in the Masai Mara. "The Serengeti is way bigger, so it's more popular. But the Masai Mara is just as stunning. It's not as if the animals know any different. The border is irrelevant during the Great Migration. And the safaris in Kenya are much cheaper."

On a map of Tanzania and Kenya, Masai Mara looks like the tiny tip of a triangular iceberg, with the expansive Serengeti sunken below a vast ocean. With an area just under 15,000 square kilometres, the Serengeti dwarfs the Masai Mara tenfold. But both parks host an abundance of wildlife and are known to be equally stunning.

The woman had paid 150 dollars for a three-day safari out of Nairobi. I was happy to learn there were regular flights from Zanzibar to Nairobi and plenty of cheap flights between Nairobi and Johannesburg.

I made up my mind: if the Serengeti wasn't in the cards for me, after Zanzibar I would make Kenya my last stop before returning to South Africa. Over the months of my journey, I had discovered that even though things didn't always work out as planned, wonderful things still happened when an unforeseen opportunity presented itself.

The next day's inclement weather forecast made my decision easy – a trip to the base of Kilimanjaro was out of the question. With 80 dollars to my name, I decided against a Serengeti safari. Even though a local agent had promised to squeeze me into a group, I wasn't about to fall victim to a scam. I decided to return to Dar and escape to Zanzibar as soon as my passport and finances were in order.

I didn't see going to Arusha as a failure. This detour opened my mind to other possibilities and gave me time to finalize my remaining days in Africa. At the very least, I was grateful to have seen a different part of the country and take in the views of Kilimanjaro.

ON THE BUS RIDE BACK TO DAR, I didn't have Phil Collins's musical magic to ease my worries, nor was I approached by any men propositioning me with their version of a "special memory." Instead, Tanzanian music videos played nonstop the first two hours of the journey back to Dar. Displays of wealth and sex – Mercedes-Benzes, high-end condominiums, short skirts and lots of thigh rubbing – reminded me of my awkward squirming session watching the B movie in Harare. Though these depictions were an interesting mix of African and Western rapper cultures, I preferred to look out the window at the scenery.

I jumped for joy when I returned to Dar: my Visa and new passport were ready for pickup. I studied the new photo in my Tanzanian-issued passport like a badge of honour. I looked more self-assured. Wiser, maybe, with a touch of badassness.

My enthusiasm, however, was quashed quickly. I arrived at the bank to be told the staff member in charge of my money transfer was on vacation. I almost burst an artery. No one checked her messages, which had the details of my request. I'd be stuck there for at least a few more days. Emotionally, I was done. With each passing hour, my patience waned. Being back in the city made me miss the South Africans even more.

I returned to the campground to pick up my belongings. When I saw a letter addressed to me from Pete, my heart grew five times bigger. In his unmistakable playful yet flawless upper-case printing, he addressed the letter to "Miss Lisa Duncan Canada" and signed it "Love the family xx." The humorous and encouraging contents of the "SA NEWSFLASH" warmed my heart. Pete's endearing insults made me chuckle as I pictured his smiling face. The letter was exactly what I needed. But reading it made me wish I'd gone with them to the coast instead of Arusha. By now they were likely en route to Kenya, and I had no way to contact them. All I could do was take comfort in the knowledge they had been thinking about me too.

The campground was far from the city, so the YWCA hostel downtown became my temporary home. It was central and spacious, but proved lonely and sterile. I frequented the Kilimanjaro Hotel to break up the monotony while waiting for the High Commission to process my bank transfer.

I recognized a few backpackers from Malawi in the hotel lounge. Xavier, an outgoing, dark-haired Spaniard, had kept himself employed by drawing tattoos and performing body piercings on paying customers in Cape Maclear. Back then, I found his skills and hygiene methods questionable, since he didn't seem to have a way to sanitize his tools. The last time our paths had crossed, he had inserted medium-sized wooden plugs into his earlobes. I thought it an odd fashion that bordered on a cultural appropriation of the Masai. Now, weeks later, his plugless earlobes were crusty and infected and looked permanently deformed. Clearly, this part of the human body wasn't forgiving of physical alterations.

Xavier was travelling with two Danes I recognized from my diving course. I watched with envy as the three of them picked up their backpacks and ambled over to the Zanzibar ferry while I stayed behind in the hotel lounge, waiting and wasting precious time.

Over a beer, I chatted with a guy who had been working as a promoter for Solomon Condoms. He invited a small group of us, including a local Tanzanian woman he worked with, over to his rented house in Oyster Bay. It was simple but modern and tastefully furnished – nothing like the simple interiors I had grown accustomed to as a backpacker.

The five of us strolled to the waterfront near an expat neighbourhood and feasted on mushroom pizzas at a popular seaside restaurant. Sade's "Paradise" was playing in the background. I *loved* Sade. It was as though she was in the room with me, trying to iron out my frustrations with her smooth voice: *Don't worry, Lisa. It'll all work out. Just wait and see.*

In just a matter of days, my contempt for the city had reached its peak. But this unexpected outing with new friends, along with Sade's music, gave me a more positive impression of Dar.

IN NINE DAYS I was scheduled to fly back to Vancouver from Johannesburg. After all the delays, I decided to extend my trip by two weeks. I didn't want to rush my time on Zanzibar, nor was I willing to miss out on visiting the Masai Mara. I made one final visit to the travel agent and booked a cheap flight to Nairobi from Zanzibar.

The next day I got the good news that my money transfer and travel visa for Zanzibar were ready. I beamed when the bank issued me a cheque for 127,000 shillings (300 Canadian dollars). All I had left to do was exchange some shillings into US dollars, since dollars were compulsory in Zanzibar.

I practically skipped and danced down the street to the foreign exchange bureau. When I asked the teller to convert my shillings, she asked for my ID. I proudly handed over my new passport. After a cursory glance, she didn't even inspect it. "Ma'am, you are *not* a resident of Tanzania. I'm not permitted to exchange shillings into US dollars for you."

I looked at her in disbelief. It was rare for me to lose my cool, but I was on the cusp of a breakdown. I forced myself to shut down the angry tirade brewing in my head. *What the hell do you mean, you can't give me American dollars?* There was no need to come off as an entitled foreigner.

My scowl had little effect on her. I spewed out, "Well, that doesn't make any sense," and rushed back to the bank. The manager sympathized with my dilemma and wrote me a cover letter. Thirty minutes later, the foreign exchange clerk carefully counted out a small wad of ten- and 20-dollar bills in front of me.

Finally. I had everything I needed to leave for Zanzibar.

These renewed plans lifted my spirits. Waiting around in Dar had made me wonder if the challenges I had faced – Matthias, dysentery, the theft, missing the South Africans, the bus ride to Arusha – had been preparing me for the unpredictable circumstances I would face back home. These setbacks tested my resilience, patience and bravery – qualities I would require when dealing with the declines of Dad and Russ. *Disce pati.* Learn to endure.

It was impossible to know what awaited me. But I knew one thing for certain: I couldn't go back home with regrets or leave my Africa trip unfinished.

Seventeen

ON THE FIRST OF JUNE, I boarded the ferry to Zanzibar. Escaping the stresses of Dar seemed too good to be true. It seemed fitting a new month had begun, a chance to have a fresh start.

I stayed outside on the deck. The salt-water smell of the ocean hit me. *Hard.* I exhaled a huge sigh of relief and took a deep breath, delighting in the balmy air filling my lungs. Even though Lake Malawi resembled a vast sea, I hadn't been near the ocean since Namibia. Of course, that memory had been tainted by the smelly seal colony.

I'd lived my whole life close to a coastline. It was a strange sensation, smelling the ocean again after an extended absence. The intoxicating scent called to me like an old friend. Calm wrapped itself around me the moment the ferry set sail. As we headed west toward the setting sun, I didn't dare look back toward Dar.

Unlike the *Ilala* experience, the 70-minute boat ride to Zanzibar was clean, fast and efficient. Nineteen-year-old Sophie, her friend Gina and some of their overland truck acquaintances joined me. Once on Zanzibari soil, a group of us piled into the cozy "Hakuna Matata" minibus. Our driver drove less than a kilometre along a dark, quiet road before dropping Sophie, Gina and I off at the charming Malindi Guest House.

The aqua blue ocean was what had enticed me to visit Zanzibar, yet it was the thick, humid air and Islamic-inspired architecture that struck me the most. Even though the Tanzanian coast sits less than 40 kilometres away, I experienced a distinct, sublime feeling the minute I arrived.

Loosely translated from Arabic as the "black coast," Zanzibar is the largest island within the archipelago and boasts a romantic mystique. In the mid-1800s, the "Spice Island" thrived as a major clove producer. However, despite its reputation as a tropical paradise retreat, much of its history is dark and disturbing. Under Omani Arab rule, Zanzibar became the largest slave-trading port on the east coast of Africa, and Stone Town the most important destination for trade.

The Malindi Guest House's quaint decor showcased a variety of arabesque, geometric designs, but the intricate furnishings and detailed fabrics of the inviting interior could not mask the pungent smell of mildew. Sophie, Gina and I set our belongings into our musty, dimly lit room then headed out to explore Stone Town.

We ventured into town in hopes of eating at the Jamituri Gardens outdoor food market. My mouth watered thinking about all the curries, roasted meat kebabs and ice cream I had read about. When we arrived, our hope and appetites were shattered: the garden area was empty, devoid of human activity and succulent aromas.

I approached some locals sitting on a nearby bench. They told us the government had shut down the market a month earlier. Jamituri Gardens had been a popular public gathering spot for residents to socialize and eat outdoors together, but it had also become a hub for political activities and protests. After this disappointing discovery, we settled on some lukewarm fried chicken and soggy chips at a nearby restaurant.

Our introductory exploration of Stone Town began with its labyrinth of ancient small streets. A disorientating series of narrow passageways and meandering alleys strung together a collection of gift shops, businesses, restaurants, places of worship and residences. With each turn, something new and unexpected appeared. Exploring under the moonlight made our experience there all the more mysterious.

I returned to Stone Town's magnificent mazes to see their brilliance in daylight. I stopped several times to admire the intricate Islamic relief patterns carved into the oversized wooden doors. Nothing in my architectural history courses had exposed me to such beauty. The geometric designs had a rich complexity I had never really observed in Western art.

As soon I turned a corner, it felt like a time warp. A beige-bearded grandfather figure was sitting on a rickety wooden chair on a concrete landing half a foot above street level. On the ground next to him sat what looked to be his cheerful baby grandson. Behind him, his toddler granddaughter pranced around, blowing a red whistle. The old man's wide, gap-toothed smile appeared to be a permanent fixture on his weathered bronze face. His black, thick-rimmed eyeglasses made his brown eyes look larger and blurry. He wore a loosely fitted turban the colour of his beard and a flowy, purple linen shirt tucked into a cream-coloured *kikoi*. Despite his old-world attire, the turquoise flip-flops on his feet reminded me I wasn't time travelling.

The open wooden doors behind them led into a small kitchen with a wooden table. Three piles of coconuts, a few dozen Roma tomatoes and a bowl of limes seemed to be the extent of the modest shop the old man was overseeing. This scene created the illusion that I was in Morocco or somewhere in the Middle East. Zanzibar's complex history includes Omani, Indian, Swahili and Islamic influences, a unique cultural milieu that made me feel I was in multiple places at once.

AFTER MY EXPLORATION OF STONE TOWN, I travelled to the northern tip of the island to spend a few days at Nungwi Beach with Sophie and Gina. Luminous turquoise waters and soft, white beaches greeted us and I was stoked to spend a few days at this unspoiled stretch of ocean.

There were few tourists at Nungwi, and the little seaside town was sparsely populated. Organizing a dive there was cheap compared to Lake Malawi's murky waters. It would have been a diver's dream to explore the pristine Indian Ocean. As enticing as it was, I needed to save my remaining money for the Kenya safari and settled on reading and writing on the beach instead. With the stresses of Dar behind me, the simple act of relaxing in this paradise setting seemed extravagant and surreal: I couldn't have asked for anything more.

We stayed in a small, clean lodge and shared one large room with three beds covered with mosquito nets. The scenery at Nungwi Beach exceeded postcard perfection. Small fishing boats and traditional sailboats known as dhows dotted the ocean shores. To the west, clear views of Tumbatu Island beckoned me. Tumbatu looked at least three kilometres in length and was known to have the occasional shark sighting. Though there were no reported attacks, I had *no* intention of swimming there.

Each day at noon, dark clouds formed above the beach. Mother Nature delivered her daily baptism, drenching us in a refreshing shower. In the heat of the midday sun, I looked forward to this ritual downpour. I stood with my arms stretched above my head toward the sky, wearing nothing but a smile and a bikini. The rains usually lasted an hour – long enough for us to soak our bodies, dry off and have some lunch at the lodge until the hot sun popped out again to burn off the cloud cover.

My second morning, I went for a walk along the beach on my own. A pair of fist-sized crabs scurried across the smooth sand as I padded toward the gentle waves. Moments later, I became mesmerized by a few lone African red knob sea stars lying on the creamy shore. Each tentacle was covered with radiating rows of shimmery, brilliant red tubercles reaching for the sun like gravity-defying, miniature cow teats. This spiny spectacle was unlike anything I had ever seen and reminded me of the upward growing stalagmites at the Sterkfontein caves in South Africa. That visit with my cousin Rika seemed so long ago now.

This simple act of watching starfish and crabs made me feel like a kid again. Though I grew up near the Richmond dyke, I was born in the small Vancouver Island town of Chemainus. After my family moved to the mainland, my parents kept the island house for several years. We sometimes stayed there when it was unrented during spring or summer break.

The house was perched above a quaint, kid-friendly park next to the ocean. It was in this grassy park where I experienced the confusing pain of my first bee sting between the toes. And it was at the nearby beach where my love of crabs and sea life unfolded. I spent hours exploring the pebbly shore, squealing in delight each time I lifted a barnacle-encrusted rock to discover a handful of thumbnail-sized crabs scurrying away from my shadow.

I was always disappointed when it was time to catch the ferry back home. During one visit, my parents let me bring four small crabs home in a small bucket of seawater. The first few days I loved playing with my miniature playmates. I gave them names and pushed them around in toy cars. By the third day, however, I grew tired of their company. After Dad announced we had to walk to the dyke to retrieve some seawater for the crabs, I decided a covert disposal was in order. The next morning, I hurled the tiny, helpless crustaceans over the fence into our neighbour's backyard. I was certain no one had seen me.

My 5-year-old logic dictated that no one would notice a few small crabs among the blades of the grass. But for the next two days my heart pounded out of control each time our neighbour leaned over the fence to chat with Mom or Dad. I was convinced my dark secret had been revealed and they were discussing my punishment in hushed voices.

By the end of the week, nothing had transpired beyond the images of my active imagination. From then on, I always left crabs at the beach where they belonged.

Observing the crabs on Nungwi, it occurred to me this was the first time in weeks I wasn't stressed about anything. I wasn't worrying about a flailing romance, my family or getting out of an undesirable city. I was free to stroll along the pristine beach and simply enjoy it. It was strange but wonderful. I wanted to hold on to this feeling as long as I could.

AFTER MY RESTFUL DAYS IN NUNGWI, I returned to Stone Town on my own to accomplish some end-of-journey shopping at a well-stocked curio shop that sold items from all over the continent. A beautiful solitaire game imported from Madagascar caught my discerning eye. Forty-seven perfectly polished marbles made of multicoloured stones rested on a smooth, round, wooden board, each one worthy of careful observation. This gorgeous game would go on to become one of my all-time prized possessions.

In Zimbabwe I had been enamoured by the delightful sounds of the metal-tined *mbira* instrument. I had planned on finding one on my way back through the country. With my change in travel plans, this shop in Zanzibar was likely my last chance to buy one. An *mbira* of a less-refined quality sang out to me from a nearby shelf. Its rudimentary diagonal line pattern and "JR" insignia added to its uniqueness. I love how plucking its metal tines can transport me back to Africa in an instant.

A decorative two-foot-long Masai gourd was the most peculiar carrying vessel I had ever seen. Integral to the daily lives of the Masai people, who rely on cattle for nourishment in the form of milk, beef and sometimes even blood, the gourds have lasted generations. Its pungent odour was evidence it had, in fact, been used to ferment and transport milk. The brown gourd's colourful, beaded leather shoulder strap was a testament to the Masai's intricate handiwork. Despite its utilitarian purpose, the care and detail put into the gourd was a true work of art.

My final purchase included not one but three striped-cotton *kikoi* wraps similar to the one Pete wore. I loved their versatility as they could be used as a sarong or towel in a pinch. I wrapped up my new purchases in the *kikois*, sealed them in a box and dropped them off at the post office. In a few months, these treasures would arrive in Vancouver: I couldn't wait to discover them again.

I travelled to the east coast of the island and stayed at a lovely lodge at Bwejuu Beach. On my second day, two backpackers from Ireland invited me for a beach walk. The three of us strolled along the desolate shore, wading in the warm water with the velvety sand massaging the soles of our feet. Towering, windblown palm trees provided shade when the heat got too much for us.

We were determined to locate a lagoon we had heard much about, but two hours and six kilometres later we turned around. Despite my Irish companions, we had no luck finding this elusive water feature.

Our failed expedition made me smile as I remembered Rowen and Simon when we couldn't find the rock paintings in the Drakensberg. But this little trip wasn't a letdown. On the return walk, six preteen boys playing with two green, football-sized coconuts appeared. We were delighted to have them accompany us for the last few kilometres. It was impressive to watch two of them swiftly balance across a diagonally swaying tree to retrieve a few more coconuts.

After the boys walked us back to the lodge, I sat on the beach alone and buried my toes in the warm, wet sand. A few dhows sailed by, reminders of Zanzibar's unsavoury past. The coastline would have been a completely different scene when it served as East Africa's busiest slave trade port a century earlier. Captives, including children, had been packed onto dhows like disposable cargo and transported to the island. If they survived the tortuous trip, they were forced to work on the plantations or brought to the Stone Town market, where they were beaten and sold by Arab traders for next to nothing.

This wasn't the first time I had experienced the strange dichotomy between calming ocean views and disturbing history. Sitting on this beach in Zanzibar reminded me of Dad's lesson during our family vacation in Europe.

After Paris, we drove to Normandy. Staying in the seaside town of Bayeux made me feel cultured and sophisticated. I loved strolling along the cobblestone streets, peering into the quaint shops, patisseries and cafes, and inhaling the sweet smell of the colourful hanging baskets. But Dad hadn't brought my sister and me to Bayeux for the crispy croissants or beautiful bouquets. We were there to pay our respects at the Canadian war cemetery and visit the beaches where so many Second World War soldiers lost their lives.

When I walked along Juno Beach, it was hard to imagine the war scene when thousands of soldiers and tons of artillery dotted the coastline. As a teenager, I couldn't fully grasp the significance of what happened on the shores of Normandy, but years later I appreciated Dad taking me there. He taught me that travelling isn't just about personal fulfillment and cultural experiences. It can be a window into the past, exposing the troubling histories we are all connected to.

MY TIME IN ZANZIBAR had to include a Mitu spice tour, so I signed up as soon as I returned to Stone Town. Mr. Mitu was a local legend on Zanzibar with over 30 years hosting the tours. He must have been taking a much-needed break that day because his nephew, Junior, acted as his competent stand-in.

Junior was a thin man of South Asian descent. He wore jeans and a beige collared shirt with the sleeves rolled up. A navy "Every Second Counts" ball cap shaded his dark, pensive eyes. Junior fulfilled his promise of bringing us to hard-to-get-to pockets of the island and making our experience immersive. The second we piled out of the minibus, he encouraged us to get hands-on with a variety of spices and fruits.

"Everyone, please take a strip of this, Zanzibar's finest, unharvested, raw cinnamon."

I rubbed the rough bark between my fingers. Its fragrance burrowed into my nose, creating a tunnel between Zanzibar and my childhood kitchen. The irresistible aroma awakened my senses: memories of Thanksgiving apple pie baking in the oven and making cinnamon rolls in junior high cooking class flooded back to me.

Junior let our group fondle the bark a bit longer before he walked over to some tall shrubs. "Please come this way. Ladies, I have something I think will be of interest to you," he said, peering out from under his big-brimmed cap with a wry grin. "This is *Bixa orellana*, commonly known as the lipstick tree."

The plant's spade-shaped green leaves were plain, but its fuzzy, red, strawberry-shaped clusters were stunning. "Many people think these are flowers, but they're actually pods." Junior skillfully cracked one open to reveal more than 20 small reddish-orange seeds the size of corn kernels. He crushed a few between his fingers. "Have a look at this red pigment. It can be used as a natural lipstick. Go ahead, try some."

A few of us sampled the pigment. I rubbed some of the red, creamy powder on my lips. Junior gave me a nod of approval. Minutes later, he passed around a few leaves from a sandpaper tree, citing its medicinal, anti-inflammatory benefits. Junior was on a roll and ensured the spice tour was equally educational and entertaining.

"Over here we have the remijia plant, which contains quinine. As some of you may know, quinine is used to treat malaria. It's what gives tonic water its distinct bitter flavour." He then pointed to some mint plants I recognized. "And did you know menthol is made from simple herbs like peppermint, and that the oils of eucalyptus trees help decongest nasal passages?"

Our group followed Junior over to a plant that looked like giant green beans. I was fascinated to discover these were vanilla pods. The natural vanilla extract I used back home in my chocolate chip cookies looked nothing like the pods in their unprocessed state.

The spice tour wouldn't have been complete without getting intimate with some fresh cloves, Zanzibar's most famous spice. I rubbed a handful of buds between the palms of my hand. The heavenly scent evoked the sugary flavours of pumpkin pie and gingersnaps. Of course, the history of cloves on Zanzibar is far from sweet. Slave labour allowed plantations to thrive on the island. In 1872, payback arrived in the form of a hurricane that destroyed most of the trees, which were eventually replanted.

The tour ended with a lunch of fluffy pilau rice smothered in rich, fragrant coconut-cinnamon curry. Unlike Likoma Island, which heavily relied on the mainland for sustenance, Zanzibar was committed to its independence. Our entire meal was prepared with fresh ingredients grown on the island, proof of its pride in its ability to provide for its people.

In the midst of our feast, a lovely woman showed up to paint decorative mehndi ink designs. I jumped at the chance to see her artistic prowess. She drew an intricate, curvy line pattern starting with three dots on my baby toe, extending an inch past my ankle. I had never had the desire to get a tattoo before, but I quickly became attached to the design and thought of making it permanent once I got home.

During the tour, I met Sam, a 21-year-old South Asian. His beautiful brown eyes, high cheekbones and flawless, clove-coloured skin were a magnet for my adoring eyes. A petite brunette who sounded British accompanied him. I didn't get a chance to talk with them until we sat down to lunch together.

"Did you enjoy the tour?" I asked Sam after swallowing my first spoonful of curry.

"Yeah, it was an eye-opener for me. I'm actually from Tanzania, so I'm not far from home. Dana's visiting from England. We met last week in Arusha where I live. I decided it'd be fun to show her around the island and be a tourist myself."

"Sam's been an amazing guide," Dana added.

Junior was making his rounds, encouraging everyone to eat seconds.

"That's a great motto, eh, on Junior's hat?" I said.

Dana and Sam looked over at Junior, who was talking with the ink artist. Dana let out a chuckle. "Oh, have you not heard of *Every Second Counts*? It's a British game show from a few years back."

"Really? No, I've never heard of it." I laughed. "I assumed it had some deeper meaning."

"Well, either way, those are great words to live by," Dana said.

"Agreed," said Sam.

The three of us chatted over a second serving of coconut curry and rice. Sam grew interested when he found out I was Canadian. "I'm going to Carleton University in Ottawa in September. Do you know it?" he asked.

"Carleton? Yeah, I was just there in October to visit my friend who's doing her MA in international relations. She showed me around the campus. It's really pretty, especially in autumn when the leaves change colour. But, just so you know, nothing can prepare you for the cold Ontario winters. Make sure you pack some wool sweaters and toques. And get yourself a pair of ice skates so you can skate on the canal!"

Sam looked so excited. For the next half-hour, he picked my brain about Canadian life. He wanted to know more about Vancouver in hopes of making a visit, and I was happy to oblige. Talking to him made me feel better about returning home with so many summer activities to look forward to and fun places to rediscover.

Later that afternoon, I bumped into Claire from Scotland, first at the Persian Baths and again in Stone Town during my final stroll. We hadn't seen each other since meeting in Arusha, and I invited her to join a group of us for dinner. At a seaside restaurant we devoured the biggest, most delicious crabs ever – the perfect way to commemorate my last night on the island.

AFTER MY SHORT-TERM TROUBLES in Tanzania, spending a week on Zanzibar felt luxurious. The next day I would board the plane to Nairobi. I couldn't ignore the fact that this short flight meant my journey was reaching its finale.

I would have to make every last second count, I thought with a chuckle.

Eighteen

I LEFT THE SECURITY of the arrivals terminal and loitered around the ticket booths, trying to figure out where the hell I was going. I honed in on a Lufthansa agent. Though I had no idea how to get to Mama Roche's, I was certain this woman could point me in the right direction.

Ms. Ali made up for her lack of experience in the backpacker realm with her knowledge of bus shuttles and public transportation in and around Nairobi. "Listen to me," she pontificated with perfectly manicured hands. "I'm telling you, that hostel – Mother Roche's, you said?"

"Mama Roche," I corrected.

"Yes, Mama Roche," she continued, her voice a beautiful blend of Indian and British accents. "That area isn't near the city centre. You'll never get there unless you take a taxi. Tell you what. I'll drive you to the hostel. Just take a seat over there and wait for me. My shift ends at three." She carefully removed a strand of her long dark hair from the sleeve of her navy blazer and called over the next customer.

An hour later, we pulled out of the airport parking lot in Ms. Ali's silver sedan. I wasn't expecting a free ride, but things turned awkward as soon as I clicked the seatbelt. "Just so we're clear, you *must* pay me the equivalent of a standard cab. Okay?"

I had no idea about taxi fares in Nairobi, or if Ms. Ali was trying to take advantage of me. At this point I had no alternative but to let her deliver me to Mama Roche's. "Um, sure…I guess that seems fair," I replied.

She turned to me and said in a motherly tone, "So what brings you to Nairobi?"

"I'm going to Masai Mara."

Her eyes lit up. I could almost see the cogs in her brain spinning. "Did you book anything yet?"

"No, I'll do that first thing tomorrow morning."

My response pleased her. "Not to worry. I have connections in the safari business. I can make the arrangements for you."

Half an hour later, we pulled into a dirt driveway leading to a large property. The sun peeked through large trees surrounding the hostel and a little house. I paid Ms. Ali 1,500 shillings and exited her car. She rolled down the window as I hurried away. "It's my day off tomorrow. I'll come back in the morning to drive you to the city…Let's say nine o'clock?"

"Thank you, but that won't be necessary. I can figure out a ride from here."

"Don't be silly. It's no trouble at all. See you tomorrow," she insisted. *Dammit.*

There were no rave reviews about Mama Roche's in *Lonely Planet.* I had heard about this lesser-known hostel through the backpacker grapevine. Fellow travellers deemed it a popular hub for motorcyclists and backpackers alike. The property was tucked away on the outskirts of Nairobi. The dorm quarters and campsites were surrounded by beautiful lush gardens.

A large-busted woman in her 70s was puttering outside when I arrived. Right away I knew this had to be Mama Roche. Her short, fine, blonde hair was streaked with silver, and her eyeglasses were the same hue. She was dressed in a cream-coloured "Jambo" T-shirt, a navy cardigan and a floral skirt that covered her knees. A lap-sized mutt stayed close to her feet, which were clad in white tube socks and grey flip-flops.

"Make yourself at home, dear," she crooned. Mama Roche had immigrated to Kenya from Poland in the 1940s. Though she had lived in the country for five decades, she couldn't mask her thick accent. "And, please, you can call me Ma," she said while hanging up towels on a clothesline strung between two small trees.

There were plenty of interesting travellers at the hostel. I was delighted when four of them invited me to walk up the dusty road after sunset to have supper at an outdoor diner. Among the group was a Spaniard named Luis, who seemed exceptionally adventurous. Over dinner he told us about his motorcycle trek from Spain to Morocco, then through West Africa to Kenya. We listened like doting children, in awe of his 9000-kilometre journey.

I was envious that Luis had seen the western part of the continent. He revealed, however, that his travels had plenty of discouraging days. Chronic motorcycle maintenance problems caused him his fair share of delays and frustrations. Being in the saddle for hours on hot, dry, dusty roads made him grow weary and exhausted. This revelation made me realize how easy it was to romanticize other people's journeys instead of appreciating my own.

Jason, a friendly American who had just landed a job with Come to Africa Safaris, was also seated at dinner. After chatting with him, I decided to book a three-day safari with his tour company. "Come by tomorrow morning, and I'll get you signed up."

My excitement soared. In two days, I would be in Masai Mara.

As PROMISED, Ms. Ali showed up the next morning, insisting she chaperone me to Jason's office after I told her my plans. Right after we arrived, Jason took me aside.

"Just so you know, she's asking me for a commission on the $150 cost of the trip." I had a hunch Ms. Ali wasn't helping me out of the goodness of her heart. Now I had proof. After she took her cut, I never saw her again.

Although my main motivation for being in Kenya was to view the wildlife of Masai Mara, I was eager to explore Nairobi. Despite my experience in Dar, my confidence and sense of security had returned. Instead of being jaded, I felt resilient. I wasn't going to let one negative encounter taint the rest of my experiences.

I hopped on a local bus to view the sprawling city before walking around. After a few stops, two young Masai men boarded the bus and sat across the aisle from me. Their pristine white T-shirts were plain against their dark skin. I smiled when I noticed their baggy jeans were several inches too short for their lanky legs.

I had never seen Masai in plain clothes before. The contrast between the men's striking features and Western clothing fascinated me. It was entertaining to watch one of them twist and tuck his stretched-out, earring-free earlobes like thick rubber bands. He pulled them around the tops of his ears, presumably to stop them from getting in the way. I winced, imagining what it would feel like to have them snag on something.

Aside from buying my ticket to Joburg, changing my Vancouver flight and phoning home, I had no agenda in Nairobi. I exited the bus, free to roam the city without my nose in a map. Ms. Ali had warned me about thieves on the lookout for gold, but I never felt targeted. No one seemed to show any interest in my silver ring, tiny stud earrings or small wooden-beaded necklace.

The cylindrical tower of the Kenyatta International Conference Centre served as my visual anchor in the big metropolis. I passed by the YWCA, Buffalo Bill's Bar and half a dozen embassies. I walked all the way to Chinatown, where I scarfed down a bowl of noodles.

Since my parents were expecting my return, I scoured the city to find somewhere to use my calling card. Up until then I had been relaxed, but a nervous flutter took hold of me as I dialled their number. The last time we'd talked, Mom wasn't very happy with me. I was hoping to hear her usual easygoing voice this time. She picked up after four rings.

"Hey, Mom!" I said cheerfully.

"Oh. Hi, Lis." I detected a hardness in her voice, and my body tensed up.

"Is everything okay?" I felt my chest tighten.

"Well, no, actually. Dad's been in the hospital for about a week now." She sounded despondent. The stress in her voice was a punch to my gut.

"Oh, no. What happened?"

"He had some kind of stress attack. He'd been acting funny for more than a week, getting really paranoid at bedtime. He was up half the night calling out to me, insisting someone was outside the house trying to kill him." Mom had been sleeping on the chesterfield in the living room for several months. It was the only way for her to get any rest.

"He claims to see people out on the street corner watching the house. It doesn't matter what I tell him…He thinks it's real. The doctors say he's hallucinating."

I wasn't prepared for this upsetting update. Hearing it over the phone made me feel helpless. Dispirited. And guilty as shit for extending my trip.

"I'm sorry, Mom. I wish I could do something. How much longer will he be in the hospital?" I tried to keep my voice steady and hopeful.

"They're trying out some new medications. The doctors said at least a few more days." These words gave me some relief. This meant Mom would have a little break from looking after Dad. Hopefully, he'd return home with his mental state improved.

"Okay. Um, I changed some of my plans. I won't be flying home for another ten days."

I'm sure it wasn't intentional, but Mom sounded annoyed that I was thousands of miles from home instead of providing support for our family. "Well, do what you have to. There's nothing you can do anyway."

I hung up the phone and wandered around Nairobi in a depressed haze. With Dad's illness heavy on my mind, my carefree explorations ceased. It felt as if I had an elephant pressing down on my chest and stomach. I had no one to talk to. No one to tell me everything would be okay. Though I can conjure up faint images of streets, storefronts and restaurants, my time in Nairobi will always be tainted by those raw emotions that took hold of me.

That night I went to bed wearing a straightjacket of fear and guilt. By morning it had loosened, but little knots in my stomach remained. *There's nothing you can do, Lisa*, I kept telling myself.

I was determined to push dread out of my mind and embrace my final days in Kenya. Stressing about Dad wasn't going to change anything. I was thankful to have the safari to keep me focused on the present. Whatever the outcome, I would face it upon my return.

I WAS SEATED UP FRONT next to the safari guide in the ten-seater Land Rover when he pulled up to a posh hotel at 10:30 a.m. sharp. Three women from Hong Kong dressed in freshly ironed polo shirts, designer jeans and spotless sneakers filed into the back of the vehicle. I turned around to say hello and was hit by the overpowering scent of perfume. I quickly rolled the cracked window all the way down to get some fresher air.

We drove to a three-star hotel to pick up four women from Norway wearing cotton shorts and T-shirts. Heidi looked around my age. She sat behind me with her mom while her aunts took the seat in front of the Hong Kongers.

For the first few hours, we had the luxury of travelling along a smooth highway. Once we were out of the city limits, the road quality deteriorated. I felt like an unwilling participant on an amusement ride each time the driver slowed down to swerve along the potholed route. Between the wafts of nauseous perfume and the bumpy road conditions, I was glad to be in the front seat where my chances of getting carsick were less likely.

The Norwegians, who seemed unaffected by the rocky ride, passed around paper bags of roasted cashews. Heidi's mom poured Danish spirits into plastic shot glasses like a seasoned bartender. The eight of us toasted a triumphant "*Skol!*" while trying not to spill our drinks. I smiled at them and took a celebratory sip, keeping my eyes forward.

Masai Mara greeted us with overcast skies and warm temperatures. Our guide drove us toward wide-open plains for a game drive. The ladies cried out in delight when they saw dozens of zebras. But a large, dark-brown mass beyond the zebra herd was what captured my attention.

Our timing in Masai Mara was fortuitous: the wildebeest were in the midst of their annual migration. At the end of the rainy season, in late May or early June, roughly a million and a half of them leave the parched savannah of the Serengeti and travel to the more fertile Masai Mara along a northwesterly loop.

I marvelled at the wildebeest grazing in the grasslands, enjoying rest and calm after their harrowing 1500-kilometre journey from Tanzania. Their astonishing feat carries incredible risk. Hungry, thirsty and exhausted, the wildebeest must cross the deadly crocodile-inhabited Mara River with their young in search of food and water. A quarter million of them don't survive the round trip. But the birth of half a million calves each year keeps their populations thriving. I admired their resilience and courage to keep moving despite fear and imminent danger.

Seeing the wildebeest made me think of the stunning cinematography in *The Serengeti*, the IMAX film I'd watched in Cape Town three months earlier with Anna. Narrator James Earl Jones had been spot-on when he called them "the clowns of the African plains." Shaggy manes and wispy beards. Boxy heads crowned with curved, pointed horns. Thick girths held up by gangly legs. I thought the wildebeest looked like a goofy but endearing cross between an antelope, moose and bison.

After our inaugural wildlife viewing, the driver dropped off the Hong Kong ladies at their five-star lodge near the park. The Norwegians and I arrived at our comfortable camp quarters of canvas tents and outdoor seating. We gathered around a campfire for dinner and feasted on succulent grilled meat kebabs and vegetables, spiced rice and *ugali*, Kenya's equivalent to *sadza*.

I headed to bed early with a full belly. We would be up at sunrise for our second game drive. I closed my eyes, thinking about my first day in Masai Mara. Seeing the wildebeest was fantastic, and I enjoyed the company of the Norwegians. And yet my experience there paled in comparison to the spectacular evening under the stars in Mikumi with the South Africans and Vanessa. It had taken me a few months to figure out the secret behind creating meaningful memories: the *who* was equally as important as the where and what.

THE HONG KONGERS were royally ticked off when our driver picked them up 25 minutes late the next morning – clearly, they had no idea that in Africa delays were par for the course and not worth getting worked up about.

After two hours of driving around the park, it seemed all the animals were asleep or simply didn't want to be found. Our guide suggested we return to camp for breakfast and try again later.

The second game drive was a huge success. In addition to more wildebeest and zebras, we were overjoyed to see a small pack of hyenas. I had only ever seen images of them as scrappy-looking scavengers. The sight of the mother and cubs peeking out of their den was adorable.

What followed was nothing short of amazing: warthogs, a giraffe, an elephant, a herd of impala, buffalo, hippos and a crocodile. Of course, a safari would not be complete without a lion sighting, but we had been told such sightings required a lot of patience. A typical male lion, the protector of the pride, often sleeps 20 hours a day. Females sleep less, since they do most of the hunting. Our guide reminded us not to get our hopes up. Lions prefer to keep cool in the shade to avoid the hot midday sun, recharging before preying on their next meal.

After driving around for an hour, I had given up on seeing any lions. Then the guide put the Land Rover in park and pointed excitedly toward some thick, green bushes. He spotted two males lounging a few feet apart under the shade, their fur camouflaged among the drier brown leaves and branches. If it weren't for his keen eye, I never would have made out their sleepy faces.

My reaction was subdued compared to those of my fresh-off-the-plane companions. Even though I'd already had my share of animal sightings, I felt lucky to see the lions. Observing them in a docile state wasn't anticlimactic but a rare chance to admire their beauty up close and see them doing what they do best when not hunting: lounging around.

Seeing the lions and the lone buffalo meant I had checked off four out of the African Big Five: elephant, lion, leopard and buffalo. All that was left was the black rhino. I wasn't holding my breath, though, since their populations had dwindled due to poaching. And, sadly, to achieve my 80 per cent "success" rate, I had to include the roadkill leopard I'd seen in Zimbabwe on the way to Bulawayo with Doug and Jake. Perhaps there isn't a strict rule that the Big Five must be alive when you see them, but that would have been my preference.

For 500 Kenyan shillings (six Canadian dollars), our guide arranged a visit to a Masai village for us. I'm sure I must have seen photos of the Masai in *National Geographic*. But it was the film *Baraka* that gave me a more intimate glimpse into Masai culture when I became transfixed by the scenes showing their traditional dance ceremony; the hypnotic swaying of their tall, thin bodies and the guttural vibrations of their singing captivated me.

Women and children wearing red-checked *shuka* fabrics and jewellery greeted us. Long, colourful earrings dangled from their stretched-out earlobes. Three Masai women were seated on the ground with their pipe-thin legs stretched out in front of them. They chatted in their native Maa, busily creating brightly coloured beaded jewellery similar to detailed patterns of the gourd I purchased.

I thought back to the plainclothes Masai men on the bus in Nairobi. Visiting this village taught me how some Masai live between two worlds. It made me realize there are few places on Earth where outside influences haven't found a way to alter or complement traditional ways of living.

The Masai community received money for our visit. I thought our presence might have been an intrusion into their lifestyle. But through my Western, 24-year-old lens, they appeared to be willing participants. I felt better when the three women smiled at me and carried on with their beadwork like it was just a regular day. Making this little side trip was a great finale to our day.

Back at camp, I was taken aback when a loud commotion erupted between Heidi and her mother at dinner. Heidi had disappeared for a few hours before dark. Without telling anyone, she had arranged a late-afternoon hot air balloon ride. Heidi's mom, aunts and the safari staff were worried about her unexplained absence. When she arrived back at camp, the tension between her and her mom escalated into a cats-in-heat-level fight.

Witnessing this mother-daughter screaming match made me squirm. I thought of my mom. We hadn't always seen eye to eye, but we had never fought like this.

This ending to an otherwise satisfying trip was a letdown. Prior to Heidi's disappearance, the five of us had really enjoyed our time together. The next morning, things had smoothed over, but it was still awkward to be around them. After breakfast I said my goodbyes and returned to Nairobi while they stayed behind to continue their trip.

BACK AT THE HOSTEL, Ma Roche appeared to be intoxicated by early evening. She was crying and cursing at anyone within a five-metre radius. Feeling puzzled, I walked over to some backpackers, who told me about the high drama that had transpired while I was gone: Mama's beloved dog had been killed.

"That goddamn Israeli mafia. Those *fuckers* poisoned him!"

Mama was referring to a group of backpackers from Israel. She claimed they had given her dog poisoned meat then finished the job with a lethal injection – of what, I wasn't sure. Ma had booted the Israelis out, but was adamant that there were still backpackers staying at the hostel who knew about the canine crime.

I thought her story sounded outlandish, yet it was indeed a strange claim to fabricate. I thought of Dad's hallucinations and paranoia. Maybe Mama was imagining all of this and had some form of mental illness. Then again, maybe the events had really unfolded the way she described. Either way, her dog was dead.

For the rest of the night, Mama was inconsolable. Her loud, incessant swearing and intermittent bouts of wailing lasted throughout the evening and prevented me from falling asleep. Around two in the morning, it became dead quiet. I assumed Mama had calmed down and gone to bed or, more likely, passed out drunk.

By the morning, Ma seemed to have forgotten about the whole incident. She was back to her old self and made no mention of the bizarre night.

Trying to change my return flight to Vancouver proved a tedious, time-consuming process. The travel agent pointed out the fine print on my flight instructions: I had to fax London, *not* Vancouver. Factor in the time change, and I was stuck in Nairobi for two more days.

Desperate to kill a few hours, I strolled over to the local movie house to catch a matinee. I located my assigned seat in the half-empty theatre. When the lights dimmed, everyone stood up to sing the national anthem. Political propaganda played on the big screen before the main feature started. Turns out *Jumanji* starring Robin Williams was playing that week – my wish to see a rhino in Africa had been granted after all.

My attempt to sort out ticket issues presented one roadblock after another. The travel agency in Nairobi didn't accept credit cards. I spent the morning in a state of panic after my reservation was cancelled. It was a tremendous relief when the manager pulled some strings and took my Visa payment. In less than 48 hours, I would be boarding the plane to Johannesburg.

I was surprised how much I enjoyed spending time in Nairobi despite the upsetting news from Mom. I moved from Mama Roche's to the more central New Kenyan Lodge next to the bustling *matatu* minibus station. There I met a fellow traveller who was at his wit's end, trying to get home to Germany. His travel agent had made an error in his booking, forcing him to stay two more days in Nairobi. His frustrations reminded me of my troubles in Dar. This time I shrugged off our setbacks and told him it would all work out. In the big scheme of things, these were minor hurdles that came with the privilege of travelling.

I walked over to the closest hostel to find someone to share a cab to the airport. A woman offered me a spot in her 5:00 a.m. taxi. I walked back to the lodge feeling reassured, yet my last night in Nairobi was anything but peaceful. A downpour hammered the lodge's tin roof all night long. The combined clamour of a wailing baby in the lobby and the blaring, unrelenting horns of the *matatus* kept me wide awake until after midnight. I fell asleep, dreamt for what seemed like an hour, then woke up with a start at 4:38 a.m., two minutes before my alarm was set to go off.

Five of us gathered with our luggage outside the lodge. The rain fell down in buckets from the pewter sky. We took cover under two flimsy umbrellas while waiting for the cab to show up. A couple of the women announced they were nervous about cramming all of us into one taxi. In the end two of us agreed to find another ride.

We flagged down a dilapidated cab that was parked in front of the *matatu* station. The car reeked of fumes and blew thick blue smoke out of its tailpipe. Given the early hour and the last-minute change, the whole scenario made me think of Chris's mugging in Harare. Something just didn't feel right. I got into the taxi anyway.

As the cabbie pulled away, raindrops the size of marula fruit bounced off the taxi like exploding guppies. I looked toward the ominous sky, then back at the foggy road. It seemed as if we were driving under murky waters. My jaw and neck muscles tensed up. Maybe my restless night had been a prelude for bad things to come.

The taxi's nonfunctioning defogger made it impossible to see what lay ahead on the highway. Watching the driver's pitiful attempts to wipe condensation from the front window with a small, damp rag made my heart pound anxiously. The cab's ill-fitting wipers moved across the steamy windshield with such speed and vigour I thought they would break off and take flight.

We made it to the airport at 6:00 a.m. without hydroplaning across the road or plowing into incoming traffic. No breakdowns. No delays. I was so relieved my premonition had been wrong. I handed the cabbie our fare. He smiled as if to say, *Of course, we arrived safely!*

As the plane flew over Tanzania, the tops of Kilimanjaro and Mount Meru poked out from the cumulus cloud cover to wave good-bye. Then again, maybe they were inviting me to come back one day.

Leaving Kenya made me think about all the places I had yet to explore. From Nairobi, it would have been so easy to keep going. I could head west to Lake Victoria, then to Uganda. But I knew my time in Africa was up. There was no point in dwelling on what-ifs.

THREE HOURS LATER, I was back in Joburg. "Well, I was surprised to get your call, but don't worry about the short notice. I'm so glad to see you again," Rika said with a beaming smile. I felt bad calling my cousin unexpectedly from the airport an hour earlier. Now I was seated next to her as though I'd never left.

"I want to hear all about your trip," she said. "But *first*, we have to make a detour. There are a couple more backpackers in need of rescuing."

Rika had befriended Franco and Remy, two Brits staying at a squatter camp run by Buddhists and Hindus on the outskirts of Joburg. Apparently, the unorthodox communal accommodations were not working out for them.

"I told them they could stay at my house for a few days until they find other arrangements."

The guys were my age, and we hit it off right away. It was great to have some fellow travellers to talk to now that I was back in the burbs. They were smitten by my travel stories, and I loved answering all their questions. As I described some of the places I visited, I felt a deep sense of pride and accomplishment about everything I had done.

Being back in Johannesburg felt strange. By the second day, I felt the familiar tug-of-war, the shifting of emotional tectonic plates moving through my body. Rationally, it made sense to go home. My savings had run out, and I needed to be there for my family. Rika didn't make it easy for me, though.

"Why don't you just stay a few more months? You'll have no problems finding a teaching job here."

Given the great distance and my family circumstances, it was doubtful I would return to Africa anytime soon. It was fun to envision a different future, one in which I remained in Africa to work for a while. I wasn't 100 per cent certain Vancouver was where I wanted to be, but it was easy to convince myself otherwise. Even though I had nothing pressing to get back to, I looked forward to seeing my friends and going climbing again.

"It's tempting, Rika, but I need to get home. My dad's not doing well. And I've decided to apply to the teaching program and I don't want to miss the university deadline."

I felt good about my decision: I was ready to move forward and take the steps necessary to make this career happen. Rika nodded in agreement and didn't bring it up again.

Two hours after dinner, I was consumed by nausea. I headed straight to bed before bouts of diarrhea and vomiting tortured me throughout the night. I woke up the next day feeling wretched and weak. I stayed in bed all day while Rika served me *rooibos* to settle my stomach. It was unlikely I had contracted dysentery a second time. We suspected malaria, but after 24 hours it seemed like food poisoning or an airplane bug was the likely culprit.

The next day I was on the mend and felt relieved I wouldn't have any more delays. Perhaps this was Africa's way of testing me one last time. *Haven't you had enough already? It's time to go home.*

MY LAST DAYS IN SOUTH AFRICA were anticlimactic after my unpredictable adventures. I tried to regain some muscle mass by working out at the fitness centre where Rika taught swim lessons. After months of being outdoors, it felt suffocating to be inside a gym, but my body craved exercise. I swam ten measly 25-metre laps. In the midst of a few tricep stretches, I felt a wave of nostalgia thinking back to my swim with Emma: I would have had to complete more than 60 pool laps to cover the same distance we swam to Thumbi Island.

On my last day, I visited friends of Rika's who had opened a pub on a rural property outside the city. They hosted a delicious *braai* for friends and family to celebrate the grand opening. Although it was fun to take part in this outdoor feast, I already missed the simple comforts of backpacking.

The next day Rika drove me to the airport. En route, we stopped at Thomas's to pick up my climbing gear. I had hoped to see him one last time before leaving, but I never got the chance. He had moved out and didn't have a new phone number yet. When his mom opened the door, I noticed how pale her olive complexion looked compared to my tan skin. She was surprised to see me and even more surprised to learn I was leaving. Driving away from her residence felt surreal. I looked around the familiar streets and gated houses that shaped my initial impressions of South Africa. Riding in Rika's reliable car, I had come full circle. Gone were the days of making friends with strangers in the comfort of a Kombi or travelling on turbulent trains, chicken buses and filthy ferries.

On June 20, I boarded the plane to Vancouver, my four months complete. A strange feeling took hold of me. I couldn't quite place it, but it felt familiar, like when a relationship gets cut short without realizing its true potential. I was proud of my big journey. And yet there was still a longing and curiosity within me. But the tug of family was stronger than my will to stay. I accepted my responsibility: life had other plans for me.

After settling into the airplane seat, I felt a shift from within. I was no longer the same woman who had gazed down at the Zambezi River, clutching her trusted guidebook. I smiled warmly thinking about everything I had done and all the wonderful people I had crossed paths with. I couldn't fully grasp what was in store for me back home. But I had no choice but to move forward and be brave as one journey ended and another began.

I would go on to have more travel adventures – of that I was certain. But deep down I knew I would *never* have another Africa.

Epilogue

GIRONA, SPAIN, 2010

MAC HELD THE DOOR OPEN FOR ME as we wheeled our carbon-framed road bikes into the narrow entryway of the apartment building. The *click clack* of our cleated shoes echoed up four flights of stairs as we carefully maneuvered our bikes to our top floor rental. This was our third ride in three days: my tired legs thanked me once we ascended the last set of stairs. I looked down at my Garmin computer. "Ninety-seven klicks," I announced proudly.

Mac nodded, "Yep." Though I would have preferred another century ride, there was no way I was willing to bike around Girona's cobblestone streets just to round it off to a hundred.

We walked into the brightly lit apartment. I leaned my bike against the wall next to the large window and peered down below to admire the sun reflecting onto the Onyar River and Eiffel's red iron pedestrian bridge. Even though Mac and I enjoyed pushing ourselves on the bike, at this point in our trip, the distance we covered wasn't what really mattered. We'd already spent two weeks cycling on the island of Tenerife and five weeks in Portugal. Now that we were half-way through our month in Spain, I was just grateful to be riding in another cycling haven.

It was hard to believe we were here, living our dream. Over the years, on many occasions, Mac had suggested we pick up and leave Vancouver for a few months or longer. Each time the usual wave of unease swelled up in my chest: I was too scared to leave for more than a few weeks. Each time my reply was the same: "We can't leave. We have work."

My husband's persistence paid off. After teaching for 11 years, I found the courage to take a leave from work. Once I committed to the trip, my fear of leaving family behind vanished. Mac and I had our share of travel adventures together, but this was my longest stint away since Africa and Mac's first time to Europe. We were beyond thrilled to be fulfilling this cycling trip of a lifetime. So far everything had gone off without a hitch.

After showering and some lunch, I logged into our laptop to check email. I scanned my inbox. My pulse quickened the instant I saw an urgent message from my sister: Russ was in the hospital.

Mac and I hurried to the closest internet cafe, my heart and legs heavy with dread. I phoned Sue and learned Russ had contracted a severe case of sepsis – the doctors didn't know if he'd pull through.

This news was crushing. My family had grown accustomed to Russ's frequent hospitalizations due to bouts of C. difficile and bladder infections caused by his catheter. But this time it was dire. Even though Mac and I still had two weeks left of our big journey, we couldn't stay. Barcelona – the city of my dreams – would have to wait.

Forty-eight hours later, we were on a flight home to Vancouver. I was sick with worry, but grateful to have Mac there for emotional support. By the time we arrived, the doctors expected Russ to fully recover from the sepsis and, thankfully, he did.

THAT SAME YEAR, there had been a lot of news highlighting the success of the "liberation treatment" for MS patients. Since Russ's early diagnosis, there were no medications to slow down his progressive form of the disease. Over the years he'd tried his share of alternative treatments – chelation therapy, hyperbaric chamber – but none of them helped.

Liberation treatment was controversial and criticized as ineffective, but Russ had nothing to lose. He could no longer speak or move his body from the neck down. The simple act of swallowing made him prone to violent coughing fits and choking. At this advanced stage, I'm sure we would have considered a witchcraft healing ceremony if we thought it might help.

In the fall of 2011, I accompanied Russ and his caregiver friend Marlene to Merida, Mexico. This was the first time he had been on a plane in over 15 years. I hid my tears when the airline staff maneuvered him out of his wheelchair and into his seat before anyone else boarded. Minutes later, passengers waddled down the aisle, few of them noticing Russ's compromised state. Without his wheelchair, he almost blended in.

Unlike the more mobile MS patients lodging at the nearby motel, Russ stayed all five days at the hospital. The nurses didn't speak English, so my role, in addition to keeping his spirits up, involved communicating his needs using my intermediate Spanish. I had always used a second language to enrich a travel experience or for work. Now it was a lifeline for my brother.

Anticipation filled the hospital room the morning Russ received his treatment. The doctors had been honest about the procedure – we were under no illusions it would work – but it was hard not to get our hopes up. The insertion of a deflated balloon catheter into the vein in Russ's neck was a straightforward procedure. Once in place, the doctor inflated the stent to open up the vein in order to increase blood flow. If it worked, the results would be immediate.

We detected some temporary wiggling in Russ's toes. Beyond that, nothing. Of course, it was disheartening to have him travel so far without any improvements. But we didn't see the trip as a waste of time or money. All things considered, Russ was in good spirits. At the very least he had a brief escape from his day-to-day reality.

On our last day, a hospital staff member took us on a little driving tour of the area. When we arrived at the beach, he urged Marlene and I to dip our feet in the ocean while Russ remained in the van. We strolled along the soft sand to the water's edge. I waded up to my knees in the warm turquoise waters with the sun on my face. But all of it felt amiss. A few minutes later I returned to the van, feeling guilty about my unfaltering mobility.

There was little pleasure to be had with Russ bound to his wheelchair.

A YEAR LATER, I was out on a mountain bike ride. It was early October. The forest floor was bursting with scents of earth and evergreen. My legs pumped like a machine as I pedalled up the steep, winding trail. I was grateful to have this break from teaching and my grad studies. Spending a few hours in my temple of towering trees was exactly what I needed. Time to balance my brain and body.

My border collie–pit bull ran circles around me. Maya had already covered twice my distance. Her icy blue eyes threw me the usual, *What? Is that all you got?* She begged me to pedal faster. Every breath exhilarated me, but it felt like my lungs would shatter into a hundred pieces if I pushed any harder.

I focused on my line, ensuring my front tire hit the greasy roots and jagged rocks at the perfect angle to avoid getting bucked off my bike or having my back wheel spin out on me. My quads burned and my calves screamed, but I loved the short-term pain. The reward of an endorphin high reminded me what a privilege it was to have a body that could be worked to exhaustion.

The truth was I thrived on a bit of suffering. My legs weren't just mine. They were the legs of Dad, who could barely walk five steps without his feet freezing, making him crash onto his bruised, bony knees with a resounding *boom!* They were the legs of Russ, who had been wheelchair-bound for over ten years. No, whining *wasn't* an option. My body worked just fine.

An hour later, I was back in cell range when the sound of my phone startled me. Mom was calling.

"Dad's in the hospital."

I explained I was out mountain biking on the North Shore trails. The usual easygoing warmth in her voice was nowhere to be found. Instead, I detected irritation. Guilt hit me like a gunshot. *How dare you do something so completely selfish.*

"I'll be there as soon as I can," was the best I could offer. My jaw clenched. Beads of sweat trickled down my forehead, stinging my eyes. I wiped my brow with the sleeve of my jersey and fumbled to put my phone back into the pocket of my CamelBak. My legs went into frantic race mode as I pedalled back to the car with Maya chasing my wheel. My adrenaline and cortisol levels peaked. That all-too-familiar sick feeling invaded my body, turning my stomach into crampy knots and crushing my chest. But I carried on like I always do.

A few hours later, I arrived at the hospital. The doctor explained Dad was being treated for an infection in his hand caused by one of his falls. From the hallway I heard him yelling, "Don't touch me! Get your hands off me. I *need* my pills." I hesitated outside the door like a nosy eavesdropper, the floor shifting below me. I took a deep breath. I'd done this drill so many times I'd lost count. Between Dad and Russ, hospital visits were not a matter of *if* but when. The fact they were routine didn't mean they got any easier.

A nurse exited the room. I walked in and sat next to Dad. He looked so small and frail. I wanted to protect him, but I felt as helpless as he looked. He lay twisted in bed, his torso movement mildly jerky like a failed dance routine. His feet slowly flapped back and forth like the wings of a resting butterfly.

"They've screwed up my meds, goddammit. They have no idea what they're doing." He was livid and inconsolable. Few of the staff grasped the complexity of his disease or how imbalanced he would become if they didn't get his pills right.

For years Dad struggled through trial and error to find the best way to mitigate his complex symptoms. When he tried electroconvulsive therapy, I thought it seemed archaic and extreme. But it worked. After shock therapy, Dad needed less medication for Parkinson's, in turn lessening the psychological effects that held him hostage.

Whenever the bouts of paranoia and hallucinations got too severe, Dad spent time in the psych ward. He always seemed happy to see me. It only took a quick game of Scrabble or a trip down Kingsway for a date square to brighten his mood.

Lying in the hospital bed, Dad appeared more distraught than usual. His eyes were glassy. Untrusting. I assumed my presence would calm him down, but his expression hardly changed. Our eyes locked. He seemed neither relieved nor happy to see me. Instead, he looked through me, lost in thought.

"I'm sure they're doing everything to get you back on track, Dad," I said, trying to sound convincing.

I licked my lips and tasted the salty sweat residue from my morning ride. I pressed into my calves to massage my achy muscles. My ride in the forest was just a few short hours ago. Already it felt like a dream.

I gnawed on my nails and studied Dad's skinny legs. Despite crawling to the kitchen to binge-eat ice cream at midnight, he couldn't keep an ounce of fat on him. Parkinson's had withered him down to 90 pounds, reducing his body to skin, bone, sinew. His tiny muscles resembled those of an athletic boy, not a 79-year-old man.

As a teen, Dad loathed his gangly body. Growing up with inspirational black-and-white images of fitness buff Charles Atlas and the sand-kicking bully comic, he cast off his insecurities and transformed his "Scrawny Ronnie" persona. The photo of him standing on Kitsilano beach, showing off his bronze, lean, muscular physique in nothing but a Speedo, his horn-rimmed glasses and a beaming smile, radiates pride and a smidgen of vanity.

Nothing calmed Dad down. His anger festered, and it scared me to see him like this. His agitated state carried on for the rest of the day, putting immense strain on his worn-out body and mind. By the evening, nothing had changed. I tried to sound reassuring. "I'll be back tomorrow, okay, Dad? You need some sleep." I assumed with rest and medication, he'd pull through like he always did. He barely acknowledged me as I walked out of the room.

On the drive home, the sick feeling in my stomach dug deeper into my tunnel of grief. Half an hour later, I pulled up to my house. Minutes later the shower's steaming water rinsed the sweat from my skin. There was little comfort, though: nothing could wash away the worry that had taken hold of me. I crawled into bed next to Mac and closed my eyes, knowing full well that Fear wouldn't let me sleep much.

The next morning, when I met Mom at the hospital, I was shocked to hear the doctor's update. Overnight, Dad had suffered a stress-induced cardiac arrest and entered a semi-unconscious state. Simply put, his body was shutting down.

Short of a miracle, a cure or effective treatment, we knew one day Dad's body would quit. Yet it still came as a surprise when his doctor told us he wouldn't recover. Dad had seven to ten days to "live." As sad as it was, there was a comfort in hearing his fate. I had grieved his death long before this day ever arrived. His struggle – this cruel life sentence – would finally be over.

Dad was moved to palliative care. The nurse hooked him up to a morphine drip to keep him comfortable. Aside from his meds, Dad never touched drugs – he could barely finish a can of Kokanee. This was the first time opiates entered his body.

Each day, members of our family sat vigil, taking turns giving Dad tiny amounts of water to moisten his mouth. There were sporadic moments when he perked up and mumbled something incoherent. Mostly he slept. A few days in, my brother Mike, who'd been living in Australia for over 15 years, called to say goodbye to Dad. We propped the phone on the pillow against Dad's ear, hoping he might be lucid enough to comprehend Mike's departing words.

On the seventh day, out of the blue, Dad whispered into Mac's ear, "Can you get me some ice cream?" Mac's hazel eyes met mine and we shared a laugh. Past boyfriends had often gotten a "run for the hills" look on their faces when they met my family. When Mac and I started dating after my return from Africa, he didn't flinch when he met Dad and Russ. As a teen, he had endured his own grief after his dad died from AIDS-related illness. Between our love of the outdoors and our imperfect family backgrounds, it was comforting to have someone in my life who understood me.

Mac spoon-fed Dad vanilla ice cream – the last morsels of food he would ever eat. It was hard not to find the humour in Dad's final request. It was a rare, bittersweet moment when we could smile and relax while death lurked in the corner.

Two days later, Mac and I spent the night and day at the hospital. We were driving Mom and Russ home late in the evening. A few minutes after dropping off Russ, my phone rang. Sue was calling from the hospital. "Dad's breathing changed for the worse. You'd better get back here quick." Mac turned the van around and sped up: we were literally racing against death. We entered the hospital room minutes after Dad exhaled his last breath.

I was buffered from death as a child. This was my first time witnessing it up close. But years of worry had prepared me for this moment. Despite feeling sad, I was embraced by calm: Dad looked like he was at peace.

The four of us gathered around the bed, hugged one another, stood in silence and supported Mom, who had just lost her partner of 49 years. Dad's illness had taken its toll on their relationship. I felt some relief that she was no longer tethered to her caregiver role and the burden she could never escape.

Minutes later, we filed out of the room like robots. I felt terrible leaving Dad all alone. But it was late. We were exhausted. There was nothing else for us to do. *He was gone.*

As we walked down the hallway, the soothing sounds of half a dozen people singing spilled out of a nearby room, signalling another death. Their foreign chants seemed to be a final rite of passage, a means to send their loved one off to the next realm. I didn't really hear sorrow in their voices. Instead, they seemed to be rejoicing in the life that was lived.

Their singing transported me back to the tragic death of the mother and baby on Likoma Island, when the community had sung their songs of lamentation. I remembered that evening with clarity. I had been distraught – a bewildered outsider, out of sorts emotionally. It was the closest to death I had ever been. Now I was facing death head-on.

This unexpected ceremony in the hospital made me feel uneasy about how we were leaving Dad. I don't have strong convictions about what happens after death. My family didn't have any end-of-life rituals to send Dad off to some sort of heaven or spiritual afterlife. All I could do was take solace in knowing that at no point was Dad left alone or in pain. And nothing indicated he'd been afraid. After 22 years, he was finally free.

Dad's death brought me relief and acceptance. I'd forgotten what it was like not to have that gnawing trepidation simmering in my chest and stomach. Now I was granted the freedom to live with less guilt, fear and worry. A chance to regain the parts of myself that got lost in illness and grief.

Now that I was 40, I couldn't help wonder if I had been denying myself one of life's greatest adventures. Maybe I was finally ready to set fear aside once and for all and add a small branch to our family tree.

THE SOLES OF MY RUNNERS crunch against the gravel and pine needles blanketing the cold ground. The morning spring air begins to work its magic. The intoxicating smell of warming, mossy earth coats my nostrils and lungs. The sun peeks through the branches of old-growth trees, casting abstract patterns onto the paved path cut into the hilly forest. I see my breath as I run back and forth to warm up my legs.

My heart isn't pounding out of control. The usual anxious gut wrench has decided to leave me alone. I feel relaxed. Strong. Ready.

I run over to Mac. He's holding our beautiful, healthy daughter. Living proof there's life after death. I wrap my arms around her and plant kisses on her cheeks, forehead and nose. Today is her second birthday. Today is her mommy's first half-marathon.

I jog over to the start of the course to join the other runners. My legs are powerful and light. Fear and guilt are no longer weighing them down. Today, my legs are mine.

AFTER YEARS OF MUSING, "we should move to Squamish," Mac and I made the leap and left Vancouver in 2017. A month later, I left the stability and security of my teaching job. After 19 years, it was time.

Within a few months of our move, Mom and Russ left Richmond. Having lived in the turquoise house for 45 years, Mom moved into a seniors' home, five minutes from Sue's neighbourhood, an hour's drive from Squamish. Russ, who no longer qualified to live in his residence of 17 years, moved into a care home down the street from Mom. Their transitions were less than perfect, but over time I worried less. Their moves made me accept that often there are no perfect solutions to life's big challenges. Sometimes all we can do is choose the best option and hope it works out.

I spent two solid months that summer setting up the house and caring for a spirited toddler full-time while Mac commuted to the city for work. Ella kept me busy, but every day we spent together was an adventure: hiking the local trails, biking with her up front in the bike seat, my heart bursting with love.

Africa taught me that, when I let go of fear, beautiful things happen. It took me 20 years to accept my journey for what it was: a once-in-a-lifetime odyssey. No longer am I driven to chase Africa, to chase the person I thought I needed to be. Imagining a different path prevents me from appreciating the phenomenal gifts that made their way into my life.

Now, whenever Ella plunks her happy self onto my little Malawi chair, plucks a tinny tune on my *mbira* or arranges the colourful marbles of my solitaire game, her unexpected connection to my African adventure is soul stirring. Uniting the two most profound journeys in my life in the same room feels sublime, almost unreal.

By the end of our first summer in Squamish, however, the adventurous part of my pre-mother identity could not be suppressed. Ella was almost 3 and a half years old, yet *not once* had I spent a night away from her. I was in dire need of a little getaway. Some time to be on my own.

I'd always regretted that, despite all my travels and road trips across North America, I had never made it to New York City. How could I call myself a seasoned traveller when I had *never* been to New York City? I began to think about going there – on my own.

The next day my inner voice wouldn't shut up: *You can't go to New York alone, Lisa. Don't be ridiculous.* I invited my best friend Cathy to join me. She was keen, but the timing didn't work for her. She suggested we wait, go in the spring. But I *knew* this trip couldn't wait.

I couldn't get New York out of my head. Mom and Russ were settling into their new homes. Ella was in capable hands with Mac as she began preschool. I didn't have a job lined up or academic commitments tying me down. Aside from my maternity leave, this was the first time in two decades I wasn't preparing for a new school year. It would be foolish to waste this opportunity. The only thing stopping me was the silly voice of doubt.

After a second day of waffling, I decided I would *really* regret it if I didn't go to New York, but I wouldn't regret it if I went by myself. After all, I'd backpacked for four months in Africa on my own. Surely I could handle four days "alone" in a city of millions.

The next day I booked my flight and hotel. *Click, click, click* and *clickety-click.* It had been so simple and satisfying. A huge blanket of relief wrapped its arms around me.

My initial excitement returned. I felt braver than ever. Adventurous. And, for the first time in my life, truly *free.*

ACKNOWLEDGEMENTS

THIS STORY WAS ONLY POSSIBLE because of the wonderful "strangers" I met and bonded with during my journey. In the same vein, this book was only possible because of those who guided and encouraged me along the way.

In January 2015, during my maternity leave, I was trying to finish my thesis. After I was told I had to make some revisions and wait a few months, I felt frustrated and disappointed: I just wanted to finish and focus on being a new mother. That unexpected delay turned into a gift of time when I realized nearly two decades had passed since I travelled to Africa. I remembered my adventures with fondness and nostalgia and felt compelled to expand my travel journals into book format.

Two years passed after I finished my first (very) rough draft. Then, in August 2018, serendipity came knocking on my door when I met the Creative Academy team: Donna Barker, Eileen Cook and Crystal Stranaghan. These talented women authors gave me the confidence to see myself as a writer. I am so thankful I trusted my gut instinct and went back to talk to Donna about my memoir, then, months later, worked with her as my trusted developmental editor and mentor. Donna, we did it!

Amanda Bidnall was the first person to read my earliest draft of the manuscript. Even in its ridiculously infantile stage, Amanda saw a glimmer of potential that encouraged me to keep writing. I am very grateful for her keen eye and thoughtful input.

A heartfelt thanks goes out to the early readers of the manuscript who were generous with their time: Cathy Clay, Carolyn Klassen, Elizabeth Gillis, Sean Nakatani and Jackie McNamara, and to Jennifer Ogilvie, who gave me invaluable feedback on some shorter pieces. It was scary putting it out there for others to read, and I am so grateful for everyone's patience when the book still needed a lot of work.

I am thankful to editor Sarah Chauncey, who exposed my blind spots when I was under the delusion the book was almost done.

I am especially grateful to fellow writer Dr. Judy Dercksen, who was my final reader. She approached each chapter with supportive words, honesty and a critical eye and helped me strengthen the book more than I thought possible.

Additionally, I am indebted to those who offered me encouraging words and support along the way: Erica Hakonson, Susan Germain, Eric Angus, Kelsey Miller, Leanne Gillies, Todd Clark, Carol Marlowe, Tina Sherlock, Linda Talstra, Stella Harvey, and everyone else who rooted for me over the last few years.

A special thank you goes out to Don Gorman, Kirsten Craven and the Rocky Mountain Books publishing team for helping me make this book a reality.

A colossal thank you to all the real life characters who appeared in this book, especially Pete, Matthias and Phyllis, who became part of my writing journey after I contacted them out of the blue two years ago.

I am indebted to my mom and dad for teaching me early on in life that you don't have be wealthy to have a rich life.

A special thanks to Sue, Russ and Mike for being part of my story even though none of you signed up to be.

Almost last, but definitely not least, I am grateful for my faithful hiking and running partner. In the forest, with Maya wagging her tail at my side, I can ponder words and ideas away from the computer screen.

And, finally, thank you Mac and Ella for your love, support and the gift of endless adventures.

Where to next?

ABOUT THE AUTHOR

LISA DUNCAN'S OUTDOOR PURSUITS have taken her all over the world. She spent over a decade climbing in Squamish, Skaha, Smith Rock, Red Rocks, Joshua Tree and the Bugaboos before she got hooked on road cycling and mountain biking. Lisa has travelled to Maui, Tenerife, Portugal and Spain to push the limits of her cycling legs, and drove from Vancouver to Cape Breton across the American Midwest with her husband in their VW van with their mountain bikes and border collie–pit bull in tow. Since the birth of her daughter, her family adventures have included backcountry camping, sailing along the Sunshine Coast and Desolation Sound, and trips to Maui, Haida Gwaii, Yosemite, the Rocky Mountains and Costa Rica. Lisa has been an educator for over two decades, teaching Japanese as a second language and visual art for most of her career. She holds a BA in art history and a MA in environmental education and communication. When she isn't teaching or writing, she spends her time hiking, running and biking the trails near her home in Squamish, BC.